The Enneagram at Work

The writer says: I have not written this work to teach people what they do not yet know, but to remind them of what they already know and what to them is very much evident. For in my words you will find only things which most people know and about which they have no doubts. But in the measure to which these things are generally known and their truth has been revealed to all, in that measure forgetfulness arises with extreme frequency.

Moshe Chayim Luzzatto,
Het pad der rechtvaardigen
[The path of the righteous]
Amsterdam, 1740

The Enneagram at Work

Towards Personal Mastery and Social Intelligence

HANNAH NATHANS

CYAN|SCRIPTUM

First published in Great Britain in 2004 by Cyan/Scriptum Books, an imprint of

Cyan Communications Limited
4.3 The Ziggurat
60–66 Saffron Hill
London EC1N 8QX
www.cyanbooks.com

A CIP record for this book is available from the British Library

ISBN 1-904879-01-2

Printed and bound in Great Britain by
TJ International, Padstow, Cornwall

CONTENTS

PART III. PHILOSOPHICAL BACKGROUND FOR WORKING WITH THE ENNEAGRAM

PART IV. WORKING WITH THE ENNEAGRAM

FIGURES

TABLES

PREFACE

It has been said already in Ecclesiastes: 'Is there any thing whereof it may be said, See, this is new? It hath been already of old time, which was before us.'[1]

This thought impresses itself on me regularly nowadays. I think I have invented something myself and subsequently it turns out that it had already been thought of a few thousand years earlier. In my first book, *Adviseren als tweede beroep* [Consultancy as a second profession], the principles of consulting well, for instance, were shown to be be practically identical with the principles of the Eastern martial art of aikido.[2] In this book this principle is represented, for example, by 're-minding': bringing back into our minds what we already know . I regarded this as a nice discovery of mine, but later found that Plato had thought of it already. That is why I have introduced the book with the quotation from Luzzatto.[3] We all know everything, or in any event a great deal, but we have also forgotten a lot. This book will therefore help to 're-mind' you of what you already knew, rather than offer you something completely new.

Another book about the enneagram?

I was uncertain for a long time about whether I should write this book. There are already so many books about the enneagram. For a number of reasons, however, I decided that I had to do it nonetheless.

My first reason was because this tool for personality analysis and personality formation is sometimes used too stereotypically in practice. Then people have labels stuck on them and, as a result, are limited in their development instead of being helped to develop by the enneagram. In my practice as trainer and consultant I have met few stereotyped people – although these certainly exist – but I have encountered countless variants of different types. I was regularly confronted with people who did not behave at all like the 'cliché' of their type and who did not recognise themselves in that stereotype, yet did recognise the basic patterns of their type. When people have developed their personality they sometimes behave completely 'a-typically'. In short, reality seemed a good deal more varied in practice than in theory, at least as it is sometimes applied in practice. The theory, however, certainly does describe the differences between people with one and the same enneagram type. For each of the nine personality types distinguished by the enneagram literally hundreds of different manifestations exist in practice. This book therefore discusses both the similarities and the differences between people with the same enneagram type.

The second reason for this book is that much of the literature only discusses the development side of the enneagram to a limited extent, whereas this tool is essentially a developmental model. In this book I discuss more extensively than is usually done how people as individuals can work on their own development, and how as professionals they can coach others in their development. To this end, and at three learning levels, I describe a number of exercises, points for attention and development themes.

Because the enneagram is a transformation model, at the same time I pay attention to the transition from the lower to the higher states distinguished per type by the enneagram system. The lower state (the enneagram of fixations) means that someone identifies himself completely with his type and is trapped there, as it were. Thus someone cannot look objectively at himself and, as a result, there can be no question of self-management. Someone in this phase of development lacks a certain flexibility of mind in his contact with others, and is also unable to put his own passions temporarily in 'cold storage' if that proves necessary. The higher state recognised by the enneagram (the enneagram of higher virtues and ideas) implies that someone can distance himself from his type and can operate independently of it, something that also brings with it the development of qualities like courage, equanimity, self-esteem, detachment and decisiveness. Between these levels lie a number of levels, each of which represents a specific development task, so forming, as it were, a 'ladder' from low to high. In this book I describe an 'anatomy of consciousness' which can help to provide insight into the development process from lower to higher within the enneagram type, and consequently bring it within reach of self-management.

In principle there is nothing against using exclusively the lower part of the enneagram as a psychologically descriptive model. It is, however, a pity to limit the application of this system in this way because the enneagram distinguishes itself from other typologies precisely through the development possibilities it offers. The essence of the enneagram is that it is a transformational model. That is why we have chosen a butterfly, the symbol of transformation, for the cover of this book. After all, that butterfly was once a caterpillar.

The third reason for this book is my wish to make a contribution to the responsible use of the enneagram. Responsible use occurs only if work is done at the right level of analysis. That level is the level of basic patterns, and this cannot be emphasised sufficiently. The enneagram offers, as a result, a more fundamental level of analysis than most personality typologies, which usually deal with behaviour and behaviour preferences. The basic patterns consist of basic motivations, the mental models and the emotional programming from which people act. Two people can have the same basic patterns and still behave differently. Conversely the same behaviour can arise from different basic patterns. Behaviour or appearance is not the level of the enneagram.

If the enneagram is used for one's own personal development, then clarity about what is precisely involved is of great importance. If we use it as a professional in an organisation then a number of professional conditions should also be fulfilled.

A psychological and a spiritual model

The enneagram is both a psychological and a spiritual tool and yields its full worth only when it is used in both capacities. Although I regard the word 'spiritual' as one of today's most misused words, I have not been able to avoid it completely. If, for whatever reason, you have problems with this concept, then it is perhaps good to remember that in ancient times (the enneagram is an old model – more about this in Chapter 4) no distinction was drawn between psychology, philosophy, ideology and religion. It was all about the same thing: namely how man is put together and how he relates himself to his origin and his future. In that sense philosophical and religious traditions represent the psychology of antiquity.

Present-day psychology has occupied itself principally with sub-optimal functioning. The higher levels of functioning are mostly left out of consideration (except by certain side branches such as transpersonal psychology). There are clear relationships between the psychology of sub-optimal functioning and the enneagram of fixations. For the higher levels of functioning I shall refer regularly both to transpersonal psychology and to knowledge from philosophical and religious systems of thought.

Background against which this book is written

The enneagram has wider applications than just in management. It may be used for self-management and personal development and, as mentioned briefly above, in all areas where human interaction is involved. Professionals who work with the enneagram recognise four application areas: organisations (management, consultancy work), teaching, psychology and social service, and spirituality.

I myself am an organisational consultant and educator/trainer with an intense interest in spiritual development. My experience lies in organisations. I have written this book from the perspective of my own work and from my personal experience.

If you find that your own type is under- or over-represented in this book, this does not mean that I find your type relatively unattractive or attractive, or alternatively relatively important or unimportant. The examples in the book are derived from my own practice and as a result of this not all the types are evenly represented. In the examples given here, various clients have been combined and all the names are fictitious. Nonetheless all the examples have been derived from the practice.

My thanks to my teachers

Newton once said that he was able to further science because he could stand on the shoulders of giants (his predecessors).[4] Much of this book builds on what others have said. After all the years in which I have worked with the enneagram, in which I have developed much course material and made hundreds of overhead transparencies, it is difficult for me to reconstruct precisely which word and which formulation I derived from which author or teacher, and which are based on my own observation. In the book I refer as carefully as possible to the publications of others, but offer my apologies to anyone who might feel I have not given him or her proper acknowledgement. Let me know, and I shall set matters right in a subsequent edition.

Naturally many thanks are due in the first place to Helen Palmer and David Daniels, my teachers in the Enneagram Professional Training Program and in post-graduate training. I first met Helen at a congress on intuition, a subject that is a passion for both of us. She is a great source of inspiration for me. I came to know David as a really outstanding tutor who teaches the enneagram with warmth, humour and the ability to put things in perspective. Helen and David trained me, and I have since had the opportunity of working with them. Much in this book is inspired by them.

Further my thanks go to:

- Karen Webb and Jürgen Gündel, my supervisors and fellow organisers in the integration of English and German activities for enneagram teachers in the narrative tradition. (The oral tradition is the method of Helen Palmer and David Daniels – see Chapter 13.)
- Rabbi Howard Addison, who let me acquaint myself with the connection between the Kabbalah and the enneagram (see Chapter 11).
- The members of the Dutch enneagram network in the narrative tradition, in which we studied the enneagram together.
- The participants in my workshops, my clients with whom I worked with the enneagram, and the participants in Helen Palmer's Enneagram Professional Training Program for whom I acted as supervisor. I may have learned more from my 'pupils' than they have from me.
- My Dutch publisher, Hans Ritman of Scriptum Management, for his enthusiasm and trust, and his efforts in so many aspects of this project.

The knowledge about the enneagram which exists at the moment is not complete. Famous enneagram teachers do not always agree with each other – far from it, in fact. This book too will not be the last word. I hope it will contribute to an ongoing dialogue. I remain open to comments on the book, critical or otherwise, with a view to mutual learning and possible improvement.

In writing I have chosen literary convenience instead of correctness in gender politics. Thus 'someone' is referred to as 'he', 'the type' as 'his', and so on. All these cases refer equally to women as well as men.

Hannah Nathans
Zeist, March 2000

INTRODUCTION

The enneagram is a diagnostic tool. It can be used to increase self-knowledge and as a guideline for personal development. As a result a person increases his personal effectiveness. At the same time, the enneagram helps provide insight into colleagues, subordinates, clients and others, and into the mechanism of human interaction. With the help of such insights, someone can communicate more effectively.

The enneagram is therefore a valuable item in the toolkit of the professional consultant, manager, trainer, coach, and others. (To simplify matters, I shall refer in this book to the 'professional', unless a point is relevant to a specific function. Within the framework of the book, 'professional' therefore means also 'manager'.) In order to be able to guide others in their own personal development one needs more than the enneagram as a diagnostic tool. The profesional development toolkits of the trainer, coach, process counsellor, change expert and others come into play. These toolkits lie beyond the scope of this book.

In this introduction the following subjects are considered:

- The enneagram: a modern management tool with ancient roots.
- The enneagram as a tool for (self-)management.
- The enneagram type as a mental model.
- Modern management and the enneagram.
- The structure of this book.
- Readers for whom the book is intended, and possible reading 'routes'.

The enneagram: a modern management tool with ancient roots

The enneagram classifies people in terms of nine personality types ('ennea' is the Greek word for 'nine' while 'gram' is derived from the Greek word 'gramma', which means 'something written'). The enneagram is represented as a figure with nine points (Figure 1). It can be applied in any situation in which human interaction is involved.

Elements of the enneagram have existed for thousands of years: in Mesopotamia long before Christ, among the Greek philosophers, and in the early Christian doctrines. These elements are also to be found in great philosophies and religions, as well as in modern psychology (see specifically Chapter 4 and Chapter 11). They can be regarded as 'archetypal' human knowledge.

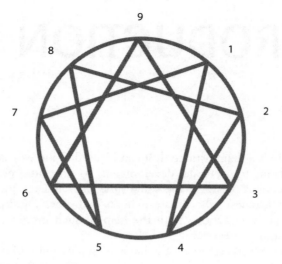

Figure 0.1 The enneagram

Now the enneagram has developed into a modern management tool. It is used frequently in organisations and taught in universities. There are various professional training courses devoted to it, as well as professional associations with thousands of members, such as the International Enneagram Association, the Association of Enneagram Teachers in the Narrative Tradition (for people who have studied with Helen Palmer) and, in Europe, an English-language and a German-language organisation for enneagram teachers in the narrative tradition.[1] There are also various professional publications, of which the *Enneagram Monthly* has the largest circulation.[2]

The enneagram: a tool for (self-)management

Knowledge of the enneagram helps people to recognise their own qualities and weak points, and to deal with these in a more effective way. With the help of the enneagram people develop consciousness of how they function and learn to see possibilities for improvement. In an interview with Wim Kayser, the concert pianist Vladimir Ashkenazy[3] stated that the aim of life was to improve oneself. Furthermore, working with the enneagram makes it clear how the world looks when it is no longer seen through the spectacles of one's own type, but from a broader perspective instead. The more someone is aware of these things the better he will be able to govern himself. Thus the enneagram is a road to *personal mastery*, a development model, and an extremely precise tool for self-management.

Besides this, the enneagram throws light on the personality types of partners in a discussion – for instance, colleagues in the management team, staff members or clients – and can be a means of achieving better results. The enneagram can offer someone insight into the way in which others might interpret a given situation. This means that one can use the enneagram to call up the best in people, to take their feelings into consideration and to fit in with that which drives them. This is the principle of *social intelligence*. Knowledge of the enneagram increases inter-personal effectiveness when (for instance) guiding, advising or training people. In this way the enneagram can also help guide people during change processes, in strengthening the way a team works, in coaching, in management and leadership, and in situations demanding co-operation. In addition it represents a tool which (for example) managers, consultants, trainers and coaches can use for supporting people in their personal development.

The enneagram type: a mental model

Personality types in a management team

A management team consists of five people. Ron, the director, sees the world through 'spectacles' which reveal everything that can go wrong. At every management team meeting the team members have to suffer statements beginning with phrases such as 'Have you thought about ...?', and 'Have you checked this or that/worked it out/controlled it/followed it up/compared it with last year/compared it with the competition/compared it with the prognosis/compared it with ... and so forth?' In this way it seems that there is always something which someone else has failed to think of. So Ron is really happy that he thought of it – after all, the whole organisation would be in the soup otherwise! His team members, on the other hand, find him tiresome and feel he delays things and slows progress.

Lisa – assistant director and business-unit manager – sees the world through spectacles which reveal opportunities and possibilities. And there are plenty of those! She comes to every team meeting with ideas about new products, new projects, new market opportunities, how to set up the organisation... and new ideas about PR, IT, HRM, financial and economic affairs, and all sorts of other fields that are not her area of work. Her colleagues don't believe in much of it, as many of the ideas are never put into practice. And anyway, why does she not keep to her own field? Everyone else does. But Lisa actually derives great satisfaction from her multiplicity of ideas because they don't come from others. Without her, she feels, they would soon fall asleep. And if her colleagues in the management team do happen to have an idea themselves, then they get their teeth into it and don't want to let it go. For Lisa an idea is just an idea: why do you have to be so deadly serious about it? Lisa thinks that things need livening up a bit; her colleagues want peace and quiet.

Business-unit manager Quentin always tries to keep himself out of the discussion as much as possible when it gets heated. All those emotions don't get you anywhere. It's much better to analyse what is really happening and base your actions on that. He does find it interesting to observe the discussions and analyse why they proceed as they do. Quentin's colleagues find him withdrawn and they don't always know what to make of him. Sometimes they try to draw him out of his shell. But Quentin likes to keep things as they are.

Team meetings irritate business manager Karina immensely. It all lasts much too long and is about nothing. Just think what she could achieve in that time! No goals are set, so of course you can't have an effective meeting. Karina has arranged things better in her own business unit. Now she tries to use her time effectively by doing other work during the meeting. That works quite well. Furthermore, she allows herself to be called regularly from the meeting so that she can arrange other affairs quickly while she is engaged in it. She has the idea that this actually makes a good impression on Ron, the director. Her colleagues, however, are upset by her behaviour. It means that the meetings last even longer.

Thomas, the head of Personnel and Organisation, worries about it all. At every meeting he sees the same patterns of interaction. To a great extent the course of the meetings is predictable and they are certainly not effective. Naturally everyone is different – and so they should be – but here they always succeed in building up the irritation level. Ron reacts to Lisa's impulsive ideas with still more control. Karina reacts to Ron's suggestions about how everything can go wrong with still more pressure for efficiency and results. Lisa reacts to Karina with ideas that seem even more impractical; in fact, it looks as if she does it in order to make Karina angry. Quentin reacts to all three by keeping his distance, now and then making a comment that is certainly relevant but does not involve him at all in the emotions which have become so heated in the meantime. Thomas thinks that something has to happen to the way the management team works. He has occasionally heard the enneagram mentioned.

The enneagram differs from other personality typologies in the *level* of analysis that it involves. Whereas most personality typologies are related to behaviour or behaviour preferences, the enneagram is concerned with basic underlying motivations and mental models. Every *enneagram type* has a different way of looking at the world and interpreting it. Each type has its own selective perception. The sociologist Merton once said that facts which are perceived as real are real in their consequences, even if the facts are not actually true themselves. Our mental conception works as a 'self-fulfilling prophecy'. Someone who finds, for example, that they cannot generally trust people – like director Ron in the case above – will tend to exert extra control on people. This can lead to them being avoided by others – some people do not want to be controlled by someone else! This kind of avoidance behaviour can further strengthen the suspicious person's distrust, making it seem even more important for him to keep an eye on others.

Another example: someone who holds the basic assumption that quarrelling means the end of a relationship will not want to quarrel and will avoid confrontation at all costs – until the tension reaches an uncontainable level and the dam bursts. Indeed, another party to discussions with this individual may be completely taken aback by the ensuing verbal violence, feel very unfairly treated (particularly if the root issue seems trivial) and end the relationship. In this way, people create situations which confirm their own views of the world.

Director Ron's belief that his colleagues always miss important matters is confirmed for him again and again. Team member Lisa tries ever harder to shake things up, while her colleagues try more and more to restrain her. With team member Quentin, the need to distance himself increases in proportion to his colleagues' efforts to draw him out of his shell. Team member Karina experiences more anxiety for efficiency and results the further the discussion goes. All these fixed reaction patterns form vicious circles. Each type lives in a world of 'self-fulfilling prophecy'.

Every type has difficulty in imagining that the world might be seen in eight other ways. Regularly I hear participants in training courses say during the discussion of other types: 'It must be really awful if you're made that way!' And others then say that in turn about this person's type. Each of the nine types sees, as it were, a ninth part of total reality. When people develop themselves, however, they learn gradually to distance themselves from their own type and to broaden their field of vision to a perspective of 360 degrees.

Each type is particularly sensitive in certain areas: for example to criticism, not being taken seriously, lack of loyalty, feelings of injustice, and so on. Now, many of these sensitive issues are things that *nobody* really likes, but with each type one or two are at the top of the priority list, as stimuli to which someone reacts allergically, as it were. Someone else only has to press briefly on these 'type-allergy buttons' to provoke a predictable and automatic reaction. These are instinctive reactions, and it will be clear that such responses are not always the most efficacious. Sometimes they actually make a bad situation worse.

Well meant but not effective

Manager Bob cannot stand it when Ali, who works in the repro department, is denigrated by his boss Albert. Ali is mentally retarded and doesn't always do things well. Albert rubs his nose in this fact in a distasteful manner, thus emphasising Ali's limited intellectual capabilities. Bob is furious when he sees this and makes short work of Albert. But as soon as Bob has left the repro Albert takes it out on Ali, who is left worse off for Bob's intervention. It is therefore important not to act automatically in response to instinctive reactions, but to consider first whether or not they constitute an effective intervention. Thereafter one can decide what to do: to act in accordance with the first impulse or do something else (or even do nothing).

Another example: a parent has said countless times that his 15-year-old son has to clear up his room, but without any result. He keeps repeating this and his irritation grows. When a strategy has not worked on a great many occasions, the chance that it will work the next time is small. When someone reacts automatically he does not think about effectiveness but acts from emotional instinct. In this example the parent calls still more angrily that the room must be cleared up *now*. If he were to think in terms of effectiveness then he would choose another strategy, for instance:

- adding his own mess ('clearly this is the place for dumping the rubbish!')
- clearing it up himself (it bothers him, but not the boy)
- throwing the things out the window (an acquaintance of mine found this strategy highly effective – the children had never gone upstairs faster than when they saw their things falling past the window)
- puting the stuff in the rubbish bin (a radical and permanent solution)
- shutting the door and not getting upset any more (when one stops seeing something as a problem it is not a problem any more)
- … and so on.

When people develop themselves they learn to distance themselves from their automatic reaction pattern. They then gain mental space to devise effective strategies. When someone becomes aware of the spectacles through which he sees the world, from his underlying motives and his reaction patterns, he can choose whether or not he wishes to continue expressing this view of the world – and these motives and automatic reaction patterns – in his behaviour, or wishes instead to adopt behaviour more in keeping with what individual situations demand.

When the team members in the example at the beginning of this chapter become aware of their individual patterns and how those affect the other members, they can discuss more effective ways of dealing with one another. Thus they could come to the conclusion that Quentin actually becomes less accessible as soon as the others come too close, and that he needs time to think. They could discuss the best way to give Ron the security he actually needs. They could ask Karina to prepare the meeting so that it would progress more efficiently. They should understand that Lisa is not as passionate in her support for every single idea she presents as they are themselves when they present an idea. For Lisa an idea that is proposed is only an idea, beside many other possible ideas, and she certainly does not feel that all ideas should be acted upon. In short, mutual tolerance would increase greatly and the meetings would become a good deal more sociable, as well as much more effective and efficient.

The enneagram type is therefore an automatic pattern of thinking and feeling related to a non-objective view of the world. It involves what are initially subconscious motives and focuses of attention. Thus Ron in the example is driven by a relatively great need for security, and his attention focuses automatically on what can go wrong. Quentin needs autonomy in his own territory above all else. His attention focuses automatically on unwanted interference by others. People feel uncomfortable when when they cannot satisfy their (subconscious) motivations, and then make still greater efforts to do so. When this behaviour prevents other people from satisfying their own inner motivations the vicious circles described above arise, and no one feels happy.

Every person has a type. Associated with each individual type are qualities and potential pitfalls. Anyone who learns to fathom his or her own type, and those of others, will function more effectively both on a personal level and in interactions with others.

Modern management and the enneagram

Modern management demands knowledge of the enneagram. My clients keep telling me that the importance of co-operation is continually increasing, and that things work better if people understand one another. This view is supported by a random selection from the bookcase of management literature.

As early as 1982 John Naisbitt called one of his 'megatrends' 'high tech, high touch'.[4] In so doing he established the connection between technological development and development in human communication, the latter being a prerequisite for being able to implement the former. It is questionable whether developments in the field of human communication have kept pace with technological developments since 1982. With regard to human communication, the enneagram offers possibilities for making a great leap forward. In the book by Starren and van de Kerkhof, *De 21 geboden van modern leiderschap* [The 21 Commandments of Modern Leadership], an important commandment is 'Thou shalt know thyself.'[5] Knowledge of the enneagram is also essential for all the core disciplines Senge considers necessary for the learning organisation:[6]

■ *Personal mastery.* The enneagram is concerned with how people function personally, how someone deals with one's personal vision, and how one can get a grip on one's own energy.
■ *Mental models.* The enneagram type is a mental model – it implies a basic assumption about what constitutes reality and a way in which a person perceives that reality.
■ *Shared vision.* This can be realised only if people are actually able to share insights in practice. The enneagram is helpful in this. Someone can understand another person, instead of interpreting what he says through one's own 'decoder'.
■ *Team learning.* Team learning starts with dialogue. A dialogue makes more sense if people understand each other. The enneagram helps people achieve this.

- *System thinking.* This fifth discipline welds the other four into a whole, according to Senge, and helps one understand how individuals see themselves and the organisation. The enneagram sheds light on this too. Senge quotes the example of the carpet salesman who sees a bulge in one of his carpets. He stands on it in order to flatten it neatly again. This succeeds briefly, but then a bulge appears somewhere else. He stands there instead, and this process is repeated a number of times – until the salesman lifts the carpet and an angry snake shoots off. People often try to stand on someone else's 'bulge' when it is more effective to study the underlying system.

This is not to say that every problem in an organisation can be solved by the enneagram. What it can do, however, is make an important contribution to optimising every aspect of an organisation, in which the way people function personally plays an essential role.

Weggeman claims that in knowledge management a heavy emphasis lies on teamwork, networking, and dialogue with clients and colleagues.[7] These are all areas in which the enneagram can lead to greater professionalism. Knowledge management is unthinkable without continuous learning by knowledge workers and staff members. Kessels says that people can learn only by developing reflective skills and acquiring communicative skills that allow access to the results of learning gained by others – which at the same time makes the learning climate more pleasant! – and by learning to regulate their inner motivations and inclinations surrounding learning.[8] These are all areas where the enneagram can make a contribution.

Daniels points out that the enneagram shares a number of principles with the concept of integral management.[9] Both underline the principle of continuous learning and are based on personal responsibility. In both cases it is recognised that people work in a dynamic system of mutually related elements and that they consequently influence each other. Both are also concerned with managing relationships and creating 'win/win' interactions. Both the enneagram and internal management are about bringing out the best in organisations and people. Both theories speak about the transformation of mental models.

Vincent Nolan's *Innovator's Handbook* has as its subtitle 'Problem Solving, Communication, and Teamwork.'[10]

This list might easily be continued for pages. From the management literature, it seems incontestable that there is ever more demand in organisations for real communication, team and project work, leadership, self-knowledge and insight into others.

Things are changing ever faster in this area. The person who once only carried out orders is now a member of a self-managing team, or an 'intrapreneur' in a dynamic organisational environment. Social skills and the ability to change are also in increasing demand. Here the enneagram can make a fundamental contribution.

The enneagram, however, is a rather complex tool. An initial investment is required in order to be able to work with it. That sometimes scares people off. They want something short and easy – preferably not more than one sheet of paper – that can be applied quickly. Such tools certainly do exist, and they can also be useful, but they cannot offer the same things as the enneagram. Nonetheless, if someone has little or no time available, these 'small' instruments provide the only option. In such a situation using the enneagram is pointless, because one really needs to invest time to reap its benefits.

Naturally, time is money. But *not* using the enneagram may also cost money. So many qualities can remain unused, so many opportunities may be missed, so many unnecessary misunderstandings may take place, so many conflicts can evade easy resolution, so many sub-optimal performances cannot be improved, and so much demotivation may result from someone being addressed in a manner that does not suit his type ... Furthermore, so many delays in change processes also cost money, although those costs are hidden. In many organisations, a great deal of 'human capital' lies in the safe without earning interest.

The structure of this book

The book consists of four parts.

Part I briefly describes the themes that are worked out further in Parts II–IV. It features short descriptions of the main features of the nine types, and an account of the enneagram's characteristics and the mechanisms that play a role in it. Thereafter there is discussion of the possibilities for applying the enneagram in management and in training and consulting work, the way the enneagram is used as process description, and finally the history of the enneagram through the centuries.

Part II provides an extensive description of the nine types. Part III provides the philosophical background without which one cannot work with the enneagram. An anatomy of consciousness is discussed, in which the lower and higher 'states' of the enneagram have their places. This anatomy provides an accurate map of the various steps involved in climbing from 'low' to 'high'. At the same time the various parts of this anatomy can function as sub-personalities. A relationship is established between the steps in the development from 'low' to 'high' and the levels of learning, which are dealt with in Part IV.

Finally, Part IV discusses working with the enneagram. For the individual, the enneagram is used as a tool for personal development and self-management. For the professional, it is a tool for working more effectively with clients, colleagues and staff members, and for guiding people in their development. Amongst the issues discussed are the way to determine a person's type, the role played by the professional's own type and adjusting to the

types of others. There are also many exercises for use in one's own development or for guiding others on the three levels of learning, and a summary of
the development themes of the various types.

Targeted readers and possible reading 'routes'

This book is intended for two audiences: for anyone who wishes to learn to
deal more effectively with himself and others, and for the professional who
wants to employ this tool in work with clients.

Some readers will be making their first acquaintance with the enneagram.
They should pursue the following reading route:

- In Part I, they should read Chapters 1 and 2.
- Then in Part II, which describes the types themselves, they should read
  the first two sections of all the type descriptions in Chapters 7–9.
- In conclusion, in Part IV they should read Chapter 13 up to the paragraph
  'The typing interview' (p. 184).

A reader wishing to deepen self-knowledge and use it for personal development should read Chapters 5 and 6, to gain insight into the working of
a type, and Part III. Anyone who has determined his own type (see Chapter 13) can subsequently follow the further working-out of this type in
Chapters 7, 8 or 9. However, reading the further working-out of all types
in Chapters 7–9 can also be helpful in finding one's own type. When
considering one's own development Part III is interesting, along with
Chapters 15–18 in Part IV.

If one wants to work with the enneagram as a professional then one
should read the remaining chapters in the book: the rest of Chapter 13 and
Chapter 14. Obviously, working professionally with the enneagram requires
professional training as well as reading a book.

Chapter 3, about the enneagram as process description, and Chapter 4,
about the history of the enneagram, are of interest to those who want to know
more about the historical background. These chapters are not necessary for
following the subsequent course of the book.

My discussions with the editor also identified a group of readers who will
probably not be interested in this book. These are the so-called reductionists:
people who distil a wider reality down to a smaller one from which they wish
to explain things.[11] However, while the results of chemical analysis of a
painting are not in themselves untrue, they do not explain why the paint is a
painting.[12] If you believe not only that measuring is knowing, but also that
only properties that can be measured actually exist – or if you are convinced
that people consist solely of physical material and chemical processes – you
had better take this book back to the bookshop.

Part

I

The Enneagram and Its Applications

This first part of the book discusses the principles of the enneagram: what it is for, where it comes from, what its characteristics are, in what way it is distinguished from other personality typologies, and how this system is applied in organisations. The enneagram offers a deeper level of analysis than most personality typologies and, as a result, is an instrument that operates at a more fundamental level.

Chapter 1 defines what the enneagram is, and how and why the same type can manifest itself in different ways. Chapter 2 throws light on various application areas in organisations and discusses how one can prevent the enneagram being used incorrectly. Chapter 3 deals with how the enneagram is used as process description. Finally, in Chapter 4, the history of the enneagram is discussed. A detailed discussion of the various types follows in Part II.

CHAPTER 1

The Enneagram

This chapter sketches an outline of what precisely the enneagram is. First there is a short description of the nine types (these are described extensively in Part II). Then it is explained what the essential characteristics of the enneagram are and how it differs from other personality typologies such as, for instance, the well-known Myers Briggs Type Indicator. The enneagram is not only a descriptive model but also a development tool, an issue considered in the following section. There follows a consideration of the often-asked question 'Is the enneagram type inborn or acquired?' The existence of many variants and manifestations of each of the nine enneagram types is explained. In conclusion, there is a consideration of why different authors provide contrasting information about the enneagram.

The nine types in brief

To ensure that the enneagram characteristics which follow in the rest of Part I are not too abstract, we begin with a short description of the nine types. These types are elaborated on extensively in Part II.

Names of the types

Each type is a whole complex of characteristics that cannot be captured in one word. For this reason different authors work with different titles. One title may emphasise one characteristic and suit one person well, while another title accentuates another quality and will fit another person better.[1] People of a certain type often recognise themselves better within one title than in another. Indeed, when dealing with different people of the same type, different characteristics come to the fore. This is why, when applying the enneagram, I prefer to work with the *numbers* of the nine types instead of the titles. A title always throws light on one specific aspect; the numbers indicate the whole complex of characteristics, however, instead of focusing on only one. In the rest of this book, therefore, numbers will be used exclusively. Using numbers also helps avoid misunderstandings, since different authors sometimes use the same name with reference to different types!

The types

In these short descriptions we use a number of names that are encountered in the literature. Thereafter, as has been said, we shall work only with numbers.

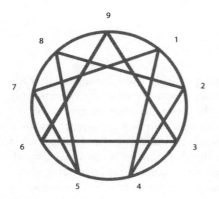

Type 1 – The perfectionist, reformer, improver, standard-setter, fulfiller, teacher, preacher, inspector, judge, entrepreneur

Basic motivation is to win affection by doing something correctly. Attention goes automatically to what is right or wrong, particularly to what can be improved. Has a permanent inner monitor. Feels strong personal responsibility: work comes before pleasure. Represses his own needs. Is convinced that there is only one 'right way'. Tends towards rigidity and to excessive control. Is afraid of making mistakes. Feels ethically superior.

Development is in the direction of accepting that the world is simply not (yet) perfect, of high morality, of being able to realise an ideal.

Type 2 – The helper, giver, nurse, manipulator, seducer, independent one, assistant, mother, lover, power behind the scenes, guardian angel

Basic motivation is to gain approval by fulfilling the needs of important people. Attention goes automatically to the needs and feelings of others. Likes to help others. Often has an attitude of service towards others, and in this tends to make himself indispensable. Sees the qualities of others and can stimulate them. Implicitly expects approval, affection and appreciation in return, and can be emotional, demanding and manipulative if this does not materialise. Is dependent on relationships. Reveals different sides of himself to different people. Has difficulty in receiving.

Development is in the direction of really caring for people and being altruistically supportive, and creating personal freedom instead of being only at the service of others.

Type 3 – The result-orientated doer, hard/successful worker, actor, performer, winner, show-off ('look at me!'), fusspot, status-seeker, producer, social climber

Basic motivation is to win acceptance through satisfactory performance. Attention goes automatically to the task in hand. Can make teams enthusiastic about carrying out a task. Is competitive. Wants to be successful and 'the best'. The goal has to be attained as efficiently as possible. Is impatient and angry if others slow things down. In this, pays little attention either to personal feelings or to those of others. Image and status are important; to acquire these he presents matters in a way that he presumes will be acceptable and in doing this he can play widely divergent roles. Expects appreciation and recognition to be based on what he achieves and not on what he is.

Development is in the direction of veracity: really 'being himself' instead of playing a role.

Type 4 – The romantic, tragic romantic, artist, individualist, blueblood, idealist, connoisseur

Basic motivation is rediscovering what is lost by being unique. Attention goes automatically to important things that are missing. Has the tendency to value more what is *not* present than what is. Is sensitive; can express this or feel it deep within himself. Is searching for a deep emotional bond and authenticity in relationships. Idealist. Is attracted by the unattainable. Feels different from others. Is empathic, especially if people are in difficulty. Does not want to be helped promptly to solve his own difficulties, however, preferring to experience the pain. Can be creative, artistic, romantic.

Development is in the direction of accepting the ordinary; equanimity; finding satisfaction in the here and now.

Type 5 – The observer, researcher, thinker, analyst, wise man/woman, philosopher, information junkie

Basic motivation is self-protection from interference by others through self-sufficiency. Attention goes automatically to observation. Analyses; researches; thinks before taking action. Wants to protect his time and energy, and thus does not like claims, dependency and too much involvement. Also keeps a distance emotionally. Finds it easier to make contact with personal feelings when alone. Avoids becoming deeply involved in situations by minimising own needs.

Development is in the direction of quiet decision-making, overall view, real independence.

Type 6 – The Devil's advocate, loyalist, cynic, sceptic, questioner, troubleshooter, guard, hero, adventurer, rebel, fanatic, pursued pursuer

Basic motivation is to ensure safety through watchfulness, imagination and doubt. Attention goes automatically to possible danger and threats, and what can go wrong. Has, in this respect, a lively imagination. Is watchful, dutiful. Is sometimes tormented by doubt. As a result has a tendency to procrastinate, also because being visible can expose oneself to attack. Tends towards identification with, and championship of, the underdog. Has a healthy distrust of people in authority; can play the Devil's advocate to challenge them, or avoids them. Has a sixth sense for hidden agendas. When personally committing themselves to something or someone, they will remain very loyal to that goal or person.

Development is in the direction of courage and trust.

Type 7 – The bon vivant, enthusiast, adventurer, optimist, dreamer, visionary, charmer, idealist, generalist, hedonist, planner

Basic motivation is avoiding fear and pain by imagining and seeking pleasant possibilities. Attention goes automatically to what is positive, and interesting possibilities for the future. Experiences are more important than results. Tends to (re)interpret negative matters as positive ones. Likes to keep all options open; dislikes limitations; commitment is difficult. Is charming, stimulating and inspires enthusiasm. Likes to have a total picture of how things fit together; links ideas with one another. Tries to stand on a level with authority, which can lead to conflicts.

Development is in the direction of making choices, not wanting everything, commitment, finishing things, taking feedback seriously.

Type 8 – The boss, leader, challenger, protector, confronter, windbag, top dog, fighter, warrior, moralist, champion, potentate

Basic motivation is to win respect by being strong and confrontational and to hide vulnerability. Attention goes automatically to power, being strong, dominating, wanting to (over)rule. Is direct, action-orientated. Displays anger and power openly; has difficulty with personal vulnerability. Respects opponents who fight. Is truthful. Has a great feeling for justice. Stands up for weaker individuals. Approaches things in an all-or-nothing manner. Cannot always distinguish between objective truth and personal interest. Has a tendency towards excessive behaviour. Needs stimulation and excitement. Refusal to recognise personal limits can be harmful to himself and others.

Development is in the direction of recognising own vulnerability, finding the real truth, facing up to the world candidly.

Type 9 – The mediator, peacemaker/protector of the peace, liberator, conserver, devotee, searcher, negotiator, saint, straightforward person

Basic motivation is to create harmony by forgetting himself and accommodating himself to others. Attention goes automatically to what are seen as the expectations and wishes of others. Tends to satisfy those expectations and wishes. Avoids conflict; strives for harmony. Can easily empathise with different standpoints. Knows how to find solutions which everyone accepts. Adapts himself superficially to others. Is often seen as engaging, laconic, accommodating, but within can be very obstinate. Has difficulty in guarding his own boundaries and realising personal needs; has difficulty in saying 'no'. Expresses anger indirectly. Tends to avoid feelings of dissatisfaction through immersion in something else.

Development is in the direction of self-acceptance, making choices, decisiveness.

These short descriptions offer a first impression of the various types. In reading them, perhaps you have thought: 'I have something of them all!' That is often the case. In principle, everyone has everything within themselves. Everyone is sometimes indecisive or decisive; is sometimes optimistic or pessimistic; has a certain feeling of justice; prefers pleasure to pain; is sometimes worried; finds recognition and appreciation pleasant; and is sometimes angry. The type, however, is something that is always present, even though it is sometimes in the background. If you are looking for your own type it is better to look at the total picture conjured up by a type description than at separate elements. More about this in Chapter 13.

Characteristics of the enneagram

In previous sections it has already been mentioned several times that the enneagram distinguishes itself from other personality typologies in the level of analysis that it offers: that of the deeper causes of behaviour. The enneagram is not a static descriptive model, although it can be used in this way, but is essentially a dynamic development model. Different levels can be distinguished: the 'lower' enneagram of fixations and the 'higher' enneagram of higher virtues and ideas. The question of whether an individual's type is inborn or acquired will never be answered definitely, but a disposition towards a certain type is probably inborn. There exist many variants and manifestations of each type. Different authors emphasise different aspects of the enneagram, and there are good reasons for this. We shall now deal successively with:

- the level of analysis of the enneagram
- the enneagram as dynamic development model
- the enneagram of fixations and the enneagram of higher virtues and ideas
- type: inborn or acquired?
- many variants and manifestations of the types
- differences amongst authors.

Level of analysis of the enneagram

The level of analysis of the enneagram is different from that of most personality typologies. Other typologies concentrate mostly on the level of behaviour or of behaviour preferences. The enneagram, however, mainly provides insight into driving forces and motivations: into the way in which – and the subject towards which – attention is automatically directed, the way in which reality is perceived, and the mental and emotional 'software' governing every type's actions.

It is important to define this analysis level clearly. Anyone who uses the enneagram at the wrong level of analysis can quickly get lost in the system, resulting in a sort of 'women's magazine' psychology. In saying this I am not being negative about women's magazines *per se*, but about a particular kind of psychology. Within its frame of reference, the type descriptions are condensed to a few behavioural traits per type (although behaviour in itself does not actually represent the type ...), a short list of questions is made up or plucked from the Internet (Chapter 13 considers the very limited value of enneagram questionnaires), and that is that. When the enneagram is worked with in such a way, an individual will have difficulty in placing himself, will attribute wrong types to other people and, on this basis, will then choose the wrong interventions.[2] For the person who wants to develop himself or work professionally with the enneagram it is essential to be clear about the right level of analysis.

Possible levels of analysis

If someone comes to me for coaching and brings along a psychological report, a behavioural assessment or the result of a test, then that report, assessment or test result usually predicts what *behaviour* can be expected of my client in different situations. That information is, of course, useful for the individual who commissioned that particular report, assessment or test, who will indeed want to know how the person concerned can be expected to behave in the future. Usually, however, someone wants to be coached out of a desire to *change* this prediction. The report said, for instance, that the client would give up quickly under pressure – the client now wants to develop greater perseverance. Maybe the assessment maintains that he pays little attention to the interests and feelings of others; now he wants to develop greater sensitivity, or show more interest in other people. Perhaps the result of the test indicated a strongly dominating and controlling style; now he wants to learn to delegate.

This can be a useful approach in training skills in the person concerned, yet this is useful only if inadequate behaviour is a consequence of a lack of skills. If the cause of the problem is at an underlying level then such a person will not gain much from skill training (and his employer will gain just as little). When someone is convinced, for instance, that other people must be taken into account, that conviction can lead to giving in too soon. When someone has a dominating and controlling personality type, then that personality type can be the cause of this behaviour. If people in such cases work only on their skills and leave the underlying levels undisturbed, there is a real risk that the problems diagnosed will keep coming to the surface again. We must therefore distinguish the levels of behaviour, skills, underlying convictions and personality type. Some convictions are connected with the personality type, others not. Thus, the conviction that 'authority is not to be trusted without question' belongs to Type 6, yet a conviction such as 'he who is born for a penny will never become a pound' (as the Dutch say) can occur with every type. Each type has some skills that come naturally and others that must be learnt with the necessary effort. Thus Type 8 is assertive by nature and has to learn to listen to others. Behaviour arises in an interaction between what the person has by nature and what the environment asks of him. Type 9 is not so assertive by nature but can be so if the situation makes it necessary.

At the level of the enneagram the following type of question is asked: *Which motivation* leads someone to give up under pressure? *Which view of the world* leads them to pay little attention to the interests and feelings of others? *Which mental or emotional software* gives him a dominating style? Working with these concepts we link up with the 'levels of learning', probably thought up originally by Argyris, which have since become a general mental framework in the world of management and training:[3]

- *First-order learning:* learning new skills through step-by-step improvement, extending the behaviour repertoire. At this level someone learns skills in areas in which he has less natural aptitude.
- *Second-order learning:* reframing, clarifying underlying thought patterns, studying the 'software'. At this level someone learns to become self-aware of the automatisms associated with a particular type, and also to see the world through spectacles other than those of his own type.
- *Third-order learning:* transformation learning. In connection with the enneagram: transcending the type.

First-order learning is certainly useful, but it does not change someone's 'software'. His automatisms remain the same and, as a result, he regularly slides back into 'old' behaviour. Studying those automatisms is second-order learning. When someone appraises his basic motivations, view of the world, attention pattern and emotional reaction pattern, he can make a conscious choice as to whether he wants to let himself be ruled by his automatic patterns or wants to liberate himself from them, to a certain extent at least. That liberation is third-order learning.

The 'software' mentioned in the context of second-order learning is the real level of the enneagram – or at least of the 'lower' enneagram, the enneagram of fixations. With third-order learning an individual can come in contact with the 'higher' enneagram, the enneagram of higher virtues and ideas. The enneagram offers the possibility of working at all three levels. Chapters 16–18 deal extensively with the three levels of learning with the enneagram.

Enneagram type is not behaviour

Thus behaviour and enneagram type are two different levels of analysis. Both levels, incidentally, are important and can complement each other well.

The fact that there are actually two different levels of analysis is clear from research in this area. Different authors have sought one-for-one correlation between one of the other 'great' personality typologies – the Myers Briggs Type Indicator (MBTI), which is concerned with people's personal behaviour preferences – and the enneagram which, as has already been pointed out, is concerned with basic patterns. Recent research indicates that these correlations have no great significance.[4] There are indeed some statistically significant correlations, but every enneagram type can in principle go hand in hand with every MBTI type, and the reverse is also true.[5] This last means that certain observations about the types, such as those that can be found in some literature, have to be reviewed with care: for example, 'Type 5 is always introvert', 'Type 1 always works in an orderly manner', or 'Type 4 always decides on the basis of people's feelings'. Apart from that, much more research will be needed to ascertain whether the statistically significant connections that have been found are also repeated in further studies. These research results agree only very partially with earlier research findings, and when you correlate enough information with enough other information there is *always* something that is statistically significant.[6] This is just in the very nature of statistical significance.[7] When I was employed in the housing sector, someone once came up with the idea of investigating which aspects of new homes correlated with which other aspects, and carried this out by correlating everything with everything else. If I remember rightly, it turned out that the placing of the light switch in the garage correlated significantly with a leak in the attic … A statistically significant relationship is not necessarily a meaningful one, let alone a causal relationship. Thus more research about the relationship between MBTI and enneagram is certainly needed.[8] In the meantime we have to assume, on the basis of available information, that every enneagram type can be combined with every MBTI type, although some combinations perhaps occur more often than others.

Enneagram type is not a role, task or culture

The enneagram type, as we have already seen, is not behaviour – nor does it equate with someone's role or task. For instance, not every leader has Type 8, even though that type is often called 'the boss'. Not every social worker has Type 2, a supportive type. Not every researcher has Type 5, associated with an analytical attitude. Not all preachers have Type 1, associated with high morals and (sometimes) an admonitory finger. Every type can come up with innovations, not just the plan-making Type 7. Every type can sell, not only the result-orientated Type 3. Different types will, however, carry out the same tasks in different ways.

In the same way the enneagram type must not be confused with the culture of a country or an organisation. In a result-orientated culture not every worker has Type 3, in a people-oriented culture not every worker has Type 2, and in a power-oriented culture it is not only Type 8 that works there.

Hofstede defined culture as 'mental programmes' or 'mental software': that is to say, 'patterns of thinking, feeling and potential acting which have been learned in the course of life'.[9] He described five indices in which different cultures score in different ways: large v. small power range, individualism v. collectivism, masculine v. feminine, tolerance of uncertainty, and Confucian dynamism. Such an index is a piece of statistical data for a whole culture. Within such a culture different people have different types. Their behaviour, however, can often be determined culturally, because particular behaviours are experienced as socially desirable. For example, I once interviewed a man from the Far East who avoided eye contact, expressed himself extremely cautiously and tended to agree with everything I said. His type, however, was not at all inclined to adaptability – a cultural 'film', as it were, lay over it.

Development model

The enneagram is not a static model but a development model.

The man as he is and the man as he can become

Ouspensky, a pupil of Gurdjieff who brought the enneagram to the West in the second decade of the twentieth century, distinguished two sorts of psychology: the study of man as he is and the study of man as he can become. When someone has found out what his type is, he can do two things: let it be or use this knowledge for self-improvement.

In the first case, a person might well say to himself:

I am happy that I know my type. Everyone has a type and mine is just as good as those of others. I was born with this type and I shall die with it. It's just the way things are, and others must take me as I am. I cannot help it if I do not always react adequately. It is irritating if people find me a cold fish, a tyrant or a manipulator – and unfair, too, because I don't mean it badly – and it is a pity that that has negative effects in the workplace atmosphere and on the tempo at which I can bring about changes but, alas, as the saying goes, 'there is a grain of truth in every story, however tall', and that is true of me too.

This is the knowledge of man as he is. It can be an important step in some-one's development to recognise his own type and to be aware of all aspects of that type. It leads to greater self-acceptance and makes it easier to recog-nise both one's own type-specific qualities and one's type-specific pitfalls.

At the same time, somebody's type will remain his boss. Thus a person has no free choice as regards his actions but acts automatically according to his type 'software'. The type can be used as an excuse: 'I can't do anything else because that is my type.' A person's effectiveness is not then as great as it could be, however. Thus someone with knowledge of his type can actually be worse off for this knowledge. Previously he perhaps thought over how he could tackle things differently – not any longer! If the type is his horse, so to speak, then this horse bolts with the rider astride it. In his perception he does not have a type: he *is* his type, and identifies with it completely.

In the second case, someone says to himself:

> I am happy that I know my type because now I can see better how to improve the way I function. I am going to make use of my type-specific qualities and work on overcoming my type-specific pitfalls.

This is knowledge of man as he can become. In this case someone becomes the boss over his type and turns into the road towards personal mastery. His type is going to be of service to him instead of running off with him. He is going to ride the horse of his type. He has a type; he is not it.

The enneagram is thus not a static model ('analyse what there is and let it be'), although it can be used in that way, but a dynamic model ('analyse what there is and subsequently use that knowledge for development'). The aim of the enneagram system is development, not imprisoning people in boxes.

The enneagram of fixations and the enneagram of higher virtues and ideas

The enneagram is a psychological and spiritual system. As was pointed out in the Preface, no distinction was made in ancient times between philosophy, psychology, ideology and religion. Old philosophies and religions are thus also old forms of psychology, albeit forms that pre-existed any western scien-tific notions. All great religions and many different philosophies – at least those in the (neo-)Platonic tradition – regard the personality of man as a deviation from his inner core, his essence, his real or higher self.[10]

There are therefore two levels in the enneagram: the *enneagram of fixa-tions* (individual psychological) and the *enneagram of higher virtues and ideas* (trans-personal). The enneagram of fixations is the enneagram of the personality type. It is concerned with limitations on human functioning. When someone's attention is directed at 'X', he pays less attention to 'Y'. When the spectacles through which he regards the world are 'A', then 'B', 'C' and 'D' are less noticeable. When someone has 'K' as basic motive force, then he will strive less for 'L', 'M' and 'N'. If the specific quality of a certain

Figure 1.1 The enneagram of fixations

type is 'Q', then the person with that specific type will be, by nature, less good at 'R'. Those limitations are completely normal: everyone has them. And behind every shadow lies a sunnier side. Usually people have developed more strongly the qualities that belong to the natural tendencies of their types. Thus someone who is strongly orientated towards creating safety can become an incomparable risk analyst. Someone who uses his brains to allay his basic fears can be a tower of strength in crisis situations. Someone who wants to avoid conflicts can become a star in the process of reaching a consensus.

The 'lower' level is called the enneagram of fixations because people have difficulty in freeing themselves from their type-specific way of focusing their attention and their type-specific motivation.

The enneagram of the higher virtues and ideas is on a transcendent (or trans-personal) level, that is to say, a level that transcends the psychological level (from the Latin *trans* = over, *scendens* = rising). This level has very practical implications. The higher virtues and ideas of a certain type form the core of that type's direction of development. Thus the higher virtue of Type 6, whose driving emotion is fear, is courage. Type 9, who tends towards self-neglect, has love or self-acceptance as higher idea. Type 3, who believes that role-playing will help win recognition, has veracity, authenticity and honesty as higher virtue.

Every type in the enneagram of fixations corresponds with higher qualities in the enneagram of higher virtues and ideas. The unique path to development for every type involves actualising the qualities concerned. In this the enneagram of higher virtues and ideas is a guideline for development. It can make clear in which direction someone's deepest desires lie. It can help people to see the difference between the 'real' reality and their type-specific way of interpreting it.[11]

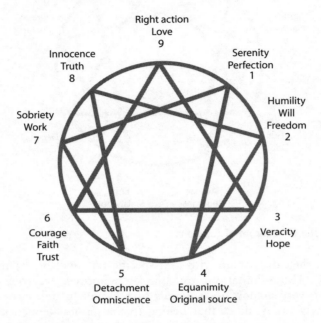

Figure 1.2 The enneagram of higher virtues and ideas

The enneagram of fixations and the enneagram of higher virtues and ideas indicate two rungs on the ladder of grades of consciousness, whereby the enneagram of fixations represents a low level of consciousness and the enneagram of higher virtues and ideas a relatively high one. Between them lies the level of the true self. The personality type is not the true self – the personality type, in fact, is sometimes called the false self. The true self is that part of ourselves that can observe our enneagram type. At the level of the true self someone does not identify himself with his type.

In Chapter 6 the higher virtues and ideas are explored further, while the steps from fixation to higher virtue and ideas are described in Part III.

Both enneagrams in practice

No matter how far one develops oneself, however, one will always have to keep dealing with the enneagram of fixations. The 'software' remains present, even if we learn not to start it automatically any more. The enneagram of fixations therefore remains just as important as the enneagram of higher virtues and ideas. Tom Condon has put this aptly into words. Here I summarise his description:[12]

> Many spiritual practices deny the subconscious will and the profit we have from lower motivations (enneagram of fixations). They emphasise combating sinful tendencies through discipline or through denial. But when we direct ourselves exclusively at higher spheres it is difficult for us to integrate that in our daily lives and work. When we deny our defences and historical dilemmas (fixations) they simply come back after meditation. We can be a meditator of world class and still have immature relationships and bouts of anger in daily life. On the other hand, when we direct ourselves exclusively at our 'lower' personality aspects (fixations) we can remain stuck in our psychological paradigm. Some people use the enneagram to make problems, excuses and limitations they did not have before they immersed themselves in the enneagram.

Condon describes here why people have to operate in practice on both levels of consciousness. Most readers of this book will not be planning to withdraw for good into a cave in the Himalayas. In the western world most people, even if they withdraw for a year, still have to return home at a given moment in order to make a living. And that is a good thing too. Admittedly there are also a few people in our society who become enlightened, but ordinary people like you and I (my assumption is that you will not read this book if you are enlightened) have to deal with normal daily life. The art for people who work in organisations, therefore, is not so much to gain contact with the higher virtues and ideas by means of meditation (although this is a great art, and certainly also a very good exercise), but, rather (and ultimately) to give these virtues and ideas an increasingly important role in daily life and work. Communications consultant and management coach Rolph Pagano put it this way: 'Flying is not an art, but landing is.' [13] Once again, this idea is not new. Francis of Assissi said in the thirteenth century: 'Contemplatio et actio!'[14]

No stereotypes: only variants and manifestations

Sometimes people protest that (contrary to their own pre-existing beliefs) the enneagram pigeon-holes people, and that the real world cannot be covered by nine personality types. These people are absolutely right. Within the enneagram system alone there are hundreds of variants and manifestations of the same type. Part II of this book deals with this extensively. In the type descriptions given there, the basic patterns of the types are explained. These basic patterns apply to everyone with the same type. The basic structure is concerned with the inner functioning: the 'software'. Thereafter it considers a number of aspects which explain why the same type can behave in so many different ways. When this book speaks of 'behaviour', what is meant is the average behaviour of a certain type. Individual representatives of a type can agree with this or diverge from it.

A book can provide a good start in the process of making acquaintance with the types. Book knowledge, however, remains subject to divergent interpretations. Everyone places what they read in a personal frame of reference. The only way to gain a really good view of the various types is to experience them personally in large numbers. In the narrative tradition in which I was trained, people talk about their types themselves, in panels for instance. In this context, a panel is a group of people of the same type. Someone who listens to a panel gains an impression of the points on which people of the same type correspond, and also of those in which they differ. Comments by panel members may also clarify a passage from a book: 'Aha, so *that's* what the author means by ...' In this way, the book knowledge becomes flesh and blood. One can form a good picture of the individual types only by associating with many live representatives of a type. The picture 'fills out' gradually. First only the theoretical contours of the type are known, but steadily these are filled with more and more living examples. In this way the theory acquires an ever-deepening meaning. It can be compared with photographs printed with rough and fine screens. The screen can be so rough that the image in the photograph is barely recognisable, although the main structure is present. The more information is added, the finer the screen and the clearer the photograph (Figure 1.3).

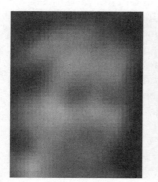

Figure 1.3 Knowledge of the types: coarse and fine screens

Inborn or acquired?

Given the impossibility of control group studies, the question of whether an individual's enneagram type is inborn or acquired may never be answered definitely. There are, however, strong indications that individuals are born with a strong predisposition towards a certain type.

David Daniels quotes Thomas and Chess in his article about nature and nurture.[15] These researchers – who seem to have been unaware of the enneagram – carried out research among children from two months old and followed them in long-term research. They found nine temperaments that could already be distinguished in very young children, with an inter-observer reliability of 90 per cent. Daniels claims in his article that there is a noticeable similarity between these temperaments and the enneagram basic patterns (Table 1.1). Thomas and Chess found nine temperaments that display clear similarities to the enneagram types in children as young as two months, according to Daniels.

Table 1.1 The nine temperaments and the similarities seen by Daniels

Temperaments	Types
Temperament 1. Rhythm and regularity, predictability	Type 1 corrects errors to make life regular and predictable
Temperament 2. Active approach, positive responses to new stimuli	Type 2 approaches others in positive ways
Temperament 3. Level of motoric activity	Type 3 focuses on tasks or goals with high activity and go-ahead energy
Temperament 4. Quality of moods, the amount of positive and negative emotional behaviour	Type 4 longs for heartfelt connection with intense feelings and changing moods
Temperament 5. Threshold of responsiveness, the intensity level of stimulation necessary to evoke a discernible response	Type 5 being highly sensitive to stimuli, detaches himself in order to observe
Temperament 6. Maintaining attention, even in the face of obstacles, vigilance	Type 6 is always aware of what can go wrong; vigilance demands persistence in attention
Temperament 7. Ability to adapt, reactions are modified in desired directions	Type 7 bears in mind multiple options and possibilities, showing changeability and ease in shifting to desired directions
Temperament 8. Intensity of reaction, the energy level of response irrespective of its quality or direction	Type 8 aims at power and control and has a high energy level
Temperament 9. Measure to which someone allows himself to be distracted	Type 9's responsiveness to environmental stimuli alters the direction of ongoing behaviour; attention is attracted by environmental claims and he accommodates himself easily to them.

Furthermore, some authors detect similarities in childhood stories told by adults with the same type. There might be several possible reasons for this. Firstly, children with different dispositions elicit different behaviour from their parents. Thus a boy who is shy, timid and introverted may be encouraged by his parents to take bold steps and stand up for himself, while his very assertive sister is told by the same parents that she cannot always be in the foreground, that she must listen, and that children who demand things are passed over.

Secondly, these stories come from the mouths of the 'victims' themselves. It is what they have seen through their 'spectacles' of perception. And every type has a specific way of interpreting the world. The timorous child just mentioned perhaps found his parents too severe, while his assertive sister who was constantly reproved had no problems with the same parents. Anyhow, she usually succeeded in getting her own way. Parents who were intimidating for a Type 6 could have been too weak for a Type 8, and not in a position to offer protection. Childhood stories do not reflect the objective reality. They reproduce the experiences of that reality just as the people concerned remember them after a number of years. The memories are conditioned by their frames of reference. And there may even be confusion about what happened and what did not. (Did mother go skating with us then? Was Uncle Pete there at father's birthday when the big row broke out? Did the youngest child get a bigger present than the older ones?) This can lead to violent disagreement among the members of the same family.

Listening to the childhood stories of people with the same type, one often hears contradictory tales. Thus one Type 5 (a type that wants to guard both physical and mental space more than most) says that he had to become a Type 5 because his parents tried to deprive him of private space, imposed themselves on him, and constantly wished to share their own and his feelings. Another person may say that she became a Type 5 because her parents were so distant, cool and uninterested. One Type 1 (the perfectionist type) thinks he became a Type 1 because his parents expressed their love by being highly critical; another because her parents were so good, loving, acquiescent and warm that she became convinced that she could never be good enough.

Whole libraries of books have been written about the influence of the environment on a child's development. The key question in these books is whether the child develops healthily or not. We could claim, in accordance with Daniels, that there are strong indications that the type is inborn, and that the degree to which someone tends towards the healthily developed or the pathological variant of his type (see Chapters 6–9) is partly determined by upbringing.

Differences among authors

Reading more books about the enneagram, one will notice that the authors are not always unanimous. There are various reasons for this. Authors, too, cannot avoid wearing the 'spectacles' of their own types. This means that they emphasise certain aspects at the expense of others. When I write that there are thousands of variants of the same type, this is typical of the kind of contribution that my type, Type 9, has to make to the discussion. Type 9 is the queen of nuance! Thus a book by a Type 1 author, who has perfection-ist traits, looks different from one by a Type 7 author, who wants it first and foremost to be interesting, pleasant or inspiring. If other people were now to say 'Oh, typical Type 9, 1 or 7!', and in so doing push aside the line of approach in question, they would be wrong. Every type enlarges, as it were, a ninth part of reality, and thus has a specific contribution to make to the discussion.

The second reason for the differences among the various authors is that some base their assertions as much as possible on factual observation, while others prefer to describe a well-integrated system. Sadly, reality does not always correspond with such a premeditated system.

The third reason why authors differ from each other is that every system description is a reduction of an endlessly complex reality. In a sense, every description is a projection of a multi-dimensional reality on a flat surface. According to one story, the Flatland people saw a sphere as a circle. When a sphere passed their flat surface they saw a growing and then a shrinking circle, which finally disappeared in a point. I had a vision one night of a multi-coloured, multi-dimensional kind of enneagram that rolled through space and time. I could only see half of it. It was the enneagram, but it was different and somehow more than the enneagram. The familiar flat ennea-gram logo was only a pale reflection of it.

Every author describes a personal projection of the original. This can be compared with the maps that are made of the world. These are created with the help of different projection systems (Figure 1.4). In the sixteenth century the Flemish cartographer Mercator used the so-called 'cylinder projection'. On his maps the most northerly territories were dispropor-tionately large, but fidelity to nature was sacrificed for the convenience of seamen: on these charts the course of a ship could be plotted in a straight line.[16] In the ninth century the mathematical geographer Habash al-Hasib placed Mecca in the centre of a map intended to indicate as accurately as possible anyone's direction to, and distance from, this centre of the Islamic

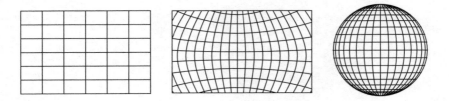

Figure 1.4 Same reality, different projections

world. This was important for establishing the direction of daily prayer, and for making the pilgrimage that every Muslim is expected to make at least once in his life.[17] Present-day atlases try to depict the form and scale of surfaces as accurately as possible. One projection may approach the original somewhat better than another, but they remain maps. The map is not the country.

So is it too with enneagram books. They are written with different purposes. All descriptions point to the same reality, but they are not that reality. Books about the enneagram help to sharpen human observation. It is of little value to argue about the different projections of different enneagram authors. It is better to use the various projections to come closer to reality.

CHAPTER 2

The Enneagram in Organisations

The enneagram can be used in situations which involve personal behaviour and inter-personal interaction. The enneagram is a diagnostic instrument. When we want to do something with the knowledge acquired in this way, we also need a toolbox with such a diagnostic instrument. A great many exercises for the 'self-developer' are described in Chapter 17. Furthermore, the enneagram is used in professional areas like education and training, consultancy work, coaching, psychotherapy and spiritual guidance, all professional areas which have such a development toolbox available. This chapter describes various application areas. After this, we shall consider how misuse of the enneagram may be prevented.

Application areas in organisations

The enneagram can be used widely in organisations. (In this connection, it does not matter if an organisation is profit-making or otherwise – the enneagram can be used to increase performance capacity in either.) Application areas in organisations include human resource management (HRM), general management, consultancy and coaching. In the field of HRM the enneagram can be used to strengthen the self-management capacity and personal development of staff, as well as being valuable in the frameworks of career development, recruitment and selection, education and training. In general management, it is relevant to such subjects as leadership style and assessment, matching leadership and coaching methods to employees' personalities and motivations, coaching, team formation, issues surrounding team-building and co-operation, change processes, time management and negotiation methods. To a great extent, consultants encounter the same subjects in advising and coaching, but (of course) in the roles of consultant or coach rather than of manager.

Here we shall address the following subjects:

- self-management
- career
- selection
- education and training
- leadership
- coaching by executives and supervisors
- team-building and co-operation
- change processes
- time management
- negotiation strategy
- consultancy and coaching by professionals.

Self-management

Self-management demands self-knowledge – otherwise one might better speak of an unguided missile than of someone who manages or directs himself. Chapter 1 has already indicated that someone who is not aware of his type is governed by that type, instead of him managing it himself. Self-management requires knowledge of one's own type mechanisms, a capacity to stand back from these mechanisms, and the will to look at reality through other than the type's characteristic 'spectacles'. This is one of the two core themes in working with the enneagram (the other being social intelligence). Part IV explains in detail how self-management can be strengthened further with the help of the enneagram.

Career

The enneagram type says something both about the qualities someone develops from nature and about those that might be developed in the course of a career. It says nothing, however, about a person's will to develop potential qualities and use them for an organisation's benefit. Some people will want to concentrate on building further on their strengths; others, however, will choose to bring their 'weaker' sides into development. This is a personal choice; people will look for a career that fits that choice. The enneagram helps in making choices about a career because people can use it to gain more insight into their qualities and points of development, and into their career motives.

The enneagram also provides insight into the way in which people deal with the choice process in relation to their careers. Thus someone might find it difficult, for instance, to make a decision about the next step in their career, or notice that they continually find themselves in the same undesirable situations. The enneagram can throw light on the reasons for this and so contribute to a wiser choice.

Yet another career move?

Carlo cannot decide whether or not he should change his job. Actually he is no longer content in his present role, but then he is not a youngster anymore and taking another major step at this stage ... He can't decide, and goes to a career consultant. From the typing interview it transpires that he has Type 9. It now becomes clear that many choices are open to him, and that there is something to be said for all of them; in fact, this is a characteristic of Type 9. No wonder he cannot reach a decision! And he certainly belongs with those Type 9s who set great store by comfort. A change involving a great element of risk, he feels, would threaten that comfort too much.

The question is now whether Carlo wants to develop himself in this respect, or wants to act on the basis of his type. In the first case the career consultant goes to work with him on the making of choices, and on addressing things that make him uncomfortable. If Carlo wants to act on the basis of his type, however, then the career consultant will talk with him about minor improvements in his present situation and about safe possibilities for changing to other work that is not too remote from his present job. The choice is Carlo's.

Selection

When managers hear about the enneagram they often want to know what types one must select for performing particular functions. In principle every type can do everything, but different types will perform a given task in different ways. In selection processes, the question of somebody's specific type is less important than the question of whether he has developed himself in his type. A person who has done so will not allow himself to be controlled completely by automatic behaviour patterns. Certainly this will be true for people-oriented functions (for instance leadership, training, consultancy). Someone who has developed himself in his type will fall less readily into automatic behaviour, will be better equipped to put an individual way of seeing things into perspective, will attune more easily to other types, and will be sooner able to choose a strategy in a particular situation that is attuned to the needs of the moment. In other words, someone who has developed himself in his type will be, in most cases, more effective.

Education and training

In education and training the enneagram is particularly relevant for learning and teaching styles, and also for learning motivation. Thus a teacher with Type 7 will find the teaching process interesting in itself, while a trainer with Type 3 will want above all to produce results. On a videotape on which teachers of different types explain how they give lessons, the teacher with

Type 3 talks with great enthusiasm about his lessons, yet the word 'student' does not appear in the whole story. A teacher with Type 5 wants to analyse the learning material, while a teacher with Type 2 prioritises creating a good atmosphere and building a good relationship with the students. A trainer with Type 4 might want to make every training course a unique event with great depth. Every type has an individual preference with regard to the style of giving lessons.

However, a group of students in a workshop, seminar, course or training programme naturally consists, in most cases, of all sorts of types. For such a group the lessons style must be sufficiently varied to fit in with the diverse learning styles and motivations of the course participants. Different types expect different things from a teacher. The ideal circumstances for learning also vary by type. Thus a Type 1 needs structure and clarity, and also respect. Sometimes it will be necessary for the teacher to make it clear that making mistakes is the best way to learn and will have to divide the lesson material into smaller pieces, each of which leads clearly to its own learning result. A Type 3 needs to learn from experience and needs concrete positive feedback. A Type 8 tends to challenge the leadership and likes action in the lesson. It is wise for a trainer to work with Type 8 interactively while taking care to retain leadership personally. Thus each type needs a different teaching style.

In addition, different types have different learning motivations. Type 3 learns with a goal in sight. For Type 5 interesting ideas must be presented in clear relationship to each other; the student's involvement is conceptual. Type 9 learns better if a subject is of personal significance.

Thus the trainer cannot simply make do with teaching from the standpoint of his own type – the types of the students must be taken into consideration, too.

Leadership

Every type has its own leadership style. A leader can be charmed or impressed by the way in which a colleague leads and decide to adopt that style. This, however, can be a pitfall if that colleague has another enneagram type. By copying that style the manager concerned underestimates the value of his own type and overvalues that of the colleague. With awareness of his own type, the leader will be better able to put his typical qualities to use and can also be more alert to his type's pitfalls and less developed areas.

In the contact with staff members a leader can fall into a similar pitfall, that of regarding one's own type as the norm (and thereby overrating it). The manager then expects the employee to be as much like him as possible and assesses him on this basis. A staff member with another type can only fail in this situation. The challenge, therefore, is to respect staff members in their own types and accept that they will do things in their own style. This need not lead to better or worse results than the chief's style does.

In order to be able to attune to the personalities of staff members one has to take account of what motivates them. Every enneagram type is motivated in a personal way and by specific circumstances. Someone with Type 5 likes to stand alone, wants to be valued for his analytical, intellectual contributions, and likes to make observations. An employee with Type 2 wants to do things with people, needs personal attention and is demotivated by solo tasks. A colleague with Type 7 wants many options, does not conform easily with rules and procedures, and wants to associate with authoritative figures on the same footing: this person needs space. But someone with Type 6 needs structure and clear leadership without pretensions. In short, every type has an individual 'handle'; thus every type demands an individual approach. On the other hand, there is also an individual mechanism for antagonising every type very rapidly! Insight into these mechanisms increases the effectiveness of leadership.

Coaching by leaders

When coaching staff members, it is important to consider both short- and long-term outcomes. In the short term one can speak of *first-order learning*. The manager in his role as coach will help an employee to learn to recognise their own type characteristics. The emphasis here lies on acquiring skills. Staff members learn skills that compensate for their typical pitfalls and learn to co-operate better with colleagues with other enneagram types. In the longer term, the worker acquires a picture of people's underlying motivations. A staff member with Type 3 becomes more and more aware that he never does anything without serious consideration of how it affects others' views of him. A colleague with Type 2 begins to recognise the aspirations behind his helpfulness. Second-order learning – investigating the underlying patterns and standing back from them – then comes in view.

In coaching, of course, the types of the coach and the person being coached both play a role. The coach has to take his own qualities and pitfalls into account, as well as considering the most effective way of working with the person being coached. More about this in Part IV.

Team-building and co-operation

When we work with the enneagram on team-building and co-operation questions, there is an exchange of information about everyone's typical qualities and pitfalls, and the individual development points of everyone involved. Generally this leads to greater mutual acceptance. Thereafter there will be general discussion about what approach each individual colleague needs, and is in a position to provide.

Personal relationship or detachment?

Tania (Type 4) complains that she has no real personal relationship with her boss, Ivan (Type 5). Ivan does not really want any 'personal' element to enter his working relationships, he does not have that many feelings and he certainly does not want to talk about them. He cannot offer Tania what she would like. But now that the subject has come up anyway, it troubles him a good deal that Tania walks in at every odd moment and seems to want something from him. After both have informed each other of their types they can, with a greater chance of success, talk out which form of co-operation is workable for them both. Ivan will make a fixed amount of time available for Tania in which they will not talk exclusively about work, and Tania will no longer walk in on Ivan every other moment.

Ruth Benedict said it of cultures, and we can say the same of enneagram types: 'A pig will never become a hippopotamus.'[1] It is of little use investing a lot of energy in unattainable wishes regarding the behaviour of others: the enneagram helps people to work with each other in a realistic manner. In this way, pleasure in co-operation increases and this also yields more in terms of results. In a team session it can be considered how team members might support each other in their individual development. Thus Tania could become Ivan's coach in talking about feelings – or at least if he asks for that. And Ivan could help Tania to concentrate her attention more on the here and now – if indeed she asks him to.

A team's work with the enneagram can be coupled with its work on a given task. For example, a team wanted to achieve more within the context of the political climate in the organisation. In considering this aim, there was both a co-operation component (how they got on together) and a change-strategy component. After co-operation had been improved with the help of the enneagram, we discussed possible strategies for change. At this point, the roles that individuals might fulfil in this process – and, in particular, what the various team members wanted to learn in this context – came onto the agenda. At the same time, the team members' enneagram types returned to the picture. Another example was developing a vision together as a team and putting it into practice. In what follows, the enneagram is applied in a conflict situation.

The controlling chief

A department calls in the help of a consultant. The staff members have been on the verge of beginning an action to get rid of their new boss, but eventually decide this would be going too far. They complain that the new boss imposes himself on them far too much, that they are given no responsibility, that management is concerned too much with details, and that they are treated like infants. People feel they are not taken seriously and are angry and hurt. The boss's first story is that the staff members were not used to being managed under the previous regime, that they are not used to working hard and that there are a few notorious troublemakers who stir up the rest. The boss feels that he has never had an honest chance; people were already against him before he was there, and naturally he feels hurt by this.

Staff members and boss agree to try and discover more workable relationships in a few team-building sessions. The types of the team members are determined in typing interviews. The boss, Pete, turns out to have Type 6: his management of details arises from his need to prevent anything going wrong. Jack, with Type 7, who wants most of all to deal with his superiors on an equal footing, and Jacqueline (Type 9), who feels unnoticed, are troubled most by this. Pete works very analytically and concentrates on the content of his work. Ernest (Type 4) reacts most strongly against this trait. He misses emotional contact with his chief, which he needs. Fatima (Type 5) does not like this aspect of Pete's behaviour either. She thinks she produces much better analyses on her own, and regards the boss's continual interventions as an unacceptable intrusion into her own territory.

After the members of this team have informed each other of their personality types, and everyone has told the others what he or she – on the basis of his or her own type – requires from the others, the discussion starts again. There is now greater mutual understanding. This makes it possible to negotiate about the way people will communicate with one another in the future. 'Negotiate' because, at the end of the day, a number of wishes do not fit in with what the boss himself is able to concede. Thus the wish that the boss follows a completely *laissez-faire* management policy is unrealistic. He is just 'not the type' for that; furthermore, such a great measure of freedom in the given situation of the department is certainly not desirable. However, the group discusses how Pete can create sufficient certainty for himself without trying to control everything, and various options for allowing this are found. The division of work is adapted slightly: more will be invested in clear agreements before projects begin, instead of Pete maintaining direct control during the work itself, and staff members will provide feedback during weekly meetings. This framework should be sufficient. *En passant*, staff members are able to clear up some friction amongst themselves. Regular evaluation must keep the process going. Besides this, Pete begins a personal coaching course in order to recognise better and overcome his own pitfalls.

With regard to the composition of teams, it must be stated clearly that no ideal team formation exists in terms of the enneagram. Furthermore, when assembling a team the team members' development levels are more important than their types. What is true in general terms, however, is that a team that is too one-sided will be less effective. Think, for instance, of the possible consequences of building a team wholly from undeveloped Type 7s (evasion of problems; presenting negative matters positively; attention directed primarily at interesting possibilities in the future and not at taking action) or Type 4s (attention for the negative sides of what is present and the positive sides of what is absent; individuals wanting to be different from others)!

A team which includes one representative of each type might seem ideal, but this is only the case if the team members can step sufficiently far back from their own types and are capable of accepting the types of other team members – otherwise they will inevitably create a variant of Sartre's 'L'Enfer, c'est les autres' [Hell, that is other people].[2]

In addition a team's membership always reflects the specific task with which it is charged. For different tasks different qualities are needed. Thus there can never be a question of one ideal team composition.

Change processes

The success of a change process stands or falls by the degree to which the management succeeds in motivating staff members and either preventing or managing any resistance. Every type deals in its own way with changes. Someone with Type 6 will reflect on everything that could go wrong and ask if the management has any hidden agendas. A Type 7 will throw himself enthusiastically into all the new possibilities that are now going to be created but can get lost in this. Someone with Type 8 can organise the various initiatives necessary for the planned change, and in so doing makes use of personal power. A Type 9 must first get used to the idea for a while before they can participate positively: inner resistance arises in response to being made to hurry in the course of the change. In short, each type demands an individual approach. With knowledge of the enneagram, a professional can anticipate better what clients, colleagues and staff members need to allow a change process to proceed smoothly.

Change process

Project leader Pim, with Type 3, is amazed that there are people who say to his face that they agree with the direction the organisation is taking and then send e-mails round behind his back saying the reorganisation is taking a wrong turn. Not only does it amaze him, it makes him furious. He'll tell them what he thinks of them! At least, that is his first, impulsive, reaction when he hears about their actions.

Yet throwing out the pair of staff members that did this would have still more negative effects on the current change process: in spite of everything, they hold key positions and it would certainly create the wrong impression with other staff. If he wants to achieve what he has planned he needs to have them on board. That is why he agrees to a meeting. It turns out that Clara (Type 7) thinks there is far too little room for individual's contribution. The train rushes on, so to speak, and soon she will end up in a situation with far too few possibilities for her to enjoy her work any more. She assumes that everyone will find the new situation just as bad as she does herself. And Bert (Type 9) is angry that he is never asked anything. He assumes that everyone who is not involved will sabotage the change.

Pim comes to the conclusion that his own strong orientation towards results remains sound, but that he will have to give Clara and Bert more of a say in how the reorganisation is tackled. At the same time he agrees to a general interim evaluation. The feelings of Clara and Bert may not apply for all types. He would like to know how things lie in a wider perspective.

Time management

Every type has individual weaknesses in the field of time management. Thus, Types 1, 6 and 9 all have problems with making decisions, but for different reasons. For Type 1 the proposition calling for action is not yet perfect; Type 6 thinks of everything that can go wrong; Type 9 sees so many sides to every alternative that it becomes difficult to choose between them. Persuading these types to make a decision therefore requires three different approaches. Finishing something is a problem for (for instance) Types 6 and 7: for Type 7 because there are always so many other interesting projects on the horizon; for Type 6 because success brings with it the risk of being attacked.

Other different types (for example, Types 3, 7 and 9) have a tendency to take too much on their plates, but with different motives. You've guessed it already – each requires a different approach. The subject of time management also underlines the fact that every type needs to be handled differently.[2]

Handling conflict, mediation, negotiation

The types diverge somewhat over the question of what constitutes a conflict. What Type 9 calls a conflict is a discussion for Type 8. Thus Type 9 can withdraw co-operation because he no longer wants those endless rows and Type 8 honestly does not understand what Type 9 is talking about. 'We've always worked well together, haven't we?' Type 8 just does not have it as a norm that differences of opinion are not allowed; Type 9, however, does lean in that direction. Simple clarification of the typical norms and expectations of the opposing parties can be an enormous help.

In the same way the types have different preferred styles for solving problems – from head-in-the-sand to wielding the blunt implement, from patching things up to the proverbial 'bull in a china shop'. Clarification of this can also lead to greater tolerance. Thus a Type 5 will want to analyse the nature of the problem and leave feelings out of it, while it is precisely the feelings involved that Type 4 wants to explore. Type 7 might let the problem be and start something somewhere else, and Type 1 will try to establish what is right.

Different types call for different negotiation strategies. With Types 2, 3 and 4, for instance, it is crucial that the people concerned do not lose face. With a Type 6 it is extra important not to give the impression that there are still cards up the sleeve, or the colleague becomes suspicious and inflexible. For Type 6, openness and transparency are important. A Type 9 reacts negatively to a sense of being put under pressure. A Type 8, on the other hand, loves a good fight and does not feel bothered by pressure nearly so quickly. Thus every type calls for an individual approach.[3]

Consultancy and coaching by professionals

In consultancy and coaching – and this applies equally to both internal and external consultants – the personal type of the consultant or coach is of first importance. A consultant with Type 8 has a tendency to assume control from the client. A consultant with Type 9 can display so much understanding that he might forget to work on change. A coach with Type 5 may seem uninvolved, while actually analysing the problems well. Each type has individual qualities and pitfalls as consultant or coach, and attuning to the personality of the client also demands attention. In short, the same subjects arise as in management, but in the context of another role. More about this in Part IV.

Preventing misuse

It will be clear from what has been said that the enneagram can be employed in all sorts of ways to improve the interaction among people in organisations. The enneagram, however, can also be misused in a number of ways, and this calls for constant vigilance.[4] For example, someone who does not want to learn and change can misuse the enneagram as an excuse for his attitude. Someone may say: 'Now I know that I have Type X, they will just have to take me as I am. I don't have to change anything, and I am not be blamed for things I cannot do because my behaviour goes with my type.' This kind of position cannot be supported from the standpoint of the enneagram. A Type 9 is not confrontational by nature, but that does not mean that such a person cannot learn to confront people and issues when appropriate. It does cost time and energy to learn it and at the start it will certainly not happen by itself. Thus a Type 5 can also learn to get along with emotional people; a Type 3 can learn to meet a Type 6 halfway with his worries, and so forth.

Conversely, it is also a form of misuse when a professional in an organisation puts people in the 'boxes' of their types – 'fixing' them in their types, as it were. 'You're a Type 5, so ...' As is discussed in Chapter 1, there are countless variations of the same type and people can develop themselves within their types. Knowledge about the enneagram types releases no one from a duty to keep looking keenly at every individual as an individual. What is crucial is appreciating how this specific person represents his or her type, and that this can vary from person to person.

One outright misuse is rigidly coupling certain types with particular tasks. 'Research? Then we have to have a Type 5.' 'Social work? Only a Type 2 will be considered.' 'Facilitating work conferences where conflicts have to be solved? Typical duty for a Type 9.' In principle every type can do anything, or learn everything, and individuals will do this in their own style. But development can also begin within this personal style. Whether someone can actually do something reflects his developmental level within his own type and the skills at his disposal, whether they are natural or consciously learned.

Finally it is important for us to realise that we cannot force people to develop themselves. What the organisation can do, however, is to lay down requirements as regards behaviour. Thus first-order learning with the enneagram can be made a requirement. Up to a certain level that applies also to second-order learning with the enneagram: certainly for some particular functions. It is difficult to imagine a professional consultant without some capacity for self-reflection, but does this also apply to the laboratory worker? Third-order learning can never be enforced; this can only be chosen personally by an individual.

The enneagram is a powerful instrument and it certainly can be used to manipulate people. For the conscientious user, it is therefore of great importance to remember constantly that people's personal boundaries must be respected.

CHAPTER 3

The Enneagram as a Process Description

As well as being used as a personality typology, the enneagram can also be used as a model that describes the steps by which a process takes place. By 'processes', one can think of establishing something, improving or renewing something, developing a vision, promoting new ideas or products, and learning new skills. However, the term can also embrace second- and third-order learning, finding a new job, organisational development, and similar endeavours.

The enneagram as process description represents its oldest application. Digesting this chapter is not necessary for an understanding of Chapter 5 and subsequent chapters, since these are all concerned with the enneagram as a personality typology. The chapter after this one, however – about the history of the enneagram – will be difficult to follow without reading it. In the literature about the history of the enneagram terms connected with the enneagram as process description – such as 'the law of 3' and 'the law of 7' – occur quite often. In this chapter we discuss the enneagram as the description of a process.

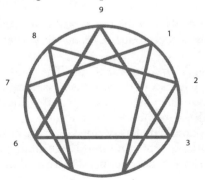

When we use the enneagram as process description each number in the enneagram represents a step in a process. The nine numbers, therefore, are not personality types but steps of a particular character. For example, step 1 is the preparation of the situation itself, step 2 the preliminary consideration of the process involved, and so on. At points 3 and 6 external input is required.

Bennett provides a process example involving the preparation of food:[1]

- *Point 1:* the kitchen must be made suitable for cooking.
- *Point 2:* someone must decide what will be cooked and in what order the activities will be carried out. In order to be able to do this the cook must:
  - Look ahead to Point 4: the preparations for cooking, such as chopping, cutting and cleaning (this is the line 1-4-2 in the enneagram diagram).
  - Look ahead to Point 8, or eating: for how many people does one have to cook, and for which occasion? Do some diners have special diet requirements, and so forth (this is the line 2-8 in the enneagram diagram).
- *Point 3:* the external input, in other words raw materials in the form of purchases from the supermarket.
- *Point 4:* the food is prepared.
- *Point 5:* the food is cooked.

So far the process has taken place in the kitchen. At Point 6 there is new input, however: the diners appear on stage. As a result, Point 6 is also a transformation point – the food acquires another meaning now that there are diners. Before Point 6 materials were processed; now the materials have become a meal. The cook knew that already because he looked forward at the beginning of the process. The process now continues as follows:

- *Point 6:* the diners appear on stage.
- *Point 7:* the meal is served.
- *Point 8:* the meal is consumed.
- *Point 9:* a new cycle begins. After the food has been served the kitchen can be restored to its original condition and made ready for preparing the next meal.

Bennett applies this process description to all kinds of processes: production processes, the creation of beauty in art, and also the development of man and humanity. Piederiet describes the same steps in the outplacement process.[2] In summary:

- *Points 9/0: intention.* The candidate intends to fulfil a responsible role in society by fulfilling a certain function in the labour market. He wishes to work towards a (new) goal.
- *Point 1: orientation towards the process of finding a new job.* The candidate clarifies his situation, specifies his wishes and the various possibilities considered, and describes as fully as possible what he can do and wishes to achieve. He visualises what his qualities might allow him to do.
- *Point 2: starting the self-analysis.* The candidate has decided in favour of outplacement. He has a learning question ('Why am I in this position?'), and a desire that has to be expressed in concrete terms. The candidate writes a self-analysis of his qualities.

- *Point 3: coaching.* The coach supports the candidate and helps him to summarise his past achievements on paper.
- *Point 4: orientation towards authentic personal qualities.* What does the candidate need to be able to start work? He is encouraged to use his imagination: which personal qualities and experiences will be useful and which not? The candidate chooses aims from a number available to him. Obstructive thoughts are identified. The candidate asks 'Who am I?', and begins searching for his authentic self.
- *Point 5: how can I take action?* The candidate starts work with the insights gained from examination of Points 1 to 4. He has to make a realistic choice and, to this end, to match what he has learned in Point 4 with the outside world.
- *Point 6: the outside world.* The candidate considers in real terms what society has to offer him, and examines what he has to offer himself. This point is characterised by thematic networking. The candidate learns to handle his fear and uncertainty. He takes the initiative in facing the outside world. He believes in himself.
- *Point 7: applications.* The candidate applies for work and presents himself to potential employers. He has various possibilities – for instance, starting his own business or taking a salaried job.
- *Point 8: to work!* The candidate knows what he wants. He is fully identified with who he is and what he has to offer. He pursues offers and finally accepts work.
- *Points 9/0: intention.* The candidate intends to fulfil a responsible role in society by fulfilling a certain function in the labour market. He wishes to work towards a (new) goal.

The movement through the diagram from Point 1 to Point 2 represents the actual start of the outplacement process. In order to reach Point 2 the candidate must first think about point 4, because Point 4 tells him who he is in the first place. He can only say this, however, when he knows what Point 8 – the ultimate goal – looks like. The candidate must therefore look ahead to Points 4 and 8.

There is a jump between Points 4 and 5. At Point 5 the wishes of the candidate must be manageable internally and also presentable externally. Up to and including Point 4 there was talk of an inner process; at Point 5, orientation towards the outside world begins. The attitude of the candidate changes with the transition from Point 4 to Point 5.

At Point 6 the candidate actually goes out into the world. His personal changes and qualities then acquire a different meaning.

According to Piederiet, Points 1, 4 and 7 are all of a similar nature, each representing a stage of preparation.

1 = orientation towards the course of outplacement
4 = orientation towards original (authentic) qualities
7 = applications.

Points 2, 5 and 8 are also of a similar nature; they indicate what is happening in the process.

2 = starting the self-investigation
5 = how can I go to work in practice?
8 = being at work.

This example has shown how the enneagram is used as an aid for examining a process closely through consciously paying attention to all nine steps. Bennett and others call this enneagram process a transformation process.[3] Thus food passes from one state to another, for instance, from inedible raw rice to edible cooked rice.

Among other writers, Ouspensky – a pupil of Gurdjieff whose doctrine he described in a more accessible manner than Gurdjieff himself – outlines 'the law of 3' and 'the law of 7'.[4] The 'law of 3' states that in every event three powers play a role: an active expanding renewing power, a passive reflective traditional power, and a third power which brings the first two powers into equilibrium. The active power tries to bring about a change, the passive power offers resistance to this change, while the third power reconciles the two opposing powers. These three powers are represented by the enneagram numbers 3, 6 and 9. This 'law of 3' can also be found in many ancient philo-sophical and spiritual systems, and also in modern philosophy. Thus Hinduism recognises the supreme deities Brahma, the creator, Shiva, the destroyer, and Vishnu, the preserver.[5] The 'tree of life' in the Jewish mystical tradition, the Kabbalah, distinguishes three 'pillars': the active, expanding pillar, the passive, traditional pillar and the central pillar of equilibrium.[6] The Chinese tradition recognises heaven as the active creative force yang, the earth as the passive receptive force yin, with mankind uniting both.[7] Chinese culture also unites Confucianism (a yang philosopy) with Taoism (a yin philosophy).[8] Christianity recognises the values of faith (the higher idea of Type 6), hope (the higher idea of Type 3) and charity (the higher idea of Type 9, which in enneagram literature is usually called love). Such nineteenth-century philosophers as Hegel, Feuerbach, Marx and Engels speak of the dialectic movement of thesis, antithesis, and synthesis.[9]

The 'law of 7' is the process described above. According to Ouspensky, every phenomenon comes about in seven steps. No process in this world proceeds in a straight line: left to itself, it will start to exhibit deviations. Similarly no processes ever take place entirely uninterrupted. At these points of deviation and/or interruption an external 'input' can keep the process lines straight. The process begins at 1; input from without comes at 3 and 6; at 9 the process is complete and a new cycle begins. The 'law of 7' is also known as the law of the octave.[10]

If one divides the number 1 by 7, one gets 0.142857142857 etc. Divide 2 by 7 and we get 0.285714285714 … If we divide 3 by 7 then we get 0.428571428571 … and so on. Behind the decimal point there is the same infinite series of numbers, beginning each time at a different place in the

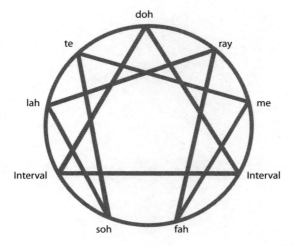

Figure 3.1 The law of the octave

series. This numerical series is the order in which, in the enneagram diagram, the points 1, 2, 4, 5, 7 and 8 are connected with one another by lines. The number 3 and its multiples are missing from this series of numbers. In the enneagram diagram the 'law of 3' and the 'law of 7' are represented as two independent figures: the internal triangle 3-6-9 and the figure formed by the lines 1-4-2-8-5-7-1.

The 'law of 3' therefore describes the relation between the three powers while the 'law of 7' describes transformation processes. The interweaving of the triangle and the lines between the remaining points in the enneagram diagram indicates how the three powers work together to overcome problems in the transformation process. In the outplacement example, this was provided at point 3 by the coach, an active power who helped the candidate maintain his course, and at point 6 the outside world, a passive power in relation to the candidate without which he cannot realise his goal – work.

CHAPTER 4

History of the Enneagram

'The modern manager hyperventilates from one fashion to another', as the Dutch newspaper *NRC Handelsblad* said on one occasion.[1] Is the enneagram also a short-lived craze? If so, it represents fairly old wine in new bottles. Elements of the enneagram were known, at least according to some sources, long before the Christian era. Scholars, however, are not agreed about its precise origins. Not being an archaeologist, I cannot participate in this discussion. What I find more important than the question of whether the enneagram originated 2500 years before Christ, or 1000 years after, is whether we can work with it now in our organisations.

In training courses I am regularly asked about the origins of the enneagram. The summary that follows here is included in response to this interest.

Earliest traces

The origin of the enneagram is shrouded in mystery to some extent. According to Gurdjieff – about whom more shortly – the theory of numbers, along with the 'law of 3' and the 'law of 7' which we discussed in Chapter 3, had its origin in 'Chaldea', a province of Babylon in Mesopotamia, about 4500 years ago.[2] Unfortunately, Gurdjieff was not clear about his sources. This dating does not correspond with the usual dating of Chaldea by present-day historians, who place this name only around 1250 BC.[3] As an indication for the area of south-west Babylon it would therefore be an anachronism, at least in the view of these scholars. Furthermore, according the Jesuit Brother Mitchell Pacwa, Professor of Holy Writ and Hebrew at the Loyola University in Chicago, there is no hard evidence of the enneagram in any form before Gurdjieff.[4] Pacwa bases this view on his studies of old literature and archaeology.

If Gurdjieff were still alive, undoubtedly he would have countered this by saying that the enneagram was a manifestation of an esoteric science and that he had had access to secret sources. In fact, he devoted a great deal of his life to searching out sources of this kind.

Be that as it may, the theory of numbers, according to Gurdjieff, was the work of a group of spiritual masters known as the Sarmoeng Brotherhood. Nygaard confines himself to saying that the oldest traces of the enneagram are probably to be found in Mesopotamia.[5]

The Greek thinker Pythagoras (sixth century BC), who according to tradition was the first to prove the famous mathematical proposition which bears his name, rediscovered this science and is thus often regarded as the discoverer of the enneagram. In Pythagoras' work, however, the connection between the 'law of 3' and the 'law of 7' was not made, whereas it was known to the Babylonians.[6] Yet it seems likely that Pythagoras had acquired his knowledge in Mesopotamia.

From the Greek philosopher Plato (fourth century BC) comes the well-known 'parable of the cave'.[7]

Plato's cave

A number of people live in an cave with an opening towards the daylight. They are bound in such a way that they can only look straight in front of them, with their backs to the opening: they have never looked directly into the daylight which enters. Behind and above them burns a fire; in front of the fire is a little wall. People carry all sorts of objects along the path between the fire and the wall which stick up behind the wall, throwing shadows on the cavern wall which the inhabitants can see directly before them. The bound inhabitants therefore only ever see the shadows of objects on the cave wall – that is their reality. If one of them were to be released and had to turn round and walk towards the light, all of these acts would be disturbing to them. Because of the brightness of the incoming light they would not be able to see the objects which until then had been perceived only as shadows. Being forced to look directly into the incoming light would hurt the eyes of the cave-dweller, who would rather look at things he could actually distinguish. Being taken outside would result in complete blindness. Only after a process of adjustment would he gradually be able to see things in the world outside the cave. If the cave-dweller were now to return to his old home, he would not at first be able to see. His previous companions would say that the trip outside had damaged his eyes. None of them would believe that a trip outside would be worthwhile.

According to Plato, the cave may be compared to the world perceptible through the senses; the trip outside symbolises the psyche's ascent to the world of thought, the so-called world of ideas. The enneagram of fixations can be compared to the cave. Everyone believes in the reality of their own images and projections. The real world outside corresponds, in this analogy, to the concept of the enneagram of higher virtues and ideas.

The desert fathers

Grün, a Benedictine who studied business economy as well as theology and philosophy, describes how from around 300 AD a number of monks – the so-called desert fathers – withdrew to the desert to live as ascetics and to fast. In this life, they made use of practices from various religious movements and philosophical trends.[8] They investigated their own thoughts and emotions, and discussed these when they met on Sundays with their spiritual father. In the second half of the fourth century their various pronouncements were gathered in book form by the early Christian theologian and mystic Evagrius Ponticus. The Greek philosophy of the time recognised three areas in man: the areas of physical desire, of the emotions, and of the soul. Evagrius placed three *logismoi* in each of these three domains. Grün states that these nine logismoi were emotionally loaded thoughts that ruled people: passions of the soul, or motivations with which they had to learn to live.

Seven of these passions identified by the monks have survived through history as the Seven Deadly Sins of Christianity: pride, covetousness, lust, envy, gluttony, anger and sloth. These passions disturbed the monks in their prayers and meditations, and so stood in the way of the contact with God that they sought. Two passions disappeared in the course of church history: vanity was equated with pride, while fear, as the fear of God, came to be seen not as a sin but as a virtue. The logismoi described by Evagrius correspond to the motivating energies of the various enneagram types that will be discussed in Chapters 7–9 inclusive.

These three human domains – the areas of physical desire, of the emotions and of the soul – correspond to the three centres discussed in Chapter 5. They may also be found in Sufism (a mystical movement in Islam), in the Jewish Kabbalistic tradition and in Hinduism. These traditions, and also Buddhism, share the view that man is blinded by his emotions and passions leading to separation from his essence, from his origin, from God.

In short, it is clear that similar concepts about the way people function and the anatomy of reality have recurred in different places and at different times.

Gurdjieff

It is not easy to characterise George Ivanovich Gurdjieff (Alexandropol 1877?–Neuilly 1949) in one word or sentence. Was he a mystic? A great teacher? A psychologist before his time? An adventurer? A musician? What is certain is that he inspired many people.

Much about his life is unknown, but various accounts of parts of his life (all by himself) have been circulated. It is assumed that he was born of Armenian and Ionic Greek parents in Alexandropol in Russian Transcaucasia (present-day Georgia), near the Persian border. The year of his birth has been reported to be 1877[9] but also as 1866.[10] In the course of his life he assumed various nationalities. In his younger years he undertook adventurous journeys in search of ancient sources of knowledge which he believed must exist, preserved in old documents and particular communities. He sought, in his own words, the Truth. Around the time of the outbreak of the First World War he began to disseminate the knowledge he had acquired in Moscow and St Petersburg. This knowledge included the enneagram. He fled from St Petersburg in 1917, first over the Caucasus to Tiflis and finally in 1922 to Paris. There he settled in the priory at Fontainebleau-Avon. From France he undertook a few journeys to the United States. In this way Gurdjieff brought the basic ideas of the enneagram to the West.

Gurdjieff claimed he had acquired these ideas in the principal monastery of a community he called the Sarmoeng Brotherhood, and in so doing suggested a continuity between the Sarmoeng Brotherhood in the Chaldea of 4500 years ago and the inhabitants of this monastery. Gurdjieff describes in his book *Meetings With Remarkable Men* how he was brought there blindfolded on a horse.[11] No one has ever been able to locate this monastery. Various writers point out that Gurdjieff wanted above all to teach, and was less concerned with producing historically accurate descriptions.[12] It is also clear from what Gurdjieff wrote about himself that he regarded his higher goal as more important than fidelity to facts. Thus he tells how, when he was in need of money, he painted sparrows and sold them as rare coloured canaries, after which he quickly left the place concerned before it began to rain. He found it quite acceptable to distort the truth because he needed money to enable him to continue his travels in search of the Truth.

As well as the Sarmoeng Brotherhood, Gurdjieff in later life cited esoteric Christianity from the Greek Orthodox tradition as the source of the enneagram. This is not improbable, for it seems that all the basic elements of Gurdjieff's system occur in this tradition.[13] Gurdjieff's enneagram figure also appears in it. According to this Greek tradition it is based on three fundamental elements: the circle as symbol of Eternity, the 'law of 3' as symbol of creation and the 'law of 7' as symbol of action.

Despite all of this, there are clear similarities between Gurdjieff's teaching and the Sufi enneagram.[14] The Sufi order Naqshbandi-Haqqani claims that Gurdjieff learned the enneagram from them: Sheik Hisham Kabbani, the leader of this order, claimed this at a conference of the International Enneagram Association in 1997. Some, however, do not exclude the possibility that exactly the opposite happened: namely, that the Naqshbandi learned the enneagram from Gurdjieff. What is certain is that there are great similarities but also differences between the standpoints of the Naqshbandi and Gurdjieff (see Chapter 11).

Thus it is unclear from whom Gurdjieff obtained his knowledge of the enneagram, and exactly who influenced whom. Perhaps historians will eventually discover the true sequence of events. But it is certainly true that the same concepts crop up in many traditions.

Ichazo

Oscar Ichazo, a teacher from Bolivia who began teaching in the United States in the 1970s, studied the doctrine of Gurdjieff in later life, but claimed he had acquired his knowledge of the enneagram earlier and from elsewhere. While still young he became a member of an esoteric group which found its sources in the Kabbalah (the mystic branch of the Jewish tradition), Sufism (the mystic branch of Islam) and in Zen, a Buddhist meditation technique and way of life.[15]

Ichazo says he encountered the enneagram figure in an old medieval text under the name 'the Chaldean seal'.[16] This text has not been found by others, however, according to Nygaard.[17] The name 'seal' is highly meaningful here. On one hand a seal closes something: a sealed house cannot be entered. The enneagram figure represents knowledge that is not freely accessible. On the other hand, to gain entry to the house one has to break the seal. When the secrets of the enneagram figure are unveiled this knowledge becomes available. What is concerned here is not the enneagram figure of Gurdjieff but a circle with, inside it, three equilateral triangles. As well as this medieval manuscript, Ichazo also referred to the books of the Catalan philosopher and Christian mystic Ramon Llull (also known as Raimundus Lullus, 1235–1316) as a source for the Chaldean seal.[18] Llull's method Ars Generalis rested on the nine properties or names of God, on which both Islamic and Jewish mystics meditate (see Chapter 11 for further information).[19] According to Roos, both the Naqshbandi (whom Gurdjieff probably emulated) and Llull (followed by Ichazo, among others) trace their roots back to a secret society established around 950, 'the pure brothers of Basra', who developed a universal system based on Greek, Persian, Chinese and Indian influences, the foundation of which was the number nine.[20] Their enneagram figures consisted of a circle with three equilateral triangles inside it (the figure of the Chaldean seal which we shall encounter again in Chapter 6) and a circle in which the nine points were connected with each other in every conceivable manner (Figure 4.1).

Besides Gurdjieff's enneagram figure and Llull's enneagrams, Ichazo used a number of other enneagram figures. He was the first to speak explicitly about 'personality types' and 'fixations', 'passions' and 'holy ideas' in the way that these terms are still used in the context of the enneagram. Like Gurdjieff, his aim in working with the enneagram was spiritual development. He used exercises from various spiritual traditions to develop Gurdjieff's three intelligence centres, which correspond to the three domains of the desert fathers. Ichazo is the founder of the Arica school, which still exists today.[21]

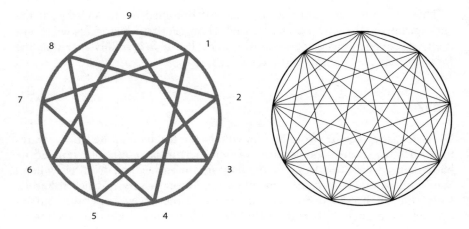

Figure 4.1 Ramon Llull's enneagram figures

Naranjo and his pupils

Various pupils of Ichazo continue to develop his teaching. The enneagram of personality types was further developed by (among others) Naranjo, a psychiatrist of Chilean origin who later moved to California. He established the connection between the enneagram and modern psychological thinking. He coupled the various types with known psycho-pathological states (for example, narcissist, paranoiac, masochistic and compulsive)[22] and with the various defence mechanisms such as projection, rationalisation and denial.[23] In this way the enneagram entered the frame of reference of modern psychology. Naranjo and his American pupils spread knowledge of the enneagram, initially in the United States. One of his pupils, Kathleen Speeth, gave workshops for many years. The Jesuit Robert Ochs taught his version of the material at the Loyola University in Chicago, whence it quickly found its way into the worldwide missionary network, mainly by word of mouth. The author Helen Palmer gave workshops, trained students at Kennedy University and wrote books on the subject. After she participated in the workshops of Naranjo in 1971, she developed an approach aimed at developing the higher aspects of the types by means of attention exercises. Together with David Daniels, a professor at Stanford University, she developed the 'Enneagram Professional Training Program', in which I and many others received our training in the enneagram.

These people and many others (for example, Riso and Hudson,[24] Hurley and Donson,[25] and Rohr and Ebert[26]) played an important role in spreading the enneagram to a wider audience. In this way the enneagram left the area of esoteric learning and this knowledge became available for everyone, both on paper and through training.

The enneagram has thus steadily come to reach a wider public in recent decades. Publicity, however, is not the same as understanding – books in

Chinese, Arabic or Sanskrit may indeed be public, but not everyone can read them. The old Kabbalists wrote 'for those who understand' with good reason. I remember reading, around 25 years ago, a little book by Rudolf Steiner, the founder of anthroposophy, with the title *Wie erlangt man Erkenntnisse der höheren Welten?* [How does one attain consciousness of higher spheres?] The first part was a feast of recognition: what I read corresponded with my own experience. After that, however, I no longer understood the text. This was not Steiner's fault, but mine. Several times since, I have also been unable to finish a book at first encounter but have been able to read it again a few years later as easily as I could a novel. That is just how it is, irritating or not. One has to have a command of certain basic material before being able to understand more advanced content. People can absorb information only when they are ready for it in terms of their development, just as a child can learn to write well only if the fine motoric system is sufficiently well developed. The enneagram is a system that can be understood at various levels.

The present situation

At present there are many schools and many pupils devoting themselves to the enneagram. We may recognise the following general fourfold division:

- the school of Gurdjieff
- the school of Ichazo
- the school of Naranjo
- the school of the Sufis.

Gurdjieff used the enneagram as a means of developing higher consciousness. Within the school of Gurdjieff we must consider people like Bennett (mentioned in Chapter 3) who use the enneagram as process description. Similarly, the school of Ichazo is aimed at attaining higher consciousness but using a different method from Gurdjieff's. In the school of Naranjo the enneagram retains its spiritual meaning, but with emphasis on its value as a psychological instrument. The enneagram is most easily applicable in daily practice within the framework of this school, although Gurdjieff and Ichazo naturally also strove for applicability. In fact, one can hardly imagine a spiritual education system that does not have implications for day-to-day practice. Sufism also aims at serving a spiritual goal with the enneagram, regarding it not as a classification system for personality types but as a series of tendencies in every person (see Chapter 11).

This book should be regarded as belonging within the school of Naranjo.

Part

II

The Types

The nine personality types of the enneagram are grouped in three centres: heart, head and belly. It is actually more correct to say that there are three centres, each of which contains three types, as stated by Evagrius Ponticus and recounted in the previous chapter.

Chapter 5 is concerned first and foremost with the nature and importance of the centres. Thereafter in Chapter 6 the framework used for detailed discussion of the separate types is explained: which aspects are characteristic for a type, why people of one and the same type can differ, and so forth.

Then it is the turn of the types themselves: the three *heart* types in Chapter 7, the three *head* types in Chapter 8 and the three *belly* types in Chapter 9.

In Part III of the book the philosophical background needed to be able to work with the enneagram is explained. Finally, Part IV discusses how one can determine one's own type, and goes deeper into the professional application of the enneagram.

CHAPTER 5

The Centres

Before explaining in Chapter 6 the framework used for detailed discussion of the separate types, we must consider the nature and function of the centres themselves. Subsequently the heart types (Types 2, 3 and 4) are described in Chapter 7, the head types (Types 5, 6 and 7) in Chapter 8, and the belly types (Types 8, 9 and 1) in Chapter 9.

Importance of the centres

In following Gurdjieff, Ouspensky divided people into seven categories.[1] The first three categories included people in whom one of the three centres dominated: the *active centre* (belly), the *emotional centre* (heart) or the *intellectual centre* (head). The fourth element in Ouspensky's vision was not an inborn property but was the product of training; his centres are in equilibrium.[2] (Ouspensky's three remaining categories represent further stages of development.)

In her book *Inner Knowing*, the American author Helen Palmer describes as highways to higher consciousness the development of the intuitive faculty, the path of the mind (meaning here meditation and attention exercises), the wisdom of the body and the knowing of the heart.[3] The three centres correspond to three development roads. The fourth road, about which Ouspensky writes, is the development of all three centres in equilibrium and in daily work and life.[4]

The three development roads and the fourth road all lead to higher levels of consciousness. We might also say they culminate in disidentification with the type, a 360 degree perspective, more contact with the real self and better-developed intuition.

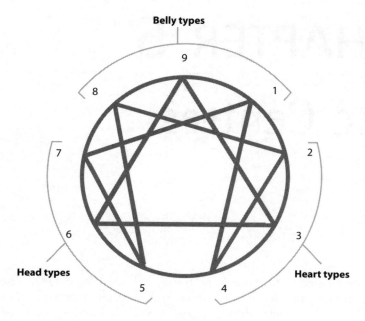

Figure 5.1 Head, heart and belly types

For every individual, irrespective of type, it is important that all centres function well. In our society, however, the various centres are not utilised properly to an equal degree.

In the Western educational tradition (both at home and at school) much attention is paid to the head centre: children have to think logically and rationally, they have to be able to reduce problems to causes, and they have to be able to think of answers to problems that really resolve them. Such skills are all related to the left half of the brain; in general, less attention is paid to the right half. While it is true that fantasy, imaginative power and intuition (also head-centre functions) are valued highly in some circles, this is far from universal.

The belly centre also receives plenty of attention in Western society. It is expected that people should be vigorous and healthy, with a healthy desire to expand.

The heart centre, by contrast, comes off relatively badly in our organisations. Both Gurdjieff and Jung, however, were of the opinion that the continued existence of humanity depended on its development.[5] The heart centre is also the centre that connects the head and belly.

In a person who functions optimally, all centres function well and in mutual balance. In practice, however, this seldom happens. 'Normal' people like you and I always have a certain imbalance in the functioning of their centres. Hurley and Donson, and also Riso and Hudson, point out that people at the level of type fixations do not use any of their centres well: some centres are less developed than others, and the centre of the type group to which the person belongs is used wrongly.[6]

Nature of the centres

Every centres has a physical, a psychological and a spiritual component. Every person has all the centres, and also needs them to be able to function well.

Physical

Physically the heart centre is to be found at the level of the heart, the head centre just above the eyebrows where the 'third eye' is located, and the belly centre a few finger-breadths below the navel.

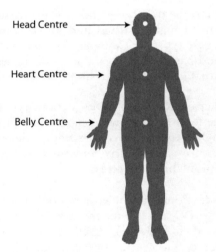

Head Centre ⟶

Heart Centre ⟶

Belly Centre ⟶

Figure 5.2 The three centres

Psychological

At a psychological level (the level of the enneagram of fixations) each centre represents a certain sort of activity, a certain kind of energy and certain themes to which attention is given. The types grouped in a centre share certain themes, with which each type deals in a different way.

■ The heart centre is connected to things like affection, love, creativity.

Heart types are concerned with others. They attach great value to recognition by others and to acquiring prestige in their eyes.

- The head centre is associated with mental activities such as thinking, imagination and vision The head types are mentally oriented first and foremost. Concepts, ideas and ways of thinking are what keep them busy.
- The belly centre is associated with vitality, instinct and emotions. The belly types have action – doing (or not doing) something – as their theme. They are also known as the 'self-forgetting' types.

Once again, every person has all the centres, and every person needs the functions of all centres. With types that belong to a given centre one can speak of an extra accent on the themes that belong to the centre concerned. This accent can manifest itself in various ways (more about this in Chapters 7, 8 and 9).

Spiritual

The spiritual – also known as the transcendental or trans-personal – level is the level of the enneagram of higher virtues and ideas. Someone who is psychologically mature (a rare type: for example, Buddha) has become free from personal fixations and has arrived on the level of higher virtues and ideas. Instead of the 'spiritual level', 'higher centres' are sometimes referred to here.[7]

At the level of the higher centres people with various types are scarcely distinguishable, but on the level of the lower centres the difference is very clear. Everyone has the higher and lower centres within themselves. Many people have had the experience of being driven by the lower centres as well as experiencing the peace of the higher centres.

The person who seeks self-development can work not only with the types but also with the centres. In Part IV exercises for this are described.

The centres are also a good aid in dealing effectively with people of different types. With knowledge of the centres one can quite literally tune to another person's wavelength. In this way mental types are receptive to concepts and ideas. Heart types pay a great deal of attention to relationships. With the belly types the generation of energy, for instance, represents an important point of contact.

The centres in various traditions

The three centres occur in many traditions. The Greek philosopher Plato talked of three kinds of intelligence. Evagrius Ponticus, who recorded the experiences of the desert fathers and is mentioned in Chapter 4, distinguished (following on the prevailing Greek philosophy) three areas within people: the areas of physical lust, of emotions and of the soul. The previous chapter has already shown, too, how Evagrius also placed in each of these three domains three *logismoi* or passions, of which there are therefore nine in all. In Taoism these centres are used in the practice of meditation. In Japanese martial arts people are trained to focus attention on the *hara*, the Japanese word for 'belly centre'.

In the Kabbalistic tree of life (about which more in Chapter 11) and also in Hinduism, the areas make their appearance as three possible ways of schooling: the way of study (head), the way of contemplation (heart) and the way of attention exercises in daily practice (belly or body).[8] Ouspensky, a pupil of Gurdjieff, also referred to these ways. He spoke of:

- *the way of the yogi* (including disciplining the mind by contemplating intellectual problems)
- *the way of the monk* (demanding control of the emotions; it was the way of devotion, the way of the heart)
- *the way of the fakir* (concerned with control of the body).

All these ways involve the control of attention. All three lead to higher levels of consciousness. However, in Ouspensky's way of thinking they demanded personal withdrawal from the world. The fourth way was concerned with the development of all three centres, in balance and in daily work and life. In Chapter 17 a number of exercises are described for each centre.

At the beginning of Chapters 7–9 inclusive, information is provided about the particular centre concerned. When subsequently you read the three relevant type descriptions, it is important to bear in mind the centre concerned. This is the background: the 'colour' of the types involved and the foundation for the mechanisms which play a role in the types. When one knows to which centre a certain type belongs, this deepens insight into the mechanisms of that type.

CHAPTER 6

The Type Descriptions

This chapter explains the categories used to describe the separate types considered in the chapters that follow.

You are best equipped to recognise the types if you see the total picture. That is why the type descriptions in the following chapters start with an impression of a certain type's perception of the world. Thereafter there is a description of how an average type may behave and can be perceived by others. But many people are not 'average'. The more closely someone is identified with a type, the more this behaviour description will apply. The less someone is identified with a type, the more this person's behaviour may depart from it. Thus a person who looks only at his behaviour to determine his type can lose his way. With regard to every behaviour trait characteristic of a type, there will also be people of that type who do not conform. Someone who looks at his own behaviour in order to determine his type may be put on the wrong track. With regard to every element of behaviour, there are exceptional individuals within a type who do not actually act in the commonly accepted way.

This chapter describes the basic patterns which all people of the same type have in common irrespective of if, and how, they have developed themselves. These include, for example, the driving energy, the basic motivation, and that to which the attention goes automatically; these traits actually corresponding with the level of the enneagram of fixations. It might therefore seem logical to look only at this level to determine someone's type. Alas, these are things most people become aware of only after undertaking the necessary work on themselves, however. Although the most correct method is to look exclusively at these basic patterns, this will not always be possible in practice. More about this in Chapter 13, in which it is explained how one can determine one's own type or that of another person.

In conclusion, we also consider the aspects which determine the variants and manifestations of a certain type. It is in this respect that people of the same type are distinguished from one another.

The type descriptions in Chapters 7–9 are therefore made up as follows:

- 'The world of ...' invariably opens the type description. This description of a 'typical' day in the life of the type concerned gives an impression of the inner dialogue characteristic of a type.
- Then follows the section 'Qualities, pitfalls and other characteristics of an average type', in which the possible behaviour of an 'average' type is described.
- The third part of the type description covers the type's basic patterns: basic motivation, focus of attention, and so forth. These form the true core of the type. These inner characteristics are not perceptible from without; one must talk with people to learn about these inner movements.
- Finally, we consider a few categories that give rise to differences among people of the same type, such as sub-types, 'wings' (adjacent types on the circle: the wings of Type 8 are Types 7 and 9), stress and relaxation points and development stages.

The world of ...

This section offers an impression of the perception of the world and inner dialogue of people of the type concerned. In most cases, it is a possible 'day' of a person with that type. Not everyone with the same type will have precisely similar days. The stories are made up of things I have heard people with that type say about themselves in interviews, workshops and panels.

This representation of an inner dialogue can be used in two ways. One may compare it with one's own inner dialogue, and in this way use it as an aid to find out if this might be your type. This inner dialogue can be used as an exercise in empathy. Someone creeps under the skin, as it were, of another person with this type and imagines how the world would appear to them.

It must be emphasised that it is the *type pattern* that is described: that is to say that someone thinks and acts in this way if, and insofar as, he is governed by his type. Individual people who have learned to distance themselves from their type patterns will do this markedly less, or even not at all. This structure applies also to all following sections.

Qualities, pitfalls and other characteristics of an average type

Every type has characteristics that will be seen in general terms as qualities or as pitfalls, and characteristics which are more or less neutral or will be seen by some people as positive and by others as negative.

Many character traits in themselves are neutral and have both a sunny and a shadowy side. Qualities and pitfalls are often two sides of the same coin. A Type 8, for instance, is assertive (quality) but will not think of leaving room for others (pitfall). A Type 3 wants above all to get results (quality), but in doing this will have little consideration for people's feelings (pitfall).

Basic patterns

The basic patterns of a type are shared by all people of that type. Basic patterns are a person's *natural direction of attention, basic motivation, how one perceives the world, emotional programming, basic assumptions, basic fears, survival strategy, type paradox* and *ideal self-image*. They also include things that *tempt* individuals with this type, and things he *avoids*, the *driving emotional energy*, the *mental preoccupation* and the *typical defence mechanism*.

All of these characteristics hang together. The basic patterns form a kind of hologram. The number of aspects of the basic patterns which we use in the type descriptions might be extended by ten, or reduced by five, without great difficulty. The total picture always remains the same, although with greater or lesser detail. In the descriptions of the basic patterns more aspects are included than usual because one reader will have more of an eye for one aspect while another reader will recognise another. Because many aspects are included, everyone with a certain type will always be able to recognise a few of them.

Focus of attention

Within the framework of the enneagram, 'focus of attention' means that to which the attention goes automatically, not that to which a person consciously directs his attention. This form of attention is, so to speak, the attention at which one catches oneself. Without any conscious wish for it to do so, a person's attention often seems to shift suddenly towards the typical focus of attention. In this way a Type 7 – whose attention shifts unconsciously onto pleasant future possibilities – may notice that his attention has shifted from a troublesome problem that has come up suddenly and must be resolved, to an attractive project with many possibilities on which he would much rather begin immediately. A Type 1 can suddenly become aware that once again he is concentrating all his attention on the single fault in a report, instead of thinking of expressing appreciation of its good sides. These are automatisms which occur unconsciously. Every type has a characteristic focus of attention. Where the attention is directed automatically is one of the important criteria for distinguishing the various types.

Focus of attention may be, for instance, what one thinks that others need, expectations of others, possible threats, options that seem rich in opportunities, or chances of scoring, control and domination. These are all things that occupy everyone on occasion. Everyone, of any type, occasionally directs his attention to these things. With a type, however, it concerns a tendency that is always there.

Basic motivation

Every type has its own characteristic basic motivation. The basic motivation is that for which people automatically, and often unconsciously, strive. Someone can deduce his or her own basic motivation from the first impulsive instinctive reaction in a certain situation. The basic motivation therefore does not embrace the (social) skills that someone has learned in the course of life. Thus, in principle, a conflict-avoiding type can learn to face up to conflicts if this is necessary. However, his typical first impulse – the basic motivation to avoid a conflict – will still be there. In practice he now knows how a conflict situation can be dealt with constructively. This behaviour in practice (tackling a conflict constructively) is not the type, however; the type has to do with the first impulse (avoiding conflict, evading, ignoring, in this example).

Basic motivations include, for instance: wanting to be seen; wanting to be approved of and valued; wanting to be loved; a longing for freedom, independence, safety and security, pleasure or control; or a desire for the unattainable. Again – everyone is motivated by these things on occasion but the basic motivation is always there, consciously or unconsciously.

How someone perceives the world

Every type has particular 'spectacles' through which reality is viewed, and an interpretation of reality arising from this which is taken to be true. These spectacles are coupled with the basic motivation, the focus of attention and (for instance) the survival strategy.

People are not always aware of those 'spectacles'. Thus a Type 2 will perceive the world through the spectacles of the needs of others ('Where can I be of service [so that I can win esteem ...]?'), but can honestly think that he is acting wholly altruistically.

The subjects that are central in someone's picture of the world are magnified, as it were, from the field of everything that can possibly be perceived: they are perceived selectively. They come to the foreground while other things recede into the background. A Type 6, for example, perceives more threats than others, and sometimes also perceives threats that do not exist. Now the world is actually a dangerous place. Even in the Netherlands (the author's country) earthquakes happen occasionally; there has been a war there and no one can guarantee that there will never be another; people die daily on the roads; every day people discover they are suffering from incurable diseases; not everyone has good intentions; and most accidents happen at home. An acquaintance of mine suffered concussion when the reading-lamp above her bed fell from the wall onto her head. Objectively, safety does not exist. Most people shut this out from their daily consciousness.[1] A Type 6 simply has not done this and is painfully aware of insecurity. The world, viewed objectively, is a dangerous place for other types too, but they are less continuously aware of it.

It is not true that someone of a particular type cannot perceive a wide range of subjects; He will certainly do so if they are pointed out. Without further indication, however, someone sees primarily and unconsciously what for him, in his own type, is important. Someone who is hungry looks for a bakery and may not realise in so doing that he passed an antique shop, a bank and an optician. Someone who has to change money will look for a bank or exchange office. In this way every type, in its perception, follows its basic motivation in selecting what is important and relevant. It is as if people look at the world in a kind of trance; as if they are hypnotised into seeing certain things a certain way.[2]

When someone is not aware of his type patterns, he has the tendency to think that everyone perceives the world in the same way. As an example, a consultant with Type 9 is asked to co-operate in a highly interesting project, along with fellow consultants from various other firms. He is very glad to integrate so many contributions in something really new. After a time, however, it transpires that some of these fellow consultants have a totally different expectation pattern. They speak about creative competition and, somewhat jokily, about colleagues fancying themselves the eventual victors. Our Type 9 consultant is very indignant, even shocked. Some fellow consultants salvage some nice side commissions, which apparently had been their intention, but because of the underlying competition between participants, little comes of the aims of the actual project. Later our Type 9 consultant realises that his colleagues apparently work from the standpoint of another world view.

Emotional programming

Emotionally, each type automatically reacts to certain signals. Those reactions are coupled to the way in which the world is perceived. They are allergies, as it were. Every type is associated with such automatic reactions. If the allergy button of the type is pressed, the person concerned is inflamed immediately. Thus a Type 9 can become furious about everything that might indicate that he is being ignored; Type 3 reacts as though stung by a wasp to even the threat of not looking good; a Type 2 cannot bear to be ignored and not to be valued; while a supposed lack of loyalty can make a Type 8 explode.

Different writers have pointed out that, to some extent, a person's 'emotional wiring' works separately from his intellectual capabilities.[3]

Emotions and thoughts can flow in completely separate circuits. Every person has emotions, and it is important to face up to them, but in general emotions are not a good guideline for people contemplating action. They colour the way people experience reality, but they are not themselves reality.

For example, I read in a newspaper once that that the Pope wanted to sanctify a number of seventeenth-century Brazilian Roman Catholics who had been killed brutally by local Calvinists for refusing to be converted to Protestantism. I literally sat bolt upright and shouted: 'What! And what about Jan de Bakker?' (In 1533 Jan de Bakker had the dubious honour of being the first Protestant in the Netherlands to be burned at the stake 'for the sake of his belief'. A great many more burnings of heretics followed.) At the same time I burst out laughing at my own reaction. On the one hand my emotional indignation was genuine; on the other the Brazilian Roman Catholics had not met happy ends either.

Another example: I read in the newspaper that German policemen in uniform, unarmed, would come that summer to help local Dutch police on the beach at Zandvoort, near Amsterdam. That was fine for the many German tourists. Germans in uniform on a Dutch beach – I saw it in front of me and panicked. Simultaneously I knew perfectly well intellectually that it could have been a brilliant idea, that it was 1999 and not 1942, that my subconscious read 'armed' where it said 'unarmed', and that those German police officers were probably all born after 1980. Yet the picture remained: helmeted goose-stepping men, uniforms, boots and shouting. I hyperventilated in this way for at least a quarter of an hour. Furthermore, I was furious that once more there was absolutely no consideration for people who still had feelings about the Second World War. Had they gone completely crazy? In short, my emotions and my thoughts were totally separate from one another. The next day there was a photograph in the newspaper of sweet young women police officers from Germany comforting children who had lost their parents. One picture gave way to another. Only then did the emotion disappear.

I make a distinction between feelings and emotions. Feelings such as joy, sorrow, happiness, interest, are not bound to types, although one type can be somewhat more 'feeling' than another. Type 4 (feelings are experienced intensely) and Type 5 (feelings are kept out of the consciousness until an appropriate moment and are often not in the foreground), for example, are opposite poles in this respect.

Emotions, on the other hand, are automatic reactions to fixed stimuli. For example:

- If I go unnoticed, I am always furious.
- Every time someone lies, I attack him.
- I cannot tolerate it if people do not treat me with respect; then I always become resentful and sulky.

Every type knows such automatic reactions. Every type has, as it were, allergy buttons. One press on such a button, and someone becomes incensed, indignant, infuriated (at least if he lets himself be ruled by his type).

Basic assumptions

The basic assumption is the false presupposition that marks the type's point of departure. Thus the presupposition of Type 3 is: 'Only if I attain results, and am admired as a result, do I have the right to exist.' This type has difficulty in understanding that he could be valued and loved simply for himself, as a person. He has to do something to earn it, however, and becomes restless when doing nothing; then his survival is endangered, at least according to his basic assumption.

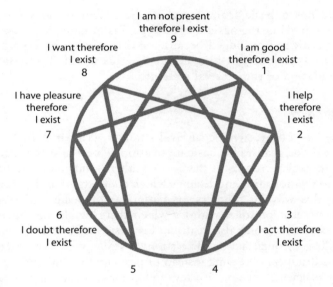

Figure 6.1 Basic assumptions

In fact we are talking here of Senge's mental models, which he defines as deep-rooted assumptions, generalisations and pictures which influence how we understand the world and how we proceed in acting.[4] According to Senge, Shell was one of the first major organisations to see that hidden mental models can have a great (negative) influence on organisational learning. Thus the first step in learning as an organisation was to 'dig up' these hidden mental models in order to investigate them and open them to discussion.

This process also works on an individual level. It is difficult to learn if a hidden basic assumption hinders the process. When someone's basic assumption is that 'he who strikes first wins', it is very difficult to give another person in a dialogue the chance to take the initiative. The unconscious basic assumption works against the other behaviour. Thus the basic assumption of Type 8 is that we live in a harsh and unjust world in which one can survive by strength of will, being hard and confrontational, and hiding vulnerability. When someone with Type 8 is totally unconscious of this basic assumption, it is difficult for him to learn from feedback in this respect. Thus I have heard many people with Type 8 saying that they were actually very vulnerable and very sensitive, and that they did not understand – and also found it hurtful – that people did not appreciate that. They were primarily aware of their soft inner core, while others were more aware of their rough exterior. When someone is conscious of his basic assumptions, he can limit the role that they play.

Basic fear

Every type has a basic fear, something he definitely does not want to happen to him. Thus the basic fear of Type 4 is of being let down; of Type 1 of being criticised or judged because he is imperfect; of Type 8 of being hurt; and of Type 6 of perishing in a dangerous world. The basic fear lies at the foundation of the survival strategy.

Survival strategy

Every type has a characteristic survival strategy with which he battles with his basic fear and realises his basic motivation. Thus the survival strategy of Type 3 is to achieve results in the eyes of others, and to devote no time or attention to relationships and feelings which could stand in the way of those results. In this way he counters his basic fear of being undervalued and having insufficient prestige, without which there would no longer be any basis for existence, while also realising his basic motivation to win acceptance and love through action. The survival strategy of Type 5 consists of keeping his distance, observing instead of participating, minimising feelings, being self-sufficient, creating privacy, and compartmentalising areas of life. In this way he counters his basic fear of not having enough energy, and realises his basic motivation to protect himself from intrusions by others and feelings of inadequacy.

The survival strategy also belongs to the automatic pattern of the type. In contrast to what the word 'strategy' might suggest, it is not something which is thought out. The survival strategy begins working impulsively and automatically, certainly in situations experienced as threatening – that is to say, threatening from the viewpoint of the basic fear and basic motivation.

Paradox

The paradox is that people do indeed succeed with their survival strategies on a superficial level, but that they do not attain their goals at a deeper level.

As an example I take my own type, Type 9. We nines strive for harmony and to this end we avoid conflict. We want to be involved, and therefore try to prevent rejection. My strategy for achieving this in earlier life was to adapt myself as much as possible and to remain out of sight. I tried to guess which answers would please people. When my grandmother died (I was then five years old) my father asked what I thought of her. In reality I was a bit frightened of grandma. In my eyes she was a big woman dressed in black who did not bother with children and talked only to grown-ups. In actual fact, I had absolutely no contact with her. But what I said was what I had always heard grown-ups saying about her: 'She was a right chatterbox, wasn't she?' I saw on father's face that that was not the answer he expected. I quickly thought up another answer that would perhaps be the right one: 'Oh, she was nice all right.' Whereupon my father said that he had not found her that pleasant. Wrong again! It is not always easy to adapt yourself, and it never worked completely. But … if it did work out, no one could take offence at what I said or did, and so I would not be rejected. This worked to some degree, at least. I felt hurt less and rejected less, and as a result I could think that I belonged, insofar as I appreciated that. But it did not make me happier. No one saw the beautiful person I was inside. I blamed people for not having the clairvoyant skills to see me as I really was. But I did not take the risk of letting myself be seen. Furthermore, because I kept seeing myself through the eyes of others, I also lost sight of the person who really lived inside myself.

This is the kind of paradox inherent in every type. The survival strategy of his type gives the person concerned what he strives for at type level, but often he succeeds so well that he loses himself at the same time and does not realise his actual desires.

Ideal self-image

Every type has an ideal image of himself. People with little self-knowledge can think that they match up to that image. Thus Type 9s like to see themselves as peace-loving, accommodating and contented. Type 9s with little self-insight also think they are actually like that. Type 9s with more self-insight also know their angry side, their tendency toward sabotage and obstruction, the way they dig in their heels, and the way they exercise silent control through passive aggression. Their ideal self-image is more the image of the person they would like to be, or hope to become sometime in the future.

People who know themselves less well expend a lot of energy to maintain the ideal self-image.[5] After all, they have to ignore a lot of information, rationalise it away or not admit it to the consciousness – and that costs energy.

The ideal self-image serves the survival strategy. Thus the ideal self-image of Type 5 is: 'I am a good observer; I am wise; I search out and possess much relevant knowledge.' This image serves the survival strategy of keeping one's distance, observing instead of participating, downplaying feelings and being self-sufficient. And in this way Type 5 counters his basic fear that his energy will be used up in contact with others.

Temptation

Every type has a specific temptation, representing what people of that type think they want and strive for. Whereas the basic motivation is an active endeavour, the temptation is more of a passive process. One is tempted. The temptation came along and one could not resist it. An opportunity arose to live out the type pattern and one did not let it slip.

Thus perfection is the temptation of Type 1, where the basic motivation is continually to track down things that can be improved. His temptation is to say something about things that come along incidentally, things that do not actually concern him. He does not actively search them out, but 'just like that' a chance to make something more perfect lies under his nose. Thus a consultant with Type 1 is sent a brochure by a client. The aim is to provide some background information about the company so that the consultant will have some idea of the kind of concern he is advising. But Type 1 cannot let it rest: 'Interesting brochure; provides the information I need. You've seen the typo on page 5, I expect? And pity about that diagram, it's difficult to distinguish the colours. I'd do it differently next time.'

What is avoided

What is avoided represents the opposite of temptation. Thus Type 4 tries to be unique and therefore avoids the commonplace. Type 1 is tempted by possibilities to perfect things and avoids errors and failings. Type 7 is fascinated and tempted by the opportunity for happiness offered by future plans and possibilities, and avoids (psychologically) painful and unpleasant situations.

Driving emotional energy

Under the heading 'emotional programming' we discussed the difference between feelings and emotions. *Driving energies* are emotions such as pride, jealousy, fear and rage. Everyone knows all these emotions. We are all sometimes angry, vain or greedy. The driving emotional energy that belongs to a type is always present underneath and provides the fuel, as it were, for the basic motivation. Thus the driving emotional energy of Type 6 is fear, which forms the foundation of the basic motivation to create safety and certainty. The driving emotional energy of Type 5 is not wanting to give himself. That forms the foundation of his basic motivation, wanting to protect himself from intrusion by others.

As we saw in Chapter 4, the driving emotional energies correspond largely to the cardinal sins of early Christendom.

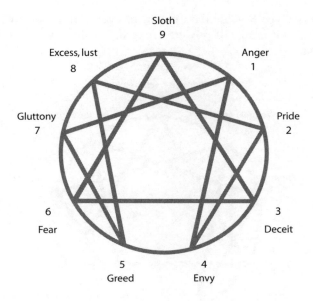

Figure 6.2 Driving energies

Mental preoccupation

A particular mental preoccupation is associated with the driving emotional energy. Thus 'fear', the driving emotional energy of Type 6, belongs with the mental preoccupation 'doubt'. Other mental preoccupations include self-neglect, revenge and planning. The driving emotional energy belongs to the heart centre, the mental preoccupation to the head centre. People are automatically busy in their heads with the mental preoccupation of their type, sometimes without being aware of it. Once more, everyone has all of these preoccupations at least sometimes, but one of them is the main theme for every type.

Defence mechanisms

Defence mechanisms serve to preserve or increase an individual's feeling of self-esteem, or offer protection against the basic fear. They usually lead to certain available information not being noticed, or being distorted when perceived. Everyone has all the defence mechanisms, and can use them all on occasion. At some time or another everyone rationalises, plans, overcompensates from his first inclinations, and so on, but every type has only one characteristic defence mechanism. Thus the 'projection' defence mechanism is characteristic of Type 6: a person seeks an external explanation for his own inner fear. The outside world must be a threatening place, then – why else would he be frightened? The defence mechanism of Type 8 is 'denial': denial of everything that does not agree with the ideal self-image of power, strength, invulnerability and readiness for anything.

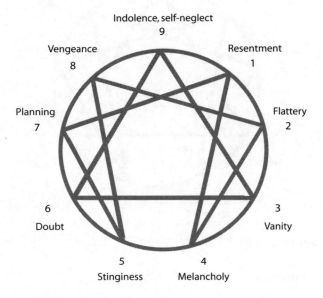

Figure 6.3 Mental preoccupations

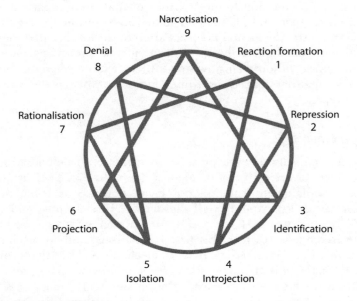

Figure 6.4 Defence mechanisms

Connections between the various aspects

The characteristics described for a certain type are connected with each other and form, as it were, different sides of the same ball of wool. Yet this ball has only one thread. These 'sides' are facets of a total image, and it is that total image we are concerned with.

As an example of the connection among the aspects we shall discuss Type 6. If someone's *basic motivation* is safety, then that person is extremely alert to everything that threatens that safety. His *attention* goes there automatically. This means that the *selective perception* of that person is attuned to possible threats. The *emotional programming* is a hypersensitivity to any signs of unreliability, imagined or not. The *basic assumption* is that safety cannot be taken for granted, and that one must therefore be watchful. The *basic fear* is that of going under in this dangerous world. The *survival strategy* therefore involves watchfulness, and being prepared for everything unpleasant that can happen. The *paradox* is that this strategy leads to an even greater feeling of insecurity. Thus the *temptation* is also safety, while risks are *avoided*. The *ideal self-image* is that people can count on the person concerned – he finds himself reliable and loyal. The *driving emotional energy* is fear, while the *mental preoccupation* is doubt: doubt as to whether people really are the way they act, and whether something or another can go wrong. The *defence mechanism* is projection: this type ascribes the cause of his fears to people and things outside himself.

Thus all these different basic characteristics hang together round the theme of safety.

We have now discussed everything that can help to determine a person's type. We have dealt with a type's perception of the world; with the qualities, pitfalls and other characteristics which can be observed in the behaviour of an average type; and with the basic patterns of a type which concern his inner workings and which everyone of the same type shares. When you have read this section about a particular type in any one of the following chapters, you will have available to you the essential information for discovering whether the type concerned could be yours.

In practice people usually recognise some of this information but not all. This is why so many basic patterns are discussed, although these all still revolve round one central core. This makes the chance of recognition greater. When you recognise one element of the information but not another, that does not mean necessarily that the type concerned is not yours. It is possible that you are more conscious of some basic patterns than of others. It is also possible that the description of the qualities, pitfalls and other characteristics of an average type do not correspond completely with your specific variant of that type. These variants are discussed in the section that follows.

Different variants and manifestations of a type

Until now we have discussed aspects that are characteristic of a type and which are shared by all people with the same type. It would be very convenient if that was all there was to it! One can still keep track of nine types, certainly if they are classified in three groups of three types and each group has a common thread which connects all their characteristics. It would be quite understandable to leave it at that. But reality is not so kind.

The enneagram provides insight not only into the similarities between people with the same type, but also into the differences that exist between them. There are literally thousands of variants of the same type. That sounds complicated, and so it is, but it is actually less complicated than it seems. When discussing the variants one should always keep at the back of one's mind that we are talking about variants of types, not about independent variables. There are still only nine types, no more.

Now we come to the reasons why people with the same type can manifest themselves differently. People can differ according to:

- sub-type
- stress or relaxation: under stress or in relaxation one sometimes takes over characteristics of another type
- wings: sometimes one can resemble the adjacent types to some extent
- an individual's degree of self-development
- difference of gender
- the content of the characteristic type mechanisms (for example, different Type 1s may express perfectionism in contrasting spheres of their lives).

Sub-types

Every type has three sub-types. These are instinctive aspirations which everyone holds, and which everyone needs in order to function well. Sub-types belong to the belly centre.

The sub-types are:

- self-preservation
- one-to-one
- social.

These sub-types are related to stages of psychological development in early childhood. The person who does not come through a development stage of this kind well may have difficulties later. The very first stage is psychological pre-occupation with physical survival. Thereafter a relationship with a single person is developed. Relating to groups comes later on the agenda.

Two variants of each sub-type exist: one in which a person goes along with the theme of the sub-type and one in which he rebels against it. Thus someone with the self-preservation sub-type may keep large stores of provisions in the house and extra bedclothes in case the central heating fails – yet someone else with the same subtype may never take any precautions, adopting the motto 'Nothing can happen to me!'

The sub-type is a channel, as it were, through which someone's basic patterns express themselves. The sub-type forms the connection between someone's inner tendencies and the way in which these manifest in the world. The sub-type has much more to do with external behaviour than the type itself.

Often one sub-type is dominant. Many people say, however, that they recognise all three tendencies strongly. When one is using the enneagram to increase self-insight, it is certainly worth the trouble to look at all three sub-types.

O'Hanrahan describes the various sub-types as follows:[6]

- *The self-preservation instinct*, or the 'one' relationship: food, shelter and warmth, physical safety. At the start of life every person is dependent on others for these things. The person who feels welcome during that stage of his development, is fed and looked after, begins life with a sense of strength and physical soundness. If this condition is not fulfilled, then someone will remain fearful for his physical survival. This can result in such a person paying too much attention to this sort of thing, or actually neglecting material well-being and personal safety.
- *The sexual or 'one-to-one' instinct*, the 'two' relationship: the attachment to one other person. After a time the baby makes a distinction between itself and the other person. Someone who feels valued as a person and also feels welcome (in terms of his or her sex) as a boy or girl feels comfortable and attached. On the other hand, a child who feels neglected (for instance, because the parents are too busy looking after their own needs) or is treated too strictly will develop psychological and emotional defence mechanisms in order not to feel this deficiency.
- *The social instinct, the 'three-or-more' relationship:* the creation of one's own place in the world, outside the home and family – a place that fulfils the need to 'belong'. In classical psychoanalysis, the father represented the relationship with the outside world. Nowadays there are all sorts of different family structures. Whatever the case, at a given moment the child becomes aware of the existence of a world beyond those who care for it directly. How the child is received in this world influences its later social relationships. When someone has a good situation in a group or community, his social instinct demands little attention. Things are different, however, if there is tension between the person someone really is and the role he or she is expected to play. A consequence of the mobility in present Western society is that people have to keep creating a place for themselves over and over again.

Chernick, who digested all the relevant literature and thereafter checked her findings in a survey, describes the sub-types as follows.

Self-preservation sub-types strive instinctively for survival. This sub-type assumes he has to rely on himself. There is a fundamental feeling that one must fight in order to survive. To this end one must remains vigilant regarding all threats to his own person or inner self. Self-protection, sometimes using aggression, is necessary. The instinctive attention goes to what is needed in order to survive: things such as safety, food, feeling good, comfort, protection, conservation of energy. In general this sub-type needs privacy. It is afraid of tension, poverty, sickness, danger, loss, destruction. The attention goes to acquiring – by whatever means – what one needs or keeping what one already has. Self-preservation sub-types have a tendency to avoid risk and safeguard things; often they are serious, a bit heavy-handed, and sometimes sombre.

As we have already seen, however, there are two variants of every sub-type. The variant just described conforms to the theme of this sub-type but the other variant actually opposes it. The underlying fear, 'If I can only survive …', is denied. This variant of the self-preservation sub-type corresponds with a 'Nothing can happen to me!' idealised self-image. This variant of this sub-type avoids every safety rule – good insurance, for instance – because 'nothing will happen anyway'.

Sexual or 'one-to-one' sub-types strive instinctively for intimacy and relationships with one person. These need not necessarily be sexual relationships. There is, however, a clear 'male' and 'female' energy and attention to strength and beauty, qualities which influence an individual's attractiveness to a partner – this is about instinct, not behaviour! This sub-type does not feel complete without a partner. The instinctive attention goes to affinity, nearness, power, the other half, love. Someone with this sub-type is afraid of being unworthy, of letting go, of breaking a bond, of not being complete. He or she dreads the break-up of a relationship, and is afraid of being powerless. Being attractive is important in order to entice a particular partner, or to be in a position to reject an unwanted relationship or to end one that is no longer desirable. There can be a tendency to sacrifice oneself for the relationship. One-to-one sub-types are energetic, intrusive and intense. They can, however, also make a playful, light-hearted, flirty impression that covers up the need for intimacy. There are also two variants of this sub-type: 'If I have a special relationship. I am very strong', and also 'I do not want to have a special relationship, and I don't need one in order to be strong.'

Social sub-types strive instinctively to belong to a community. There they find safety. They also find status in the group important; one's self-esteem depends on how one is regarded by the group. How one is seen by others is enacted, to some extent, in one's own head. Recognition, fame, honour and popularity are all important. The instinctive attention goes to subjects such as superiority and inferiority, being 'in' or 'out',

succeeding or failing. These sub-types see themselves as friendly, self-
sacrificing, and considerate of others. They fear loneliness, a lowly place
in the pecking order, failure, rejection, inferiority, isolation. Social sub-
types have divided energies: half for themselves and half for the group.
They have no clear idea of their own limits. They try to pick up the
prevailing trend in the group in order to follow it or oppose it. It is vital
to make a good impression and not to miss anything important. In fact,
making an impression is even more important than being part of things.
Here the social sub-type experiences an area of tension because he also
wants to be part of things, and being conspicuous and being part of
things can result in an inner tension between wanting to attract attention
and wanting to belong.

Two variants of this sub-type also exist. Some people are social, join in
everywhere, and try to behave in a way that makes them universally acceptable; others make themselves asocial, do not want to belong anywhere, and
rebel actively.[7]

People with the same sub-type therefore have something in common, irrespective of their type. The energy of the sub-type can actually be stronger
than that of the type. Table 6.1 provides a survey of the three sub-types of
the nine types. Each sub-type of every type has its own theme. This theme is
identified in Table 6.1 and explained further in the descriptions of the types
in Chapters 7, 8 and 9.[8]

Table 6.1 Survey of the sub-types

Self-preservation	One-to-one	Social
1 Fear, anxiety, worry	Jealousy	Unadaptibility
2 Me first, privilege	Seduction, aggression	Ambition
3 Security	Male/female image	Prestige
4 Recklessness	Rivalry	Shame
5 Haven of refuge, castle	Confidence	Totems
6 Affection, warmth	Strength/beauty	Duty
7 Defence of like-minded	Fascination, suggestibility	Sacrificial inclination
8 Satisfactory survival	Possession/surrender	Friendship
9 Appetite	Union	Participation

As we have already seen, the type basic pattern manifests itself via the sub-type. Every type therefore has three ways (or hybrids of them) in which the driving energy and the basic motivation based on it are converted into behaviour. Thus the basic motivation of Type 3 is to win recognition by performing well. The self-preservation sub-type of Type 3 does this through success in acquiring material prosperity, which must naturally be visible. The one-to-one sub-type of Type 3 assumes that his or her prestige is dependent on the personal male or female image. He or she attempts to play a presti-gious role and to compete with others; the social sub-type of Type 3 tries to acquire prestige by knowing the right people and acquiring power in politics, in business circles or in social groups.

When we are involved with sub-types, it is essential always to remember that the sub-type is an expression of the type, and of the same core that also retains the basic characteristics. It is the typical energy that expresses itself via the sub-type. If we forget this, we become hopelessly confused with 27 sub-types that are partly similar to one another.

With some people, one can speak of so-called 'cross-overs'. Here one has a certain sub-type with the theme of another sub-type: for instance a self-preservation sub-type of Type 8 with friendship as theme, although this theme really belongs to the social sub-type of Type 8; or a one-to-one sub-type of Type 1 who displays strong unadaptability (the theme of the social sub-type), particularly in his intimate relationships.

Through the sub-type, people with the same type can therefore differ markedly, while people of different types but the same sub-type can display great simi-larities in some ways. On one hand this seems to make the enneagram pretty complicated. On the other, the description of the sub-types often makes it easier to recognise one's own variant of a type as one's own type. I have encountered many people who had trouble with the fact that the description of their type in enneagram publications did not accord with the way in which this type manifested itself in their work and life. They wondered if they missed something in their self-analysis, if they had actually 'typed' themselves correctly, or if they actually understood the type properly. Acquaintance with the variants of the type – of which sub-type is one – was often enlightening.

Type shifts under stress and relaxation/emotional safety

Under stress or when relaxed and feeling emotionally safe, people tend to adopt characteristics and basic features of other types. These are the so-called stress and relaxation types.[9] Every type has its own stress factors. Thus possible threats cause stress in Type 6, while the same possible threats can represent a welcome challenge for Type 8. For a Type 9 a possible difference of opinion can cause stress, while that same difference of opinion may lead to an interesting discussion for Type 4.

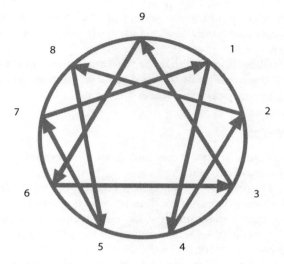

Figure 6.5 Stress and relaxation points

Under moderate stress, first one often strengthens identification with one's own type. Under severe stress one can adopt characteristics and basic patterns of the next type along the arrow in the enneagram diagram (Figure 6.5). Thus Type 5 under stress can go to 7, Type 2 to 8, and Type 1 to 4. On the other hand, if someone feels emotionally safe and relaxed then he can in the first instance either de-identify himself a little from his own type or move to its positive side. If the relaxation (or emotional safety) is deep and radical, one can shift in the opposite direction of the arrow and take over characteristics and basic patterns of the type one reaches by moving *against* the arrow. When relaxed Type 5, for instance, can go to 8, Type 2 to 4 and Type 1 to 7.

In either situation – stress and relaxation – an individual does not change his type, but rather adopts a number of aspects of the other type. In doing this one can adopt positive as well as negative aspects of the other type. Importantly, one can learn useful lessons from both these shifts. Thus a Type 9 who goes to 6 under stress can take over the negative aspect of fear, but as a result can also learn to overcome his fear. He can also develop further his loyalty to something, a positive side of Type 6. In relaxation in Type 3, Type 9 can adopt the quality of self-presentation in a positive sense and thereby learn to develop a face towards the outside world. However, this person may also be confronted with a Type 3 pitfall, the need to distinguish oneself in the eyes of others, and let this take precedence over issues of vital personal importance. Learning to deal with this tendency can also be extremely instructive. Both stress and relaxation points thus provide possibilities for development.

In practice it appears that not everyone moves towards his own stress and/or relaxation type. Some people have never experienced sufficient stress to reach their stress point; some are never really relaxed (or emotionally safe). Some people move only towards the more positive or negative sides of their own types.

Some older publications say that the relaxation point indicates the road to integration and the stress point the road to disintegration. This hypothesis is not confirmed by practical experience, however.

The nine-pointed star

Types 6, 8, 9, 1 and 3 have stress and relaxation points in the other two centres that are not their own.

Types 2, 4, 5, and 7, however, lack a connection with the third centre. Types 2 and 4 – heart types – have lines to belly types and other heart types, but in the enneagram diagram they lack connection with the head types. Types 5 and 7 – head types – are connected to belly types and other head types, and therefore lack connection with the heart types. This suggests that they lack the development possibilities of the third centre. Practical experience indicates, however, that important development possibilities can certainly lie there for these types.

When a Type 2 develops himself, a need for time for himself – a Type 5 quality – becomes important. When Type 5 develops himself he acquires more sensitivity to the feelings of other people and develops his 'Type 2' empathic capacity. There are Type 4s with an explicit 'Type 7' aura, and Type 7s with a

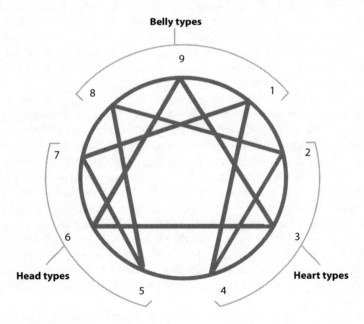

Figure 6.6 Head, heart and belly types

'Type 4' kind of energy. Some Type 4s who have developed themselves regard themselves as generally optimistic (a Type 7 quality) and certainly not melancholic. A Type 7 who develops himself no longer evades pain but starts to experience it (a strong side of Type 4 was being able to live with pain).

The nine-pointed star consists of three equilateral triangles in a circle, and so features both the line connecting Types 4 and 7 and that connecting Types 5 and 2 (Figure 6.7). The nine-pointed star is in accordance with one of Ramon Llull's diagrams, which Ichazo cites as one of the sources of his enneagram knowledge (Chapter 4).[10] Ichazo called this diagram the Chaldean seal.

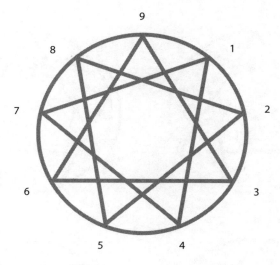

Figure 6.7 The nine-pointed star

Wings

The wings are the adjacent types in the circle of the enneagram diagram. The wings of Type 1 are Type 9 and Type 2, the wings of Type 2 are Type 1 and Type 3, and so on. Some people tend towards one wing, some towards both wings, some to neither of the two.

A tendency towards a particular wing can confer on a type the 'colour' of an adjacent type. That is to say, one preserves one's own type but is also somewhat similar to the adjacent type. Thus a Type 7 with an 8 wing can tend to take on too many projects at once, forcefully encourage people to participate, impulsively seize opportunities that come along, let alarming information go unnoticed and be a strong leader. A Type 7 with a Type 6 wing, by contrast, can be somewhat more cautious, notice worrying signs sooner, be active in explaining the positive aspects of a 'negative' situation, and be more defensive. The underlying fear that plays a role with all Type 7s can be present a little more visibly in a Type 7 with a Type 6 wing.

The circle round the enneagram diagram is a continuum, as it were. People 'can take a larger or smaller bite out of the circle' (Figure 6.8). In other words, someone can have the prototype of his own type and not tend towards either wing, or he can tend, to various degrees, towards one or both wings. Thus in some cases it is very difficult to work out if someone has a Type A with a B wing, or a Type B with an A wing. He then displays characteristics of both types. The way to resolve this is to search again for the basic type patterns, the automatic attention pattern, and the perception of the world.

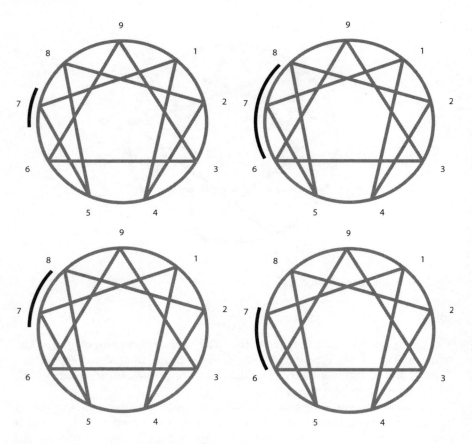

Figure 6.8 Four variants: wings of Type 7

Development stages/states of consciousness

People develop themselves in the course of their lives.[11] Thus, with many people, the type does not keep manifesting itself in the same way throughout their lives.

Roughly speaking, the following development stages can be distinguished:

- *The developed side of the type:* a person who is at this stage experiences above all the positive sides of his type and has circumvented its most important pitfalls.
- *The average type:* a person at this stage experiences both the qualities and the pitfalls of his type.
- *The pathological side of the type:* a person who is here displays above all the negative characteristics of his type and needs professional help.

There is, of course, no question here of three intermittent situations but of a continuum (Figure 6.9).

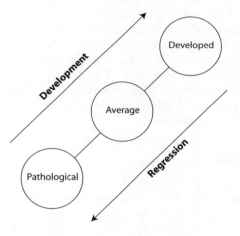

Figure 6.9 Development states/states of consciousness

Not all people begin their lives in the same development stage. Some begin in the middle area, some more on the pathological side and some on the positive side. Further, not everyone's life proceeds in the same way. Some people go through a healthy development, others encounter problems on the path of life that lead their development to stagnate. No parent can fulfil the unlimited needs of the small child. Frustrations are therefore unavoidable, even in an ideal situation with parents who are well developed psychologically and spiritually and can offer the child a materially safe environment. Most people, however, find themselves with parents who still need to develop psychologically themselves, while material poverty and war still affect many.

We can see the three positions in the scheme – pathological, average and developed – in two ways. For someone who is on the pathological side these are only stages of development: such a person has no freedom to choose another position in the continuum, even if he would like to. People who incline more to the developed side can also regard the various positions in the scheme as states of consciousness or attention. At one moment they can find themselves in one position in the scheme, and at another moment in another.

Thus, for instance, someone with Type 1 (the type that strives for perfection) who finds himself in the pathological stage is hard to please, intolerant, rigid, moralising and angry, and cannot free himself of this. He is convinced he is right and that the others are wrong, and finds his own frustration about the others' inappropriate way of working quite justifiable. Freedom from this pattern requires self-development. A Type 1 in the developed stage displays wisdom, is certainly idealistic but with a high measure of realism, and is tolerant: a true teacher. But this person can also have days – for example under high stress – when he is angry, demanding and intolerant. At these moments he is perhaps not able to distance himself from the situation, but later on he can reflect and look at the same situation with wisdom. At different moments, therefore, he takes up different positions in the scheme; This is why those positions for him are more various states of consciousness.

In general terms, people tend to shift under stress towards the negative side in the scheme, and under ideal circumstances towards the developed side. In Chapters 16, 17 and 18 we discuss how someone with a certain type can work on his own development.

Higher virtues and ideas

The developed stage from the previous section represents optimal psychological functioning. But the enneagram goes further. The enneagram also has something to offer to people who are psychologically 'ripe'. We already spoke in Chapter 1 of the existence of the enneagram of fixations and the enneagram of higher virtues and ideas.

The enneagram of higher virtues and ideas goes a step beyond the highest psychological level spoken of in the previous section.[12]

The higher virtues and ideas represent the transformation of the driving emotional energy and the mental preoccupation. Thus the fear of Type 6 is transformed into courage, and his doubt into trust. Someone begins to experience the essence of these concepts. A person who is at first driven by fear (his driving emotional energy) and doubt (his mental preoccupation) develops himself so that he becomes someone who has a great inner sense of certainty.

The scheme in Table 6.2 displays the relationship between driving emotional energy and higher virtue, and between mental preoccupation and higher idea.

The enneagram of higher virtues and ideas represents a different level of experiencing reality than that offered by the enneagram of fixations. Old traditions describe the level of fixations as the world of illusions, and the level of higher virtues and ideas as actual reality.

Table 6.2 Driving emotional energies and mental preoccupations and the corresponding higher virtues and ideas

Emotional			Mental		
1 Anger	⟶	Serenity	Resentment	⟶	Perfection
2 Pride	⟶	Humility	Flattery	⟶	Will/freedom
3 Deceit, veracity	⟶	Honesty	Vanity	⟶	Hope
4 Envy	⟶	Equanimity	Melancholy	⟶	Original source
5 Greed	⟶	Detachment	Stinginess	⟶	Omniscience
6 Fear	⟶	Courage	Doubt	⟶	Faith/trust
7 Gluttony	⟶	Sobriety	Planning	⟶	Work
8 Excess, lust extravagance	⟶	Innocence	Vengeance	⟶	Truth
9 Laziness	⟶	Right action	Indolence, self-neglect	⟶	Love (charity)

One must, however, be aware that the level of higher virtues and ideas is seen continually through psychological 'spectacles', and therefore also described from that perspective. (I myself cannot claim exemption from this rule.)

As a result, it is often asked what the real difference is between the higher virtues and ideas and the highest psychological level. In Chapter 11 this difference is explained precisely.

Going along with the type theme or opposing it

In enneagram publications we usually encounter descriptions of people who go along with their type theme. In practice, however, we also encounter people in whom the accent lies more on fighting their natural tendencies. In this behaviour they can be nearly as compulsive as those who go along with the type theme.

The most described example of this is provided by the contrast between the phobic and contraphobic Type 6. Someone with a phobic Type 6 goes along with the fear, avoiding possibly threatening situations and people. Someone with a contraphobic Type 6 does everything possible to avoid feeling the fear.

This person can take great risks and can plunge into challenging situations without allowing time for fear to arise.

Yet this phenomenon – going along with a type theme or going against it – also occurs with other types. A theme for Type 9, for instance, is that of guarding personal boundaries poorly. Many people with Type 9 are therefore compliant and accommodating. There are also people with Type 9, however, who guard their boundaries to an extreme degree, cannot be pushed into anything and hold inflexibly to their standpoints. With Type 2 we see extremely caring people and people who want more clearly to be at the centre of things. With Type 4 there are people who behave very eccentrically and people who actually present themselves outwardly as being very ordinary. And so on.

Many people experience both tendencies: going along with the type theme and going against it. In some situations they do one, in other situations the other.

Sometimes people who go against their type tendencies honestly believe they are developing themselves. This is only the case, however, if going against the type tendencies amounts to a conscious choice whereby other behaviour is practised. If this other behaviour is just as automatic and almost as compulsive as going along with the type theme, however, there is usually no question of development taking place.

Gender difference

There are sometimes more male and more female manifestations of the same type. Some types are more suited to a classical male role pattern; other types are more suited to a classical female role. Type 8, for instance, is suited to a typical male role pattern, and Type 2 to a typical female role pattern. People of the opposite sex – thus, in this case, women with Type 8 and men with Type 2 – must find a way round the fact that their types do not agree with what their environment expects in terms of male–female role behaviour. Naturally, this does not apply for all representatives of a type; it applies only if the environment expects a particular role pattern. Some women with Type 8 hide their Type 8 nature from themselves and others for a long time. They try to behave in a 'ladylike' manner and be sociable. Often they see themselves as Type 2, only to discover their real type in later life. In the same way men with Type 2 can act in a highly masculine manner and only discover they are Type 2 when they are older.

The same problem can arise if someone goes to work in an environment or culture that does not suit his type so well. In a macho environment, Type 2 can behave in a strongly masculine manner in order to survive; Type 8 can be a little more sociable in a social environment.

Content

The enneagram is an empty model. It describes mechanisms but not the content of those mechanisms. Thus Type 1 has high standards, but the enneagram does not say what the subject of those high standards is. There are Type 1s who are orderly and tidy, because their norms are connected with orderliness and tidiness. But there are also Type 1s who look shabby and cause despair in the administrative field. Their norms are related to other subjects: for instance, to the content of their work as manager or consultant. Type 3 is often described as a macho career-builder, but in reality can also manifest as the sensitive helper, the single-minded scholar, the environmental activist or the ideal son-in-law. What is characteristic of this person is a desire for identification with what the surrounding environment finds important and values, irrespective of what that is.

The enneagram deals with the mechanisms of the basic patterns, not with their content.

Do not stereotype!

As we have seen, the types can vary according to:

- Emphasis on one or more of the three sub-types, each with two variants.
- Accent on one or two wings, or none at all.
- Development stage.
- Position: someone can occupy the position of his type, the position of his stress or relaxation point, or of the opposite corner of the nine-pointed star.
- Going along with the type theme, or going against it.
- Gender difference.
- Filling in the content of the model.

Simply on the basis of the criteria discussed in this chapter, literally hundreds of manifestations per type can therefore be distinguished.

One of the sub-types may dominate, but it is also possible that two of the three sub-types are clearly present, or even all three. Each sub-type occurs in two variants. Within each type there are four wing variants to be distinguished: one of the two wings can be dominant (two possibilities), both wings can be clearly present, or neither of the two wings can be recognisable. Indeed here we are actually concerned with a continuum rather than discontinuous entities. Thus someone can tend a little towards a certain wing, or this tendency may be stronger to varying degrees. Add to this the possible stress and relaxation positions, and then the various development stages and the possibility of going along with or opposing the type theme, and it is clear that it is no exaggeration to speak of hundreds of variants and manifestations of a type. Indeed the options can be multiplied one on another.

Someone with a certain type with a certain wing (four options) can have one of six sub-type variants (six options), can be shifted to his or her stress type or relaxation type (three options), can have a low or a high degree of development (three options), can go along with his type theme or oppose it (two options), can have gender problems with his type or not (two options), and can fill in the basic patterns of his type in a certain manner. And all these options are, in fact, continua.

In addition, people with the same type can score very differently in terms of another system, for instance the personality types of Jung or Kirton.

Myers Briggs Type Indicator

In Chapter 1 we discussed the fact that the enneagram and the Myers Briggs Type Indicator (MBTI), according to recent research, are not related to each other. To illustrate this we shall go slightly deeper into the MBTI, which is based on the personality typology of the Swiss psychiatrist Jung.[13] The MBTI consists of four dimensions:

- Where is the attention preferably directed?
- Where does a person obtain information?
- How are decisions made?
- What is a person's attitude towards the world?

Where is attention directed?

Extrovert people (E) prefer to direct attention to people and affairs outside themselves. They need other people to activate their own energy, thought processes and deeds. The outside world provides energy. They like to have people around them, like talking, and have to take action and experience the world in order to be able to understand it. They like action and change.

Introvert people (I) prefer to inhabit their own inner world. The outside world costs energy. They would rather work alone in a restful environment without being interrupted, preferring to communicate in writing and thinking before they act. Their preference is to understand the world first and only afterwards to experience it.

Where does one obtain one's information?

Sensory types (S for Sensing) direct themselves towards actual reality here and now. They are realistic and practical, good with facts and figures, precise and careful with details. They can work continuously for a long time. Their preference is for what has already been proved to work.

Intuitive types (N for INtuition) are oriented towards challenge, significance, and possibilities, and they value imaginative power and inspiration. They open a current situation to discussion, draw conclusions quickly, and do not like routine and details. Their work rhythm varies: bursts of energy if they are enthusiastic, punctuated by slack periods.

How are decisions made?

Thinkers (T for Thinking) make decisions on the basis of logic, analysis of information and causality, and consider the consequences of a certain decision. They seek the best objective solution and direct themselves more readily to ideas than to people.

Feelers (F for Feeling) make decisions on the basis of personal values. They ask themselves how important decisions are for themselves or others. They are prepared to sacrifice quality if, as a result, a firm foundation can be created.

How does one deal with the outside world?

Judgers (J for Judging) like an orderly, regulated life. They keep lists of work that has to be done. They make plans and also carry them out according to schedule. They do not like to interrupt a project for something that is more urgent at that moment. Judgers prefer to make decisions.

Perceivers (P for Perceiving) live flexibly and spontaneously, are open to experience and new information and like to keep options open. They deal with changing situations easily but have difficulty in making decisions because they tend to think that they do not have sufficient information yet. They are not oriented towards controlling their lives, and trust in their capabilities to deal with situations as they arise. Perceivers have a preference for collecting information.

In reading these descriptions you may have thought of enneagram types in connection with certain descriptions. And, indeed, at first sight you would think that there is a connection. The introvert (MBTI) type looks rather like Type 5, and doesn't that J type look a lot like enneagram Type 1? As we already said in Chapter 1, this is illusory. There are also extrovert enneagram Type 5s, and many enneagram Type 1s have a P score in the MBTI.

Every enneagram type can be combined with every MBTI type, although certain combinations occur more frequently than others.

Kirton's Adaption Innovation Inventory

This test is concerned with only one dimension: improving or innovating.[14] This is not a division into two but a continuum. There are few extreme improvers and few extreme innovators, while there are many people who sit somewhere in between. Improvers hold on to generally known theories, lines of behaviour and standpoints. They look for solutions within a certain framework. They like rules and structure, which give them something to hold on to. Innovators look for solutions outside the defined problem field. Structures and rules form a challenge: they can be circumvented, evaded or sabotaged. Table 6.3 shows what is involved in a strong improving or strong innovating style.[15]

Table 6.3 Kirton's improving and innovating styles

Strong improving style	Strong innovating style
Painstaking, systematic, methodic, reliable, disciplined	Undisciplined, jumps from one thing to another
Attention to details	Broad lines, leaves attention to detail to others
Conforming, contravenes rules seldom and only with powerful support	Pays little attention to rules, habits, assumptions, ideas and methods
Cautious, avoids risks	Presents ideas self-confidently, also without support, does not evade conflicts
Known and tried methods for solving problems	Unexpected viewpoints, strong in finding problems and solutions
Problem-solving by improvements and more efficiency	Problem solution through new approaches
Ensures stability, order, continuity	Creates dissonance, dynamics, change
Few but relevant healthy, safe ideas that can be applied immediately	Many ideas, including those seen as wild, unreal, impractical, irrelevant

Enneagram Type 9 is often described as conservative and improving, but innovative Type 9s do not recognise themselves in this. Thus enneagram Type 7 is continually described as innovative, a characterisation in which improving Type 7s once more do not recognise in themselves. Every enneagram type can be innovative *or* conservative.

These are only two examples of personality systems other than the enneagram. And there are countless other systems related to behaviour or behaviour preferences. Until it is proved otherwise – and up to now there have been no indications of this – one must assume that there is little correlation between other personality systems and the enneagram.

It is therefore quite clear that every type can manifest in a great many ways.

How to read the type descriptions

When you are reading the following chapters in order to discover what your type is, it is good to bear in mind that the type itself is determined by the aspects that are shared by all people of the same type.

Descriptions cannot avoid stereotyping to some extent, and thus fall short of reality.[16] When reading one or more of the type descriptions in the following chapters, it is possible to think: 'Much of this type does apply to me, but some of it does not.' It is possible that a reader will be unaware of the unrecognised characteristic in himself. It is also possible that a small element indeed does not apply. To some extent, I can only describe an average type – and when dealing with averages one must be careful. As the English statesman Benjamin Disraeli once said: 'There are three kinds of lies: lies, damned lies and statistics.'[17] Averages represent a kind of reality that does not exist in concrete form. There is no family with 1.6 children, the average temperature in a month hardly ever occurs, and the average income per head in a country is generally divided very unequally.

How to proceed after reading a type

Here are some hints for readers who are going to study the type descriptions in the following chapters in order to discover their own types.

David Daniels and Virginia Price did research with a tool they designed for determining one's own enneagram type, the Stanford Enneagram Discovery Inventory and Guide (SEDIG): this is considered further in Chapter 13. In this, they drew conclusions representing certain statistical probabilities.[18] When someone thought he had Type 9 after using this tool, there was a 68 per cent chance that this was true. If someone thought after studying with the tool that he had Type 8, however, then the chance of correct identification was only 37 per cent. The remaining types lay in between these extremes. Because the types in the SEDIG are described much more concisely than in this book we cannot simply adopt these percentages. Individuals' chances of success will probably be higher when they can form a personal assessment on the basis of more extensive information.

At the end of each of the type descriptions in Chapters 7–9 we include the hints of Daniels and Price as to what other types might be considered if someone thinks he has a certain type. Sometimes there are a few types in this list; sometimes there are several. This has to do with the perceived desirability of a type. The more a type is seen as socially desirable the more frequently people will identify themselves incorrectly with it.

In addition, when identifying one's type it is always useful to see if stress and relaxation points are recognisable, and if one can identify the wings.

For the reader who wants to use this book for his own development we provide a few early handles to assist at the end of every type description in Chapters 7–9. Self-development is explored further in Part IV, where we also offer a helping hand to the professional who wants to explore the enneagram with other people.

Chapter 7

The Heart Types

The heart centre embraces Types 2, 3 and 4. The heart centre is the home of feelings, of love and affection, and of attachment to others. Heart types are oriented towards others. The image that others have of them plays an important role in their lives. Their attention is directed at gaining approval. They aim at creating or maintaining prestige and a positive image in the eyes of others. Failing is terrible, at least if others see it. This makes shame an issue for heart types. Shame is not the same as a feeling of guilt; it has to do with how someone thinks that another sees their behaviour. Someone 'loses face' in the eyes of the other. Guilt, by contrast, is the feeling of having done something terrible, whether or not other people know. Someone can feel guilty even when the whole world says that nothing else could have been done in the situation concerned, that anyone else would have done the same in that situation, or that the other party was actually responsible for a misfortune that befell them. Feelings of guilt are more associated with belly types.

Feelings play an important role with heart types, but the different types deal with them in contrasting ways. Type 3 represses feelings in the first instance. This person is so task-oriented that he has no useful place for feelings – they would stand in the way of the result that needs to be attained. Type 2 is directed towards the feelings of others. In fact, Type 2 is the caring and supportive individual who senses what others need and supplies it. Type 4 is concerned with internal feelings, and experiences both dizzy heights and profound depths.

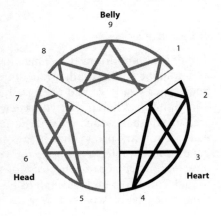

The heart types have a longing for fulfilment through others. When others value them and recognise them, then this feels good.

Development for heart types means, first and foremost, that they learn to do things for themselves instead of for the eyes of the world and find fulfilment without being dependent on others for it – naturally, this must be achieved without giving up their qualities as heart types. What is important is relinquishing a certain one-sidedness in order to find a better balance between the attention paid to others and that available for oneself.

Type 2

In Chapter 6 we dealt with all the concepts that occur in this type description. Here we discuss:

- The world of a Type 2: this is an exercise to let you experience the inner dialogue of this type.
- Qualities, pitfalls, and characteristics of an average Type 2.
- Basic patterns of Type 2: these are shared by everyone with Type 2.
- Variants and manifestations of Type 2: these illustrate how people with Type 2 can differ from one another.

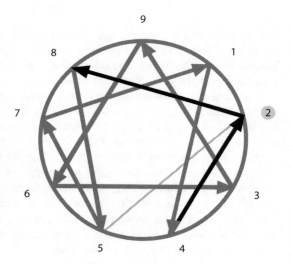

The world of a Type 2

Today is an important day. This afternoon your partner is receiving his PhD and tonight is the graduation dinner. It actually has happened, after all! Sometimes you have had to chase him off to the computer when – yet again – he didn't feel like it, but you knew how desperately he wanted his doctorate, so you have done everything possible to help bring things to fruition. And so you are proud that it says in the Foreword: 'This thesis would not have been completed without the continuous support of my partner.' And now he can become a professor, at least. There too, by the way, you will have to make an effort on his behalf as he will never demand anything for himself. Even when he was passed over for a nomination for the MBA course – by the husband of that horrible Veronica, who always preened herself on her husband's successes – he said that it was fair.

Your colleagues' reaction to this major event has been a big disappointment to you. You had expected at least some admiration and congratulations, and a bunch of flowers would have been nice as well. And rightly so: after all, you too worked hard for this. They could only manage a lukewarm 'How nice for you.' They're jealous, of course. You are particularly furious with the colleague with whom you share a room. You thought she was a good friend and so you have told her very, very clearly how terribly disappointed you were in her.

It really bothers you. Last night you phoned a friend to pour your heart out about your colleagues. But she started off immediately about the problems she had herself with her own boss. You were full of understanding and your own problems seemed smaller. When she thanked you for the talk you felt happy you had been able to help her.

But now to work. You had really wanted to take the whole day off because you want to look good this afternoon. But your boss is waiting for a memo that only you can write. He can't go further without your work, so you have come in this morning after all. He is a fantastic man to work for and he appreciates it tremendously if you take something off his hands. He always says: 'Without you I couldn't do this work.' He is very busy, attends lots of meetings at home and abroad and is regularly in the papers. You hope you can finish the memo before he is back and you really have to go.

Qualities, pitfalls and other characteristics of an average Type 2

The qualities of a Type 2 are consideration, attentiveness and helpfulness, trying to stimulate the qualities in others, empathy, and paying constant attention to relationships. Helping others provides fulfilment. Feelings, particularly the feelings of others, occupy a central place.

A Type 2 is always energetic, expressive and lively. A Type 2 takes action if he thinks it is necessary, or if another person needs it, and does not wait on the initiative of others.

This type is dependent on relationships. After all, one cannot give if there is no one who wants to receive, cannot take care of someone if no one wants to be taken care of, and cannot build up relationships if others do not want them. An undeveloped Type 2 does not like being alone: this person exists only in relationship to someone else. Because his identity depends on the relationship with another there can be a tendency to manipulate the other into playing the desired role, to make himself indispensable, and to flatter others to obtain the desired approval and acceptance. This type is proud of being needed and indispensable ('They asked specially for me!') and wants recognition of this, or can make displays of (false) modesty ('That's nothing special, is it?'; 'Anyone else would have done the same.'). Sometimes a Type 2 pushes people into things they do not really want. I once asked someone with Type 2 for an address.

He came back with a complete plan of action, in which he had already made contact with all kinds of people. This had not been my intention and I felt a little awkward with the people concerned. But it was actually well meant – I hadn't asked for that address for nothing, had I?

There can be a field of tension between wanting to give, on one hand, and on the other, resentment at a feeling of hardly being taken into account by others. People with Type 2, in fact, expect implicitly that others will do for them what they do for others. Because other types are less attentive to those around them, however, this often does not happen.

This dependency on relationships leaves Type 2 vulnerable to rejection and disapproval, and this person sometimes regards professional criticism as a more personal rejection. Thus a Type 2, in the eyes of others, can overreact, with a good deal of anger and dramatic behaviour, to a mild suggestion that something might be improved. Providing feedback to a Type 2 therefore requires tact. Because image, recognition and being seen provide the ultimate motivation for their giving, Type 2 is over-sensitive to failure in the eyes of others.

Type 2 works for people. Work that has to do exclusively with content and does not involve contact with others is less attractive. In a team this type wants a good atmosphere; work must not be solely about business.

Type 2's orientation towards others can lead to neglect of personal needs. A Type 2 can easily take on too much work – after all, there are so many people with so many needs, aren't there?

Type 2 tends to show different sides to different people – doesn't everyone need something different? Thus someone with Type 2 recalled that, when she came home, her mother always knew which friend she had been playing with. This tendency can be a problem in working in a team, for how can you adapt yourself to more than one person at the same time? Type 2 can therefore have a preference for working in pairs. Because of this automatic adaptation process, Type 2 people sometimes do not know who they really are themselves.

This type sees the potential in people and stimulates them to develop it. He is good at seeing what others need, but something is then expected from the other person in turn. According to Type 2, one should at least be able to expect that someone else will really develop himself if Type 2 takes the trouble to spend energy on it.

Type 2 can become incensed in a situation where another party is unaware of any harm done. Somehow this other person has paid too little regard for something for which Type 2 had wanted acknowledgement. Type 2's behaviour can then be angry, hysterical, manipulative or vengeful, or he can try to smear or discredit others.

A Type 2 derives status from authorities with whom he associates himself, for instance in the role of secretary, adviser or 'life partner'. A Type 2 can exert influence without having to come to the forefront personally; he can be the power behind the scenes but wants recognition of his role. Standing in the spotlight can be difficult, certainly if there is a chance of this leading to conspicuous failure. On the other hand, people sometimes have the experience of Type 2 actually wanting to be at the centre of things, and there are many examples of Type 2s who take on executive positions.

Networking suits this type well. In this environment a Type 2 can gain a great deal of information, which can lead to influence. Type 2 can sense where the power lies. This person's preferred orientation is towards important people, and this is not necessarily limited to his own superiors. Type 2 tends to have favourites and people who are not in favour.

Basic patterns of Type 2

The *attention* goes to the needs of others who are important. The *basic motivation* is generating approval, affection and love by satisfying the needs of others who are important, with the object of them giving in return. Thus the *world is perceived* through the 'spectacles' of what others need; here, the question of whether this will provide recognition, honour or acceptance is always important. The *emotional programming* is an over-sensitivity to criticism, to rejection and to not receiving recognition. The *basic assumption* is that one can only be noticed and receive attention, recognition and affection by first giving attention, recognition and affection themselves. A Type 2 presumes that other people will love him only if they need him. The *basic fear* is, therefore, of not receiving enough attention and appreciation. In order to prevent this, the *survival strategy* is to make oneself indispensable by paying attention to others and and supporting and helping them, so that they will value the helper highly and fulfil his needs in turn. The *paradox* is then that the basic motivation – 'give in order to receive' – does not ultimately bring what a Type 2 really needs: freedom and contact with what he, in the depths of his soul, wants for himself. The *temptation* is therefore to help others and to run away from oneself; recognition and expression of one's own needs is thereby *avoided*. A Type 2 projects his own needs on others and does not reveal himself as a person. The *ideal self-image* is: 'I am helpful, altruistic, self-sacrificing, a good friend for everyone.' The *driving emotional energy* is pride: when others need him Type 2 is proud of it. The *mental preoccupation* is flattering people to make them aware that they need him. The *defence mechanism* of Type 2 is repression. A Type 2's own needs are repressed to enable him to maintain the ideal self-image.

Variants and manifestations of Type 2

Different variants and manifestations of Type 2 arise from (among other things):

- sub-types
- stress and relaxation

- the nine-pointed star
- development stages or states of consciousness
- higher virtue and idea.

Sub-types[1]

The basic patterns of Type 2 – the inner mechanisms – express themselves via the sub-types. The sub-type themes of Type 2 are the following:

- *Self-preservation – 'me first', privilege.* People of this sub-type believe that others are dependent on their help. They create warm personal relationships in which they act supportively and warmly. However, this costs so much attention that they feel they have a right to have their own needs fulfilled. Become angry if not rewarded for helping others to be successful. Can appear shameless in the expectation of receiving attention. Uncertainty and fear about whether own needs will be fulfilled. There is an attitude of pride or false modesty ('I don't mind going last').
- *One-to-one – seduction/aggression.* Type 2's great capacity for empathy and attunement to others used to establish a relationship with important people and to obtain approval as an individual from them. This can be seen as seduction – which does not have to be sexual but sometimes is, in fact. Has a talent for making people feel good about themselves and for satisfying difficult people. Personal attention and recognition can be demanded in an aggressive manner. Has to feel loved. Attracts the attention of interesting prospects by displaying common tastes and interests. Resistance must be overcome. This is achieved sometimes by choosing another strategy, sometimes by being coercive, and sometimes through seduction.
- *Social – ambition.* This sub-type maintains a sense of pride by filling ambitious social positions and winning over people with status. Has a perfect instinct for who is important and knows how to provide an indispensable contribution in an organisation. The capacity for empathy and attunement to others is used in order to associate with important people and coalitions. Being allied with the right people can be more important than being in the forefront personally. Qualities also used to bring people into contact with one another, thus exercising influence. Being noticed for being troublesome is better than not being seen at all.

Stress and relaxation

Type 2 goes under stress to 8; there, on the positive side, they can be clearer about what they want themselves. On the negative side, they can quite impulsively become very angry or want to take control of things by force. In relaxation Type 2 goes to 4. On the positive side, the person can then pay more attention to his own feelings and develop his aptitude for aesthetics. On the negative side he can be consumed by melancholy and have the feeling that his needs will never be fulfilled.

Nine-pointed star

The triangle is closed by Type 5. A Type 2 who develops learns to be alone, to be independent of others, and to concentrate on content instead of relationship.

Development stages or states of consciousness

The development stages or states of consciousness are:

- *Developed:* helping without self-interest, really caring about people and supporting them, knowing his own needs and fulfilling them.
- *Average:* wholehearted friendship, central significance of relationships, seeing qualities of others and helping them to develop, self-sacrifice and repression of own needs in expectation of being noticed and valued, using flattery to achieve this, aggression towards those who do not show sufficient appreciation, adapting oneself to the needs of others, making oneself indispensable.
- *Pathological:* theatrical, hysterical, egocentric, manipulative, drawing attention to oneself, forceful, emotional outbursts, dependent, victim behaviour, seductive, aggressive.

Higher virtue and idea

The *higher idea* of Type 2 is freedom – freedom in the sense of faith that one's own needs will be fulfilled. Other people do not have to be manipulated in order to obtain fulfilment of one's own needs. These are fulfilled by a person being able to take care of oneself, or by being able to receive. Higher qualities are also a will of one's own and particularly recognising a higher Will and being part of it. The *higher virtue* is humility. Humility represents a transformation of the pride which is the driving energy of Type 2. That pride comes from always being the giver and not having any needs oneself. When humility is realised, self-respect is no longer dependent on the capacity for giving something to others, and one's own needs are fully accepted.

How to proceed

For the reader making first acquaintance with the enneagram:

If you think this is your type, then check also Types 1, 4, 7 and 9. See if you recognise the stress Type 8 in pressure situations, and the relaxation

Type 4 in situations in which you feel emotionally secure. Find out also if you recognise anything of the wings, Type 1 and Type 3.

The 'self-developer' and the professional will find detailed information in Part IV. Here are a few very brief tips:

- For the 'self-developer': find out what your own needs are and make room for them.
- For the professional with Type 2, the personal pitfall is wanting to be irreplaceable. When working with others with Type 2 attention to the relationship aspect is essential, but without letting oneself be tempted to neediness. Asking about the actual needs of Type 2 is also important.

Type 3

In Chapter 6 we dealt with all the concepts that occur in this type description. Here we discuss:

- The world of a Type 3: this is an exercise to allow the reader to experience the inner dialogue of this type.
- Qualities, pitfalls, and characteristics of an average Type 3.
- Basic patterns of Type 3; these are shared by everyone with Type 3.
- Variants and manifestations of Type 3; these show how people with Type 3 can differ from one another.

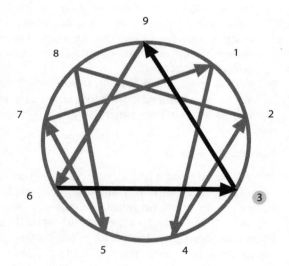

The world of a Type 3

It is going to be another busy day today. As you climb into the car at 7 am to drive to your first appointment (you are glad that you bought this Rover – you could not really have driven up to the clients in a cheap Japanese car) you think about what is on the agenda for the day. It is completely full. You are project leader on three prestigious projects. The first is going splendidly. You have got the team off to a good start and today you will present the first results to the client. You worked late yesterday adapting the presentation the team had designed so that it matched the client's expectations completely, and you are pretty sure you are going to score with this project. The other team members will be there at the presentation and it will certainly make a good impression to give them the credit. Then you had better inform the client now about your own contribution. You pick up the car telephone to call him. At this time of the morning he will also be sitting in the car.

There are problems with the second project. Some team members want to involve all sorts of things as well. Well, if you think about it, the whole world is bound up with the whole world, and you always end up with the kitchen sink too, but that's not the way to meet deadlines. You have to define a project and point it at a goal. The simplest solution is probably to replace these people. But how do you get rid of them without those around you thinking that you don't have your team under control? Ah, that's it! A little research job! You grab the car telephone again and call one of their bosses (someone also driving ahead of the traffic jam). You say that those staff members would be much more usefully employed if they did some research for a project you are starting in a few months – and couldn't you get me Ken for this project? The boss can't spare Ken. Okay, no problem, you get on faster with fewer people but without troublemakers. There is sure to be a kitty somewhere for hiring manpower from outside. Just call the financial man.

The telephone rings in the car. Your partner is asking about the little dinner the two of you are giving tonight for select company. Asparagus or avocado? You decide on asparagus, remind her to pick up your suit from the cleaners, and then you call the financial specialist.

You are going to open a nice wine tonight. Let's have the St Emilion – you have enough bottles of that (it would be very embarrassing if you had too little). And it's a good year – you can score with that too. It would be a good idea to leave that fantastic wine book by the famous chef lying nonchalantly on the coffee table; then you will have an excuse for talking about wine.

You are worried about a colleague in another company who appears in the papers a lot. Too much for your taste, and in too positive a light. You get stomach-ache just thinking about it. True enough, he has twice as much experience, but you are pretty good yourself. And then he has also suggested working together! Naturally you said no; it would just look as if you were a second-rater in this field of operation. What can you think of in order to get as much publicity as he does? Perhaps you could use your third project for that. You begin to think of how you can fix the attention of the press on this project and how you can present it such a way that your own role catches the eye. You would like your photograph on the front page as well.

Qualities, pitfalls and other characteristics of an average Type 3

Qualities of Type 3 are getting things done efficiently and practically, inspiring and enthusing people, and creating strong task-oriented teams. Type 3 is result-oriented, and is capable of high productivity. To join a team as a motivated member, this person must be clear about the goal and must be able to achieve results. Looking after the shop is not motivating. Time without a task is time lost. As a result Type 3 finds it difficult to relax and do nothing. I once heard a Type 3 say: 'I know only two situations: exerting myself and recovering.' Spare time may also be filled with projects such as building a house, leading the hockey team to victory, or running the household efficiently.

A Type 3 can work on more than one project at the same time, and is quite willing to do dull work if that is necessary to attain a result with which he can score. As long as he is on the way to a goal he has a great deal of energy. A Type 3 can take on many tasks, and sometimes overestimates his own qualities and physical capabilities. Type 3s are geared to initiating projects and delegating responsibility for carrying them out. They can make quick decisions on executive matters. Efficiency – in the sense of attaining the goal as quickly as possible with no more effort than necessary – can take precedence over quality.

Type 3s want to win. To this end they can confront and compete. They are often good at promoting and selling a product and themselves. This type also has a tendency to join in when it is almost harvest time and then to make off with the crop. Colleagues and workers can sometimes feel that a Type 3 shows off with their work.

Type 3s want to exercise authority personally, and thus sometimes circumvent other authorities. They tend to occupy someone else's territory or, if that does not succeed, to establish a personal territory in which they can rule. (For example, a trainer with Type 3 may say 'you do the projects and then the training is my area' to a consultant who can do both things.) Type 3 tends to take command. This person can keep new opportunities secret until he can profit from them himself. Self-interest is paramount.

Type 3 works, like the other heart types, for image and status. This can become more important than the content of a project, and something that can lead to a certain shallowness. Type 3 is one of the relationship-oriented types. The outcome of a project will be good enough if the clients, or other people whose judgement is important, are satisfied. What is 'good' will be decided by them.

A Type 3 has a tendency not to see problems; if they occur, he may prefer not to name them as such, but to avoid them by beginning another project in which no problems are involved. Negative feedback is reformulated to preserve one's own image. Type 3 does not like failure, and breaks off before things reach that point. In consequence, this person does not begin a project if the chance of success is not reasonably good.

Type 3 is often called the 'performer'. This word encapsulates the double meaning of obtaining results and acting. Type 3 can alter role and image like a chameleon. If the situation changes, then he adapts his presentation to suit. Although often described as a tough career-builder, in reality Type 3 can also manifest as a sensitive helper, or as a fanatical leader of a squatter movement. Characteristic of Type 3 is a desire to score in areas that are important to the people around them – whoever they are. Type 3 can also create projects and roles in private situations: super-mother or -father, the ideal partner, the sensitive friend. Making unpopular or controversial decisions will be difficult, however.

Achieving results is more important than people's feelings. People tend to be used as pawns. Type 3's presupposition is that people will adapt themselves to the work in hand. It is not surprising, therefore, that Type 3 occasionally seems tactless.

A Type 3 can be angry and impatient if there are hindrances on the way to the goal, or if his time schedule is upset (well, who wouldn't be?); people's feelings may go unnoticed as a result. In these situations Type 3 has difficulty in absorbing new information – after all, that delays the project.

A Type 3 is afraid of not being able to cope with his own feelings, and is not very good at making contact. He is also afraid of what others might think if he were to display his feelings. What he can do is display feelings that suit various situations or roles that arise, and also feelings he does not necessarily experience in reality.

Type 3 has active energy – this person really goes for it!

Basic patterns of Type 3

The *attention* goes to action, to tasks and projects, to results, to winning. *Motivators* are performance, success, prestige, image, being the best. The *world* is *perceived* through the 'spectacles' of what is good or bad for one's image. There is a sharp eye for what can go down well or not in different environments, and for possible competition on the way to the top (whatever 'top' that may be). The *emotional programming* is an over-sensitivity to low esteem in the eyes of others. The *basic assumption* is 'I will be accepted and loved only if I produce results.' To this belongs the *basic fear* of being insufficiently valued and of having insufficient standing, so that there is no longer any basis for existence. The *survival strategy* is therefore producing results, having success and creating a good image in order thereby to have a secure basis for existence. This occupies all the attention, and thus there is no time left for feelings. The *paradox* now is that if this 'role-playing' by Type 3 succeeds and people value the image created, the person in question is still not accepted and loved *as the person he is*. Furthermore, any feeling of self-esteem remains dependent on others. Thus success does not lead to his ultimate wish to be able to be himself. Efficiency and action are Type 3's great *temptation*: 'If I do my best consistently enough and operate efficiently, I can climb higher.' Failing in the eyes of others is *avoided* at all costs. Type 3s also avoid their own deeper feelings and those of others. After all, they would get in the way of achieving results. Doing nothing is also avoided. The *ideal self-image* is: 'I am efficient and successful, I get things done and am a real winner.' The *driving emotional energy* is a tendency to deceit: in the first place self-deception (deceit in the sense that people of this type like to believe in their own roles and wants to make others believe in them as well). Much energy is expended on this. Moreover, vanity is a *mental preoccupation*. The *defence mechanism* of Type 3 is identification: creating safety by identifying oneself with a role.

Variants and manifestations of Type 3

Different variants and manifestations of Type 3 arise from (among other things):

- sub-types
- stress and relaxation
- development stages or states of consciousness
- higher virtue and idea.

Sub-types

The basic patterns of Type 3, the inner mechanisms, express themselves via the *sub-types*. The sub-type themes of Type 3 are the following:

- *Self-preservation – security.* Emotional self-preservation is coupled with income and increasing possessions. Money gives security; the worth of a person is associated with material things. The ability to work hard, to build up a good image and to perform well is used to obtain material security: filling the bank account, surrounding oneself with visible material prosperity and thereby countering the fear of lacking something. This sub-type can, however still be afraid – despite a healthy bank account – of becoming unable to work or going bankrupt in the future, while the image projected to the outside world continues to radiate self-confidence.
- *One-to-one – male/female image.* Personal power and charisma rest on this sub-type's perception of attractiveness as a man or a woman. They will adapt themselves to conform to what others find attractive, and then present himself in this way: the top manager, the strong competitor, the courteous colleague, and so on. There is a tendency to continue playing a perfect, prestigious role both at work and in private relationships. The emphasis lies on appearances.
- *Social – prestige.* Anonymity inspires fear. It is painful if others are the centre of attention. Knowing the right people and having power in politics, work or social groups lead to success. This can involve real social leadership, or inflating oneself by creating an image. This sub-type feels a great tension between desiring to be seen in a positive light, on one hand, and following social norms of behaviour and propriety, on the other – in other words, between standing out and adapting. A Type 3 is preoccupied with a positive social image and adapts to different groups accordingly. 'Being the best' is often confused with 'being the best known'.

Stress and relaxation

Type 3 goes under stress to 9. On the positive side he is then better able to see things from different perspectives and to take the interests of others into account. On the negative side he can become indecisive and evade subjects likely to cause conflict. In relaxation and emotional security type 3 goes to 6. On the positive side this means allowing justifiable doubt (not every type 3 experiences this as positive) and the development of loyalty to people. On the negative side defeatism can set in, a fear of success and an unjustifiable suspicion of authority.

Development stages or states of consciousness

The development stages or states of consciousness are:

- *Developed:* honesty, feeling of self-esteem, excellence.
- *Average:* motivating, competitive, active, pragmatic, image-builder (in terms both of physical appearance and performance), self-promoting, dominant, entertaining, result-oriented, need for recognition, no attention to feelings, impatient on the road to the goal.
- *Pathological:* insensitive to the feelings of others, no access to own feelings, chameleon, over-active, vigilant, vindictive, unreliable, opportunistic, coolly calculating in relationships.

Higher virtue and idea

The *higher virtue* of Type 3 is honesty, genuineness. No deceit – playing a role, acting in a particular manner or being seen to achieve something by others in order to be accepted – is required. One does not have to be the best, the most important, or the most attractive to be of value as a person. The *higher idea* is hope. Hope is the ability to relax in the knowledge that life pursues its course according to universal laws and that individuals, in accordance with those laws, receive what their soul needs without having to set the universe in motion themselves. That is why someone at this level can admit his own feelings, for they cannot stand in the way of anything.

How to proceed

For the reader making first acquaintance with the enneagram:

If you think this is your type, then check also Types 1, 2, 7, 8 and 9. See if you recognise the stress Type 9 in pressure situations and the relaxation Type 6 in situations in which you feel emotionally secure. Find out also if you recognise anything of the wings, Type 2 and Type 4.

The 'self-developer' and the professional will find detailed information in Part IV. Here are a few very brief tips:

- For the 'self-developer': consider your own motives for doing anything, slow down, make room for feelings.
- For the professional with Type 3 the personal pitfall is wanting to make a good impression (and wanting to achieve results too quickly) so much that quality may suffer as a result. In working with others with Type 3 one has to attune to their orientation towards results. At the same time it is important to accept the person instead of exclusively the results for which he is responsible. To help development the attention is directed towards feelings.

Type 4

In Chapter 6 we dealt with all the concepts that occur in this type description. Here we discuss:

- The world of a Type 4: this is an exercise to let you experience the inner dialogue of this type.
- Qualities, pitfalls, and characteristics of an average Type 4.
- Basic patterns of Type 4; these are shared by everyone with Type 4.
- Variants and manifestations of Type 4; these show how people with Type 4 can differ from one another.

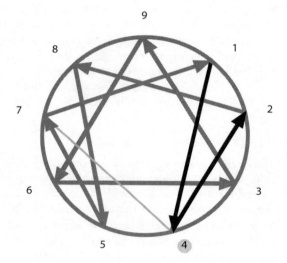

The world of a Type 4

For a while now you have gone to work reluctantly. Your colleagues are real clock-watchers, although you work in a commercial office. They are those '9-to-5' types. Have to be home on time, otherwise the dinner will be cold. You yourself work if you have inspiration, and then you go on day and night. And if you have no inspiration, it is pointless to hang around in this lifeless office building. You would be better off going to a museum or into the country, or taking a walk through the town. Then you get new inspiration. Yes, you are quite different from your colleagues. You are even moved by beauty. Not just the beauty of art: a report can also have beauty. Recently you were actually moved by the beauty of a client's staircase. Magnificent –

with those lines and the fall of the light. But your colleagues understand nothing of that. In fact, you have had about enough of it here. You belong now among the best in your professional field and as a result there is no real challenge any more. Everything you do is good, or it is maligned, something you regard as a compliment. It is time for a completely new career.

You look outside. The thundery sky above the oak tree in its autumn colours is incredibly beautiful. You feel it already – this will not be a day for working. First of all you go to the park. Perhaps this afternoon you will look for the present for the director who is leaving. They have asked you to find it because you always have unique ideas. For your part, you think you are the only one who can do it. At the same time you feel hurt that they asked you for this, but not for a contribution to the New Building work group. There you could make a particularly good contribution, but naturally the outcome will have to be a dull functional office box, with cubicles again.

Leaving is also a solution for your conflict with one of the project leaders. He is purely a businessman and interested only in progress and results, and above all in his own little star in the firmament. As far as he is concerned you could just as well be a machine. His only topic of conversation is deadlines; the content doesn't interest him at all, and neither do people. You are on good terms with his secretary who comes to you regularly to pour her heart out. That is someone you can really talk to; she is really herself. You have tried everything with the project leader: talking, provocation, sarcasm, rebellion, trying to hear him out about his ideals, about what troubles him and about his private life, but nothing helps. How can you go through life without feelings?

Qualities, pitfalls and other characteristics of an average Type 4

A Type 4 can be sensitive, empathic, creative, impassioned, romantic, artistic, idealistic. The romantic and artistic aspects are not always outwardly visible; all of this can take place solely in the inner world. This person can be an innovator and can make original contributions.

Type 4 finds authenticity in key relationships and makes a positive effort to create this. Even conflict can be used to summon up authentic feelings in others. A characteristic statement is: 'I see to it that the relationship stays interesting.' People are more important than rules. This type believes that work must be a reflection of the person.

A Type 4 is good at supporting people in difficult circumstances. They can be strongly empathic, certainly when people are in difficulties. They do not have the tendency to evade these difficulties or to resolve them as quickly as possible, but can persevere and help people through such difficult periods without themselves repudiating, evading or obscuring anything. They can inspire timid people to be successful.

Type 4's primary tendency is to find attractive what is *not* present in a situation. Whatever is present at the moment loses its power of attraction. There can be an aversion for ordinary, everyday things, which can be coupled with sarcasm if something is too commonplace. That can mean an aversion to ordinary work, and certainly to work that is monotonous. In relationships there can be a cycle of attraction and rejection. The further away the partner is, the more attractive he or she will be. If he or she is present again, however, the relationship becomes mundane and quickly loses its shine. The same can happen with jobs and projects. But that does not mean that a Type 4 cannot have a long-lasting relationship or is always a 'job-hopper'.

Type 4 can feel that others have things that he does not: 'Others are content, happy, fulfilled; I am not.' This can lead to jealousy, competition or a feeling of shame. The fear of loss or abandonment can also lead to feelings of jealousy, or the urge to possess material things.

Type 4 tries to counter feelings of personal inferiority by being unique in a positive or negative sense. This person can indulge this in a dramatic way, or quietly feel 'different' within himself. When a participant demonstrated this very well in a training course, the other participants got the feeling he would regard them as grey mice. Type 4 can have a deep feeling of shame if he cannot be unique. For the social sub-type in particular, being socially visible is outweighed by the risk of being denigrated. Evaluation can be a threatening.

Type 4s also belong among the relationship-oriented types. Because they feel different, they want special treatment and personal recognition. They may tend to gather round themselves a group consisting only of interesting people. They sometimes feel that rules do not apply to them. They can react exaggeratedly to a lack of attention from others, and are capable of creating chaos in order to attract that attention. They can become vengeful if they fall from favour, or take on the role of victim with great feeling for effect.

This person can be reckless and obstinate, and may relinquish or sabotage success. Success, after all, can lead to the mundane. Further, the result of 'having made it' is that there is no longer any desire; the unattainable has been attained and consequently loses its power of attraction. Type 4 can therefore lose interest in a project in its final phase.

Type 4 can be extremely competitive, and is then like Type 3. Emotional moods influence style and tempo, but this person can be strongly result-oriented without always being consistent in this. At one moment he can strive for success and at the next lose every sort of interest. But a Type 4 can also be a tower of strength and save a project.

A Type 4 is inclined towards intense feelings, and experiences them as well. These can be both great heights and profound depths. He can sometimes abandon himself to these and so lose contact with the here and now. Melancholy is sometimes a negative feeling, but it can also be comfortable or involve beauty. Pressure of work drives off depression.

Type 4 individuals are interested in the meaning of life in general, and in the purpose of their own lives. They can feel intensely bound up with nature, and with everything that exists.

A Type 4 can give the impression of being extremely intense, striving for an ideal, melancholic or *himmelhoch jauchzend* (exulting to the heavens), but sometimes also strongly introverted. Others can experience a feeling of drama.

Basic patterns of Type 4

The attention goes to what is missing in life, to feelings of loss. There is a search for the essentials in life and for unrealised ideals. There is always a sense of longing. The *basic motivation* is therefore rediscovering what one feels is missing. How Type 4 *perceives* the *world* is governed by this. Is this relationship, this contact really authentic enough? Is there sufficient depth? Are feelings displayed and explored? Is it special enough? Am I seen as being special? The *emotional programming* is an over-sensitivity to feelings of being abandoned, and also for superficiality and the commonplace. The *basic assumption* is that there is something essential missing from oneself. As a result, a Type 4 feels unworthy of being loved. Feelings constitute what is real. The *basic fear* is of being abandoned and of losing essential elements of one's own person. Type 4s prevent themselves from being abandoned with a *survival strategy* that involves being special or unique while personally rejecting others.

In the absence of desirable contact with others, intense feelings of longing, sadness and melancholy are experienced; in this way the longing is perpetuated. Type 4 keeps looking for the ideal relationship or the ideal circumstances, and these are always somewhere else. The *paradox* is that by continually seeking the ideal future and wanting to maintain longing, this prevents the present from ever being fulfilling; thus there is always a reason for melancholy, and melancholy perpetuates the longing. The object of the longing thus remains, by definition, unattainable. The more a Type 4 strives for genuineness, the more he can appear to be artificial. The *temptation* of Type 4 is authenticity, genuineness, originality, uniqueness. Things that are *avoided* are the ordinary, abandonment, loss. The *ideal self-image* is: 'I am sensitive, authentic and special, different from others; I have an aesthetic feeling for beauty.' Type 4's *driving emotional energy* is envy: others have things that I do not. This leads to the *mental preoccupation* of melancholy, and a continuous longing for what is missing. Type 4's *defence mechanism* is introjection. Introjection means that the expressed, unexpressed or presumed views and judgements of others – tutors, for instance – are absorbed in one's own system of thinking and feeling and are experienced as one's own.

Variants and manifestations of Type 4

Different variants and manifestations of Type 4 arise from (among other things):

- sub-types
- stress and relaxation
- nine-pointed star
- development stages or states of consciousness
- higher virtue and idea.

Sub-types

The basic patterns of Type 4, the inner mechanisms, express themselves via the sub-types. The sub-type themes of Type 4 are the following:

- *Self-preservation – recklessness concerning personal survival.* This sub-type is prepared to take risks, to let go of what currently exists and to jump into unfamiliar waters, or to abandon all thought of survival in order to realise a dream. Can express this flamboyantly or dramatically or, on the contrary, in a withdrawn and self-chastising manner. Can be like a contraphobic Type 6 (see type description in Chapter 8) in the way in which risky projects are undertaken seemingly without fear. In this way this sub-type escapes the routines of normal existence. There is tension between the need for material security and the impossibility of having one's material well-being secured. If a dream is realised and proves disappointing, everything can be demolished in order to begin anew. Throwing caution to the winds sometimes works out well in an unorthodox or creative manner.
- *One-to-one – rivalry, hate.* Competition is a way of overcoming one's own sense of deficiency. The power of others is seen as a personal challenge. This sub-type hates everyone who activates these feelings of deficiency and envy: for instance successful rivals, or people who receive the recognition he wants for himself. He boosts his self-esteem by comparing himself with others and competing with them: 'If he feels less good about himself, then I can feel better myself!' Can be eaten up by professional jealousy. Wants the respect of the very best people or people with the most status. Can also contend for approval. Even ending a relationship can be used to prevent the feeling of being abandoned. This sub-type can be like Type 8.
- *Social – shame.* Shame arises from a feeling of inferiority. Social situations can activate the sense of inadequacy, which causes shame and envy of others on account of their status, membership of a group, or success. There is a fear that one's own weak spot or own deficiency will be discovered. There is a continuous striving for higher status. If this is achieved, however, then this is never enough and this sub-type strives for the next rung on the ladder. In this process, the tension between individual authenticity and uniqueness on one hand and social acceptance on the other must be resolved. There is always a fear of falling short, of not satisfying a group's expectations or one's own standards. This sub-type is very

sensitive to not receiving appreciation, recognition, acceptance and status. Individuals will work on their own image in order to prevent such hurt. Can cover shame with charm or withdraw into solitude.

Stress and relaxation

Type 4 goes under stress to 2. On the positive side this means more attention for others; on the negative side neglect of one's own needs. In relaxation Type 4 goes to 1. On the positive side this means idealism and wanting to do things really well; on the negative side it means not finding anything good enough, and also a certain intolerance.

Nine-pointed star

The point that completes the triangle of the nine-pointed star is 7. Type 4 can learn a more optimistic attitude to life from 7.

Development stages or states of consciousness

The development stages or states of consciousness are:

- *Developed:* placid, self-aware, with a natural sense of connectedness.
- *Average:* powerfully imaginative, empathic, aesthetic, capable of playing emotional roles, tasteful, exhibits a pattern of attraction and rejection, wants to be special, tendency to extremes, idealist, pays attention to what is missing, jealous of others who appear to have that which is missing (which can lead to shame or competition), regards feelings as more real than facts.
- *Pathological:* envious, wants to be someone else, suffers feelings of worthlessness, depressive, alienated, self-hating, self-tormenting, self-destructive, cynical, feels that love must compensate for lack of self-recognition, actor, behaves like prima donna or misunderstood genius.

Higher virtue and idea

The ultimate goal of Type 4 is a fulfilling and fulfilled life in the here and now. The *higher virtue* of equanimity means fully accepting oneself and one's own life in the here and now, and no longer yearning for what others have or what might be possible. There is no need to be different or unique any more because there is already complete fulfilment in the here and now. The *higher idea* of the source, the origin, means that one no longer has the feeling of having lost something and of having to look for it. One is, as it were, reunited with what was lost. There is a feeling of wholeness and of union with the source from which one has come. When this unity exists, there is no further need to be unique.

How to proceed

For the reader making first acquaintance with the enneagram:

If you think this is your type, then check also Types 1, 6, 7 and 9. See if you recognise the stress Type 2 in pressure situations, and the relaxation Type 1 in situations in which you feel emotionally secure. Find out also if you recognise anything of the wings, Type 3 and Type 5.

The 'self-developer' and the professional will find detailed information in Part IV. Here are a few very brief tips:

- For the 'self-developer': direct attention to what is positive in the present; before acting, wait until any strong feelings have subsided a little.
- For the professional with Type 4 the personal pitfall is expecting that others will have feelings as intense as one's own, and that they too want to be unique. When working with someone else with Type 4 it is important for the professional to be able to stay with the feelings of that person without wanting to identify the cause of those feelings immediately, and to direct the person's attention to positive aspects of the present situation while at the same time respecting his idealism.

CHAPTER 8

The Head Types

The head centre is the seat of human thinking. Head types want to think first before reacting. They have a lively imagination and fantasy and a preference for analysis, thinking things out thoroughly, conceptualising and linking mental images with each other. These are all mental activities. It is not true that head types have no feelings. They often develop feelings, however, through thinking. Thinking is a defence against the underlying fear of a dangerous world. The development task for the head types is to develop a direct relationship with their own feelings and to come to believe in themselves and in others. The head types are oriented towards different kinds of mental image:

- Type 5 tries to gather neutral, objective information and use this to form an objectively correct judgement. In this way he counters his fear and stays in control.
- Type 6 has mental images of all the things that can go wrong, thinks in terms of 'worst-case scenarios' and projects his own fear on others, who are assumed to be threatening.
- Type 7 combats his own fear by turning attention to positive ideas about pleasant future options instead of facing the situation and events of the moment.

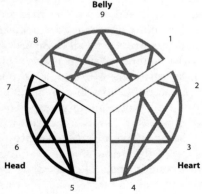

Type 5

In Chapter 6 we dealt with all the concepts that occur in this type description. Here we discuss:

- The world of a Type 5: this is an exercise to let you experience the inner dialogue of this type.
- Qualities, pitfalls, and characteristics of an average Type 5.
- Basic patterns of Type 5; these are shared by everyone with Type 5.
- Variants and manifestations of Type 5; these show how people with Type 5 can differ from one another.

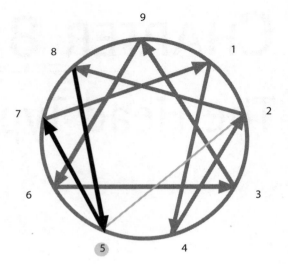

The world of a Type 5

The children whined this morning when you went to do something with them again. You find your children very important and always observe them acutely. You really have far more interest in them than your parents ever had in you. But in your precious free time you feel a great need to withdraw to your room with your books and magazines, or to download information from the web. There is so much that is interesting. And you also want to train for the marathon. You only have to run on your own like this to recover completely. You wonder if the child minder couldn't go with them to the gorilla park if they want an outing – you wouldn't have to go along with them there, would you? Eating together and putting them to bed swallows up a major part of your spare time.

At the office it is a hectic time with the merger. You see it all going wrong, with a number of colleagues letting themselves be led by their emotions. Of course, this means that they can't think clearly any more and then make strategic mistakes. You see that people are busy withdrawing from the game or becoming overstressed. Luckily this doesn't trouble you at all. Actually it is interesting, seeing all those processes. You have made a good contribution, with a number of sharp analyses of what is going on. It's amazing to see how little logic there is in people's thinking in this sort of situation. Because you keep a cool head you can also intervene very well at a strategic level. Then you don't worry about your position. Not that you don't find it exciting. But that makes it doubly important to keep a clear head.

Some of your staff have problems, however. They blame you for not supporting them. But if you look at the situation objectively, keeping everyone in their old functions would be the stupidest option possible. It would make a merger like this totally pointless. One must see how one can structure the new organisation best and then fit the people into it. It's very irritating that they now try to walk in at every odd moment to talk about their feelings, because now it is especially important to go through things systematically, and you need all your attention for that. You wonder how you can keep them out of your room without being rude.

Qualities, pitfalls and other characteristics of an average Type 5

A Type 5 is reliable, soothing, cautious, firm, studious. Secrets are safe with them. They value simplicity. They stay calm in critical situations. They can be good negotiators when they have thought things out thoroughly before- hand. They are good at strategy. A Type 5 undertakes research, gathers infor- mation and analyses things before dealing with them. Thinking and observing can take the place of acting and participation (this can happen, but not always). Designing a project can be more interesting than its execution. Type 5 is interested in knowledge for its own sake. New, unexpected things are interesting and deserve study. He can have a passion for ideas and for communicating these enthusiastically. The lack of rational thinking in others can come as a surprise.

Contact with people is made through ideas and mutual interests. In general Type 5s pays more attention to the content of the work than to people. They are logical and provide factual reports and information more readily than support in relationships. The introvert Type 5 can work well alone and often prefers this. The extrovert Type 5 needs others in order to develop his ideas and is less of a soloist. With the extrovert Type 5, however, discussions are also primarily about content, not about feelings. Type 5 does not like quick changes in plan and needs time beforehand in order to digest new information. As a result, this person can be inclined to ignore signals which call for an immediate reaction.

Type 5s do not like people intruding into their space, physically or psycho- logically, without asking permission. That costs energy. They can create private space by minimising contact, feelings and needs. The dreamwish of a Type 5 to live in a water tower one day was highly symbolic. Some Type 5s are satisfied with little furniture, few clothes and very simple food, but that is certainly not true of all. Even so, the fewer the needs, the greater the independence.

Type 5 values autonomy. As a result, they tend to keep different areas of life, such as work, sport and private circumstances, strictly separate. In personal relationships they are less expressive than in professional ones. They can hide themselves in a professional attitude. Others can perceive them as intellectually critical or superior. A need to maintain a distance can be interpreted by others as lack of interest in them as people, or as neglect. They are not always available for others. For example, someone once said that he sometimes needed to withdraw and be alone for a few days. He had learned to reassure his wife that he would be back again, however, because this behaviour worried her. A Type 5 can appear blunt without realising that someone else may feel humiliated by this. This person tends to avoid conflict and can be (exaggeratedly) watchful for possible threats, overestimating the power of potential competitors or opponents.

A Type 5 can be generous with time and energy if a task in which he is interested is involved, but he may also only do what is asked and make information available in response to a specific request.

Type 5 holds back energy.

Basic patterns of Type 5

The *attention* goes to observing and thinking, and the reduction of feelings and possible intrusion of others into his own private space. The *basic motivation* of Type 5 is to protect himself from intrusion by others and from feelings of inadequacy through maintaining privacy and self-sufficiency, minimising one's own needs and separating different areas of life. The *world is perceived* through the 'spectacles' of possible intrusions into one's own territory and the presumed expectations of others. Type 5 tries to keep the perceived world and the world of personal experience under control by thinking. The *emotional programming* is an over-sensitivity to others overstepping boundaries, and also to emotional appeals. The *basic assumption* is that the world wants too much. If a Type 5 has to fulfil all these needs his energy will be exhausted. By restraining himself and choosing the position of observer and thinker, he can prevent this. The *basic fear* of Type 5 is that his energy will be exhausted. This person tries to avoid this with a *survival strategy* involving keeping a distance, observing instead of participating, minimising feelings, being self-sufficient, creating privacy and keeping different areas of life separate. The *paradox* is that this withdrawal invites invasion. People, after all, have a tendency to fill a vacuum. Self-sufficiency actually involves depriving oneself of available resources. The *temptation* is knowledge, and knowledge is power. What is *avoided* is dependence on people and things, being overrun and a feeling of emptiness – not being worth enough. The ideal self-image is 'I am a good observer; I am wise; I seek out and hold much relevant knowledge.' The *driving emotional energy* is to keep vital energy, time and knowledge to oneself. As a result, his *mental preoccupation* is to be self-sufficient, not to need anyone, and not to be troubled by his feelings. The *defence mechanism* of Type 5 is isolation.

Variants and manifestations of Type 5

Different variants and manifestations of Type 5 arise from (among other things):

- sub-types
- stress and relaxation

- the nine-pointed star
- development stages or states of consciousness
- higher virtue and idea.

Sub-types

The basic patterns of Type 5, the inner mechanisms, express themselves via the sub-types. The sub-type themes of Type 5 are the following:

- *Self-preservation – (castle of refuge)*. 'My house is my castle'; one's own home is the safe place to which one can withdraw from the world, surrounded by one's own trusted things; where one is safe from those who would invade one's privacy, and from troublesome encounters and responsibilities. But people of this sub-type need not be bound to one particular location: everything they need is in the rucksack. The 'house' can therefore be material or psychological. There is always a feeling of scarcity. This sub-type sometimes stockpiles, because this gives a feeling of independence. There is a field of tension between wanting the good things in life and wanting to be able to make do with as little as possible. This sub-type does not want to create dependency and is acutely aware of the expectations of others; in this there is a resemblance to Type 9. Time spent with others costs a great deal of energy.
- *One-to-one – confidentiality*. The inner world can be shared with carefully selected people in a one-to-one relationship: with a personal adviser, for instance, or a 'significant other'. Within the relationship information must remain confidential ('Only the two of us know this ...'). This sub-type prefers to keep different relationships separate from one another and likes having short intensive encounters, which can be recreated continually in his thoughts.
- *Social – totems*. The totem of a tribe bound the limited human spirit and personal consciousness with the powers of nature and the larger consciousness of the world, and symbolised the relationship with the knowledge of the ancestors. This sub-type is hungry for knowledge. Wanting to belong to the group transforms itself into wanting to speak the group language, to know the shared group symbols, to be one of the important people in a group or professional field, or to belong to an elite group. The link is made by providing or receiving knowledge. The more confidential or more exclusive the knowledge is, the better. There is a field of tension between the longing for social involvement and the need for isolation.

Stress and relaxation

Type 5 goes under stress to 7. On the positive side, he can reduce tension by means of humour and by seeing many possibilities. On the negative

side, he can avoid unpleasant affairs by explaining them in positive terms.
In relaxation, Type 5 goes to 8. On the positive side he then becomes
action-oriented. On the negative side, he can harp on excessively about
something.

Nine-pointed star

The triangle of the nine-pointed star is closed by Type 2. A developed Type
5 learns to pay attention both to his own personal needs and feelings and to
those of others.

Development stages or states of consciousness

The development stages or states of consciousness are:

- *Developed:* attentive, acute observer. Expert who can also share own
  knowledge. Visionary qualities. Can let go of things.
- *Average:* intense need for autonomy; a clear cognitive and analytic orientation and a theoretical interest. There is a tendency to reduce feelings
  and needs and to shut out the world.
- *Pathological:* insensitive to the needs of others, emotionally cold.
  Conserves energy and compulsively avoids giving. There is a compulsion
  not to do what is expected. There is a feeling of emptiness and a fear of
  being swallowed up.

Higher virtue and idea

The *higher virtue* of Type 5 is detachment. This involves trusting that
there is always sufficient life energy and realising that it does not have to
be hoarded: and, indeed, that it cannot be. In this way it is possible to
pay heartfelt attachment to others without threatening one's own energy
reserves. The *higher idea* is omniscience. This involves trusting that the
right knowledge will be there at the right moment. On this transcendental level, where everything is connected with everything else, there is
transparency.

How to proceed

For the reader making first acquaintance with the enneagram:
   If you think this is your type, then check also Types 6 and 9. See if you
recognise the stress Type 7 in pressure situations, and the relaxation Type
8 in situations in which you feel emotionally secure. Find out also if you
recognise anything of the wings, Type 4 and Type 6.
   The 'self-developer' and the professional will find detailed information in
Part IV. Here are a few very brief tips:

- For the 'self-developer': consciously devote attention to feelings; reveal things that are more personal in conversation; be more explicit about the space you yourself need and the space you can give others.
- For the professional with Type 5 the personal pitfall is analysis without paying attention to feelings. In working with others with Type 5 it is important to respect their need for their own space, to make a clear distinction between one's own demands and requests to them, and to offer very carefully rationed invitations to them to discuss their feelings.

Type 6

In Chapter 6 we dealt with all the concepts that occur in this type description. Here we discuss:

- The world of a Type 6: this is an exercise to let you experience the inner dialogue of this type.
- Qualities, pitfalls, and characteristics of an average Type 6.
- Basic patterns of Type 6; these are shared by everyone with Type 6.
- Variants and manifestations of Type 6; these show how people with Type 6 can differ from one another.

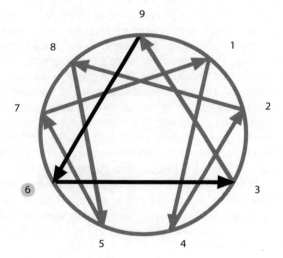

The world of a Type 6

Today you have a first meeting with a company you have just acquired as a client. You have left home in plenty of time because you definitely don't want to be late. You can't count on anything these days. If there isn't an ordinary traffic jam then a truck will topple over. Last time out it took you two hours to cover 30 miles! And your car isn't getting any younger; you imagine yourself standing at the roadside with burnt-out valves waiting on the AA. Let's just hope that the motorway telephones work. Have you got your own phone with you?

You only hope you can find the place. You don't entirely trust the route description. He said that it wasn't difficult and that you couldn't miss it, but will that really be true? You never know if people count the little streets when they're talking about the 'fourth on the right'; you've just had a problem with that. They don't always count the number of traffic lights properly either. Did he count the lights at the slip-road or not? It puts you in a lather. Just imagine if you were to arrive late! In that case, you'd better give up. He talked about a car park behind the building ('You'll see the entrance for yourself'). Well, you'll just have to wait and see about that. Not long ago you had to make a first visit to a client who said that too. The building was quite obvious, for sure, but the client's name wasn't displayed on it. You only realised there was something wrong 15 miles further on. And what if the car park is full? Can you still park somewhere near there? That's another typical example of the government's misuse of power: allowing too few parking places while they provide no acceptable alternative for using the car.

This client is quite high up in the organisation. On the telephone he said that the middle management had to be trained. Perhaps this is his strategy for covering up his own faults. In your own organisation you have agitated successfully against this kind of thing. The partners did not bring in enough work, which is their job, and tried to fob this off on the juniors by claiming that they generated too few spin-off commissions. You really went to work on that. Your concern wasn't for yourself, because you have quite enough work, but there are a few juniors who show promise but have not yet attracted any work themselves. If the partner for whom they work on projects never puts in an appearance in those projects and loses clients as a result, he mustn't complain that there aren't any follow-up commissions. You gave them a piece of your mind and that has helped. There are now clear agreements about the division between the partners' responsibility and the juniors', and no juniors have been fired.

When you think about it, there are often people high up in the organisation who can't be trusted completely. They mess things up themselves and then decide that people lower down have to be fired or trained. You are curious about the client you are going to see. In any event you'll keep a sharp eye on him.

Qualities, pitfalls and other characteristics of an average Type 6

Qualities of Type 6 are loyalty to and protection of friends and underdogs, tackling authority on their behalf, creativity, and sensitivity (also for hidden intentions).

A Type 6 values loyalty to family, friends and the group(s) to which they belong. They tend to stand up for the underdog, doing this often within a group. Within such a group it is the good cause that matters. Thus a Type 6 once related that after a number of years he realised that he scarcely knew the members of his action group as people: they were always concerned with the cause. Type 6 tests people out to see who acts solely out of self-interest and who stands up for others. This can involve 'Devil's advocate' behaviour in relations with authority.

Safety is an important motivator. There is a tendency to see threats and to suspect hidden intentions. The threats can be real, but Type 6 can also imagine threats that are not present objectively, or ascribe to people intentions they do not have. When someone departs from previous ideas or agreements Type 6 can sometimes explain this in terms of bad intentions. Doing nothing can be interpreted as deliberate sabotage or involvement in a hidden agenda. Type 6 tends to distrust others.

Type 6s tend to imagine constantly what might go wrong, and what the 'worst-case scenarios' are. They are therefore good at risk analysis and preparation for possible setbacks. They have a tendency to raise the alarm. In their imagination, the power of a party can be exaggerated. They can worry about the consequences of rash actions by others, and exaggerate in this regard.

Type 6 is strong in the pioneer phase of a project but can have difficulty in building it up and finishing it off. This person is alert and creative in solving problems. He looks for analytical solutions. Strategy and planning are strong suits. His creative power is sharpened further by setbacks.

Type 6 has difficulty with success. Success means being conspicuous and thereby vulnerable to attacks by others. Without exaggerating too much, one might say that the worse things are going objectively, the better Type 6 functions. In real danger situations, Type 6 can be extremely effective. If there is nothing the matter, however, doubt can rule him. This can result in him postponing actions and decisions, and asking the opinion of all those involved before taking a definitive personal standpoint. An alternative behaviour is exaggerated care. If in doubt he will sometimes change his opinions and he talks a great deal with people, bilaterally and in groups. He needs time to control his sense of doubt. Type 6 is sometimes called an 'evidence junkie'. After a decision has been made he can re-open discussion on a topic, not because he really wants to return to the subject but to seek reassurance that the decision has rested on sound arguments.

Authorities and rules are distrusted. This can express itself in obedience, reliability and a sense of duty with regard to authority, or rebellion. Type 6 fights or flies, looking for a protector or becoming leader of the opposition. Type 6 distrusts power.

Type 6s expect consistency, transparency, clarity and reliability from people in authority. They have an aversion to censorship. Trust is built up slowly. A Type 6 can provide good leadership when provided with reliable feedback. In positions of responsibility he can be too indulgent (the role of authority is not pleasant) or too controlling. There is a tendency to take comments as criticism.

The energy of Type 6 is actively vigilant.

Basic patterns of Type 6

The *attention* goes to 'worst-case scenarios', to what might go wrong, and to possible hidden agendas. The inner feeling of being threatened has to be dealt with by thinking. Attention also goes to control of everything that can go wrong. The *basic motivation* is to create safety in a dangerous world through exercising vigilance, imaginative power and doubt. The world is perceived through 'spectacles' of distrust and possible threats. The *emotional programming* is an over-sensitivity to lack of loyalty, a lack of transparency, and situations in which people end up in the position of underdog and are badly treated. The *basic assumption* is that the world is dangerous; one must be vigilant and doubting in order to survive. Thus the *basic fear* is one of perishing in a dangerous world. The *survival strategy* is being vigilant and prepared for anything that might happen, avoiding possible danger, and either associating oneself with authority or taking action in possibly danger-ous situations and rebelling against authority. The *paradox* is that the continual attention paid to the struggle for safety in an unsafe world leads to a still greater feeling of insecurity. The *temptation* is thus to strive constantly for safety. Things *avoided* are risk (in the phobic variant), fear (in the contra-phobic variant) and helplessness. The *ideal self-image* is: 'I am loyal and trustworthy; people can rely on me.' The *driving emotional energy* of Type 6 is fear. Thus the *mental preoccupation* is doubt. Lack of courage is also an issue for Type 6. The *defence mechanism* of Type 6 is projection. The reasons for one's own fear are sought in the outside word instead of in one's own inner world. As a result Type 6 sometimes assumes bad intentions when none exist, or sees imaginary dangers.

Variants and manifestations of Type 6

Different variants and manifestation forms of Type 6 arise from (among other things):

- sub-types
- stress and relaxation
- development stages or states of consciousness
- higher virtue and idea.

Sub-types

The basic patterns of Type 6, the inner mechanisms, express themselves via the sub-types. The sub-type themes of Type 6 are the following:

- *Self-preservation – warmth, affection.* This sub-type counters fear by using personal warmth in forming relationships and concluding agree-ments. They feel comfortable and safe with people who like them, and threatened if not liked. Can flatter like Type 2. When this sub-type receives warmth in return, they feel safe. When this is not the case, the other person is regarded as dangerous and thus rejected. Lack of warmth is a threat to safety. Without constant reassurance about a relationship their imagination quickly runs away with them ('What is happening?'; 'Why hasn't that person phoned?'; 'What are they organising behind my back?'). Needs a safe home and protection against the outside world.

- *One-to-one – being strong and beautiful.* Strength and looking good are a mask that hides inner doubt. Willpower and physical strength are used to overcome fear. This sub-type does not want to appear weak. Can also attach himself to another powerful person. This sub-type can use attractiveness to obtain protection: 'If I am attractive, no one sees that I am afraid and then I can feel strong.' Can appear outwardly just as powerful as Type 8 or 3. The preoccupation with being strong flows from the need to develop personal power to counteract fear. Even a fearful person can feel powerful if he is attractive, strong and clever.

- *Social – duty, comradeship.* Clarity about one's own role in the group, knowledge of the rules and clear agreements with others about mutual responsibilities and involvement counteract fear and prevent rejection. Innovation is therefore not very welcome. The collective authority of the group confirms existing concepts and convictions, thereby diminishing the doubt and reducing the danger of being attacked. This sub-type can be passively aggressive, just like Type 9. Doing one's duty can be both a calling and a burden. This sub-type can sacrifice himself for a good cause. He wavers between phobic and contraphobic reaction: if an authority uses its power well, he adapts himself; on the contrary, if an authority cannot be trusted, this sub-type rebels and calls on others to do so as well.

Stress and relaxation

Type 6 goes under stress to 3. On the positive side he becomes result-oriented, and is less given to doubt and procrastination. On the negative side, he can worry too much about the impression he makes. In relaxation and emotional security Type 6 goes to 9. On the positive side he can then identify himself better with different standpoints. On the negative side he may no longer feel any need to make decisions, and can interpret differences of opinion as possible conflicts which have to be avoided.

Development stages or states of consciousness

The development stages or states of consciousness are:

- *Developed:* the developed type is courageous and has developed trust.
- *Average:* is loyal, has a love-hate relationship with authority, stands up for the underdog, is worried and unsure, can be militant, is sensitive to possible hidden agendas.

- *Pathological:* paranoid. There is excessive vigilance, distrust and belligerence; cynicism; a mixture of aggression towards, hate for and submissive behaviour towards authority; and over-sensitivity. Feelings of guilt are countered by self-justification, projection, submissive behaviour and assertive bragging. Can also be his own enemy through self-accusation and drawing attention to his own shortcomings.

Higher virtue and idea

The *higher idea* of Type 6 is trust and belief in himself, in others, in the world and in the universe. Trust and belief arise from the perception of being supported and borne along by the universe. The *higher virtue* is courage, the courage to pursue his way in spite of fear and doubt. In fact, only someone who knows fear can be courageous.

How to proceed

For the reader making first acquaintance with the enneagram:

If you think this is your type, then check also Types 4, 5, 7, and 9. See if you recognise the stress Type 3 in pressure situations and the relaxation Type 9 in situations in which you feel emotionally secure. Find out also if you recognise anything of the wings, Type 5 and Type 7.

The 'self-developer' and the professional will find detailed information in Part IV. Here are a few very brief tips:

- For the 'self-developer': check your own tendency towards mistrust and 'worst-case scenarios'; find out if these apprehensions are justified.
- For the professional with Type 6 the personal pitfall is excessive concern about everything that can go wrong. When working with others with Type 6 it is important for the professional to encourage them to check this against reality, and to be transparent himself, clear about his intentions and trustworthy.

Type 7

In Chapter 6 we dealt with all the concepts that occur in this type description. Here we discuss:

- The world of a Type 7: this is an exercise to let you experience the inner dialogue of this type.
- Qualities, pitfalls, and characteristics of an average Type 7.
- Basic patterns of Type 7; these are shared by everyone with Type 7.
- Variants and manifestations of Type 7; these show how people with Type 7 can differ from one another.

The world of a Type 7

You've been landed with the third negative assessment of one of your projects. Your boss won't like that. You get an uneasy feeling in your stomach when you think about the discussion you now have to have with him. But no, you won't let them get you down. You're going to work really hard at improving your perform-ance. It *has* to work. Let's get this straight – it *will* work! You imagine how wonderfully well it will go the next time. It's simple for

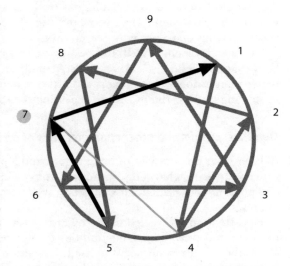

someone with your capabilities. Anyway, there is a great opportunity coming up to work on a tremendously interesting project with another organisation that you would really like to take. It is very innovative, really never having been done before anywhere. You would meet lots of different, interesting people. You have spoken already to a few of them and you are fascinated by all the possibilities. Well, actually it wouldn't be all that bad if your boss took you off this project. You've seen it all already, and then you would have your hands free to take on a number of new jobs in which you could let yourself go completely.

You have lots of ideas about all the things you could do. Improve the pres-entation of this organisation, for instance. The website, for example, is far too dull. That can really be done much better. You can do so many interest-ing things with it! You already see clearly before you how the website could look, with a lot of movement and with cartoons in it. And humour naturally: that works well on the Web. Incidentally, you also fancy being involved for a time with the control function. It must be possible to do that responsibly without people being constantly bothered by it. What's more, you recently met someone at a congress who wanted to have a talk sometime about possi-ble co-operation. The two of you had had a lively and pleasant conversation over lunch, and afterwards he had said: 'Come along sometime: there's a lot to be done in our company.' That's the way these things go. If you build up good contacts the work comes in by itself. Actually, it wouldn't be such a bad thing if you had a bit less work for a while. There are still so many exhibi-tions you haven't seen. Immediately you plan to take in a few special ones this weekend. You have seen the catalogues – really fascinating. And while you are at one gallery you might take in a museum nearby and visit some friends in the neighbourhood whom you haven't seen in months. Perhaps they would like to go to the gallery as well – that would be nice. And then a walk in the park there. Then you can fit in a cosy meal together. Then, since you're driving that way, why not go on to ...?

Ah, that project ... Well, the best thing you can do is to suggest to your boss that someone else take it over. Actually it suits your colleagues much better than it does you. There is too little excitement in it. Your strength lies in starting up new things, not in repeating the same thing again and again.

Qualities, pitfalls and other characteristics of an average Type 7

A Type 7 has great power of imagination and a positive attitude. This person is lively, creative, charming, enthusing, convincing, adventurous, self-assured and good at networking. He can get on well with most people and has broad interests.

His attention is directed more towards positive future possibilities than to the here and now. Those possibilities do not have to be realised; thinking about them is often sufficient in itself. Execution means making choices, and is therefore limiting. Type 7 would rather have ten birds in the bush than one in the hand: better to keep all options open rather than choosing any of them. There is a predilection for new experiences. New ideas and concepts are attractive. Possibilities are more interesting than actual work.

First and foremost, work must be interesting; this is more important than producing results. That is not to say that Type 7s do not finish their work, or allow it to be finished: usually they do, or at least the Type 7s that I encounter in my work. They can produce a great deal and be highly efficient, sometimes at the expense of quality. They can become overloaded by the number of projects that arouse their interest, and these are the ones they tend to take on. They cannot always distinguish main from secondary affairs; focus is difficult. Because Type 7s tend to spread their interest over many subjects, people around them can feel that they are not taken seriously, or that they neglect them ('We had an appointment, didn't we? But now you're doing something else!'). This is usually not Type 7's intention. Type 7 is good at linking various projects and possible choices and synthesising them. He likes a high energy level and invests in it.

Type 7s can have difficulty with commitment, not in the short term perhaps, but certainly over longer periods. If a project lasts longer than they would prefer, they soon busy themselves again with other options. There is a fear of becoming stuck; everything has to keep moving and must not become predictable. Type 7 does not like hindrances and limitations, and will evade them whenever possible. Flexibility is very important for him.

Type 7s want to feel on a level with those in authority. Not every boss is happy about that, and then conflicts can arise. They relinquish their own leadership roles easily if they hinder their personal freedom. Colleagues may sometimes find them hard to follow because they are constantly changing plans or direction – with no ill intentions, of course. Decisions are often made at the last minute.

Painful incidents are repudiated; problems reasoned away. Type 7 can react to feedback with excuses and avoidance, but also with assurances that all will be well in the future, without him having any idea of how he is going to achieve this. Criticism disturbs the positive self-image. Type 7 tends to reduce tension within a group, with a joke or by pointing out the positive side of a grim situation. Once, in a team session I was facilitating, a participant burst into tears, upon which the Type 7 chief responded at once with: 'But that's exactly what we are now solving.' Type 7s finds it difficult to recognise painful experiences, both their own and those of others. They tend to re-label unpleasant experiences. For example a Type 7, while he was unemployed, talked about his dismissal in the following manner:

> I now have a great chance to start something new. It's a fascinating period in which I talk to lots of interesting people. Networking is enormously interesting. I come into organisations where I would never go otherwise; my field of vision is being broadened. Now I can go and do what I really want; it gets me out of the rut I always wanted to escape from.

In this way the unpleasant aspect of being fired is kept out of the consciousness. The result is that a Type 7 sometimes feels that people do not see the deeper side of his character.

People of this type feel they have a right to satisfaction, to a good life, to the nicest work, to being treated well, and they are convinced that they are always welcome everywhere. Needs should be fulfilled immediately, and delay in this area is not tolerated. They can behave as if limitations do not apply to them personally and they are exempt from routine work. This can irritate colleagues. They can feel superior, or at least give that impression.

Type 7 has active energy; there is a quality of fascination.

Basic patterns of Type 7

The *attention* goes to thinking about as many options and opportunities as possible, imagining positive future possibilities and exciting action. The *basic motivation* is to avoid fear and pain by imagining pleasant future possibilities and seeking interesting occupations. Type 7 *perceives a world* full of bright possibilities. The *emotional programming* is an over-sensitivity to limitations and hindrances. These have to be dealt with. The *basic assumption* is that the world limits people and causes pain. Type 7s can extract themselves from this by applying their power of thought to positive possibilities. The *basic fear* is therefore suffering pain. The *survival strategy* is imagining positive possibilities to avoid feeling pain, and interpreting unpleasant things as positive. The *paradox* is that admitting only the positive side of life is actually a limitation in itself. The *temptation* is having to be happy, and also idealism. What is *avoided* is psychological and physical pain and unpleasant situations. The *ideal self-image* is: 'I am committed; I go for things 100 per cent; I am pleasant and see the positive side of things.' The *driving emotional energy* of Type 7 is gluttony. The *mental preoccupation* is making plans. Type 7 is constantly busy with all possibilities which lie open and which lie within reach. Type 7's defence mechanism is rationalisation, or finding so-called rational 'reasons' for what one does which need not necessarily be authentic: for instance, buying something useless 'because it was so cheap that I can always make a profit if I sell it'.

Different variants and manifestations of Type 7

Variants and manifestation forms arise from (among other things):

- sub-types
- stress and relaxation
- the nine-pointed star
- development stages or states of consciousness
- higher virtue and idea.

Sub-types

The basic patterns of Type 7, the inner mechanisms, express themselves via the sub-types. The sub-type themes of Type 7 are the following:

- *Self-preservation – group safety, defence of like-minded, family*. This sub-type combats fear of perishing by assembling round him a 'family' of selected people who see the same possibilities or share the same dream, or can contribute to Type 7's vision. The 'family' defends this sub-Type 7. This person has an exuberant life style: ideas are shared, elaborate meals are prepared and pleasant projects planned. Everyone must be happy. Safety arises through sharing positive future plans; in this respect this sub-type's attitude is immoderate. There is great need to amuse and be amused.
- *One-to-one – fascination, suggestibility*. This sub-type is easily attracted by new ideas, people and adventures and makes many one-to-one contacts through his charm. In his fantasy he imagines everything that could come from such a contact: the possibilities are endless. He has a great need for change; as a result it is easy for him to become distracted from what he had taken on himself. The tasks assumed must therefore remain very interesting. This person is genuinely interested in something, but soon it will be time to start on something else. He sees the world through the spectacles of his own imagination. He is also good at influencing others to start something new.

- *Social – sacrificial inclination.* Immediate pleasure is sacrificed in order to realise a dream of the future. This sub-type needs his friends and group projects; he feels attracted to people and groups who have the same ideas and take pleasure in the same activities. But at the same time, group life and responsibility for the people around him limit real pleasure, personal ambitions and possibilities for the future. He cannot go on alone if the group is not ready for the next step. The honourable role of martyr makes the limitations acceptable, as does the view that all limitations are temporary. Carrying out the good intentions, however, can be difficult, especially if something has to be given up for this. The individual wants to belong to the group, but authority, coercion and control are all unacceptable.

Stress and relaxation

Type 7 goes under stress to 1. On the positive side he then experiences a greater need to finish things off at a high level. On the negative side he can become negatively critical. In relaxation Type 7 goes to 5. On the positive side this leads to a more reflective attitude and more thought before taking action. On the negative side he can come to lack initiative.

Nine-pointed star

The point that completes the triangle is Type 4. Type 7 can learn from Type 4 how to experience the less pleasant sides of life, and so acquire a more complete world of experience.

Development stages or states of consciousness

The development stages or states of consciousness are:

- *Developed:* the developed Type 7 can take on commitments, choose a focus in his work and maintain it, and when necessary restrict himself in what he wants.
- *Average:* the average Type 7 is oriented towards positive future possibilities, new experiences and exciting action. Is interested in many things. Always wants to keep options open. Re-frames negative matters as positive. Is indulgent to himself and others. Has an unconventional outlook and sometimes has revolutionary ideas. Hates limitations and is not well disposed towards authority. Charms and disarms. Assumes a personal right to the good things in life.
- *Pathological:* narcissistic. Lacks discipline. Has something 'playboyish/girlish' about them, is manic, can be led by wishful thinking. Seduces and manipulates through charm. Avoids and represses pain and fear. Maintains an implicit superiority over others in the guise of equality. A charlatan who rationalises and idealises.

Higher virtue and idea

The *higher virtue* of Type 7 is sobriety. This means making choices instead of wanting everything. Work, the *higher idea* of Type 7, means carrying out the choice in the here and now, instead of leaving it among future possibilities. Work also means accepting in the present the whole of life instead of just the positive side, thus embracing joy and sorrow, pleasure and pain, options and limitations. Work in order to realise one's true self can only take place in the present.

How to proceed

For the reader making first acquaintance with the enneagram:

If you think this is your type, then check also Types 1, 2, 4, 5, 6, 8 and 9 (this type is seen by many as sociably desirable, hence the large number of other possible types to be considered). See if you recognise the stress Type 1 in situations in which you are under pressure and the relaxation Type 5 in situations in which you feel emotionally secure. Find out also if you recognise anything of the wings, Type 6 and Type 8.

The 'self-developer' and the professional will find detailed information in Part IV. Here are a few very brief tips:

- For the 'self-developer': note when you avoid unpleasant things by occupying yourself with more attractive subjects. Then do what has to be done with the less pleasant subject. Finish something before you start on something new.
- For the professional with Type 7 the personal pitfalls are wanting to make things exciting when this is not appropriate, and wanting to be rid of painful subjects. When working with someone else with Type 7 it is important always to be clear oneself, to ask for commitment explicitly, to support him in finishing things off and in enduring difficult situations without walking away from them.

CHAPTER 9

The Belly Types

The belly centre is the source of the vitality and energy of every person, and the source of awareness of one's very being. The belly types tend to act on the basis of intuition, gut feeling and non-verbal signals. Doing is their way of dealing with the world, or at least their preoccupation (Type 9 sometimes actually does not 'do'). The belly types have a tendency to turn against others. Power, control, justice and anger are common themes, as is an underlying feeling of worthlessness which is compensated for through these themes. The belly types are also called the 'self-forgetting' types. Where the heart types had problems with shame, the belly types have feelings of guilt. They feel that intrinsically they fall too far short of the ideal. These types have loving – primarily loving themselves – as a development task. This can then replace a desire to keep everything under control, a theme common to all belly types.

The three belly types deal with their common themes in different ways. First, anger:

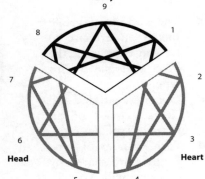

- Type 8 directs anger at others, can be explosively furious, and denies feelings of guilt (of which he may, in fact, remain unaware himself) by blaming others.
- Type 9 expresses anger indirectly through passive aggression. Passive aggression is letting anger show through without making it explicit, while disavowing this anger when spoken to about it.

- Type 1 feels he should not be angry, and suppresses rage. He can feel guilty about his anger, and about his lack of perfection if he becomes angry nonetheless. This type, however, can be aggressively critical, and even furious, if he feels his anger is legitimate.

The second common theme is that the belly types have a tendency to 'forget themselves'. This theme also expresses itself in different ways with the separate types:

- With Type 8 'forgetting oneself' plays a role in investing in power, in being strong and in control.
- Type 9 can 'forget himself' by going along with the agendas of others.
- Type 1 'forgets himself' by repressing his own impulses, wishes and needs.

A third common theme is control, as follows:

- Type 8 exercises explicit control by his physical presence, by the way he expresses himself and by his impulsive way of communicating emotions.
- Type 9 exercises indirect control by communicating disagreement in a veiled manner, by silent sabotage, by sulking and by avoiding things.
- Type 1 controls by being critical and proclaiming standards, or sometimes merely by radiating this implicitly, in which case he does not say anything but others feel judged or condemned.

Type 8

In Chapter 6 we dealt with all the concepts that occur in this type description. Here we discuss:

- The world of a Type 8: this is an exercise to let you experience the inner dialogue of this type.
- Qualities, pitfalls, and characteristics of an average Type 8.
- Basic patterns of Type 8; these are shared by everyone with Type 8.

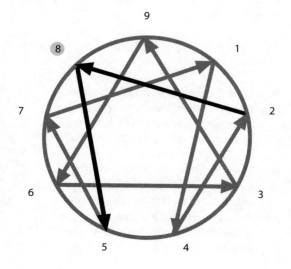

- Variants and manifestations of Type 8; these show how people with Type 8 can differ from one another.

The world of a Type 8

Your dream is of a fairer world and you are prepared to do a lot to help achieve it. With your organisation, and under your leadership, it must be possible to make a considerable contribution. So it irritates you a good deal when staff members do not commit themselves 200 per cent, and then you don't keep quiet about it. You can't stand it if they then avoid you. One must be able to speak the truth. Incidentally, you also expect that of your colleagues. Direct communication and taking personal responsibility – that's what you expect. You find all that gossip – and certainly gossip about you – unacceptable. They can simply discuss it with you if they have anything to say, can't they? But although your door is always open, people seldom enter. Yesterday you blew up. It was really out of order, but then he shouldn't have asked such a stupid question. They say that you are overpowering. Nonsense! They should just say something back again.

That grumbling about the odd-job lad must stop too. The boy is not all there mentally and, admittedly, he is always putting things in the wrong place. But if you can't have a job in your organisation for someone like that? It's unthinkable. A lad like that must also have a place. He stays here on your personal say-so. Why else do you run your own business?

You suddenly have a wonderful idea about a project you could do with your company. The thought is the deed, so you grab the telephone and begin to organise it. This will be a real topper! This will really have impact! It will be a tough haul for a while, but you are prepared to accept that. The last time you did something like this, you worked night and day for months. Now, that's no problem: if you have something in your head it will happen, whatever the cost. They're not happy at home but you were straight with your partner when you started courting: you don't want her complaining 'you weren't there when we wanted to eat at six o'clock'. A relationship with you means a total packet, not taking a bit of you here and leaving a bit of you there. You are just someone who does a lot and achieves a lot. If you work, then you work hard; if you have a drink, then it's not just one; if you're angry, then you're very, very angry; and if you take over new companies, then you have lots of them. There's no caution involved – you can't put up with that.

Qualities, pitfalls and other characteristics of an average Type 8

This type is by nature direct, assertive, does not avoid confrontation and is courageous. He likes the truth and has a strong feeling of justice. He has a great deal of energy. Many Type 8s say that others find them overwhelming, or that others think they take up (too) much space. Actually, the Type 8 is just being himself. This type does not naturally empathise with others. He expects others to stand up for themselves, just as he does. He has difficulty understanding that his directness can lead to others trying to avoid him. Letting something glimmer through or giving subtle hints is not an effective strategy with Type 8, who will probably not pick up the signals. Type 8 tends to take things literally.

Type 8s use their energy in pursuit of their own pleasure and interests, but also in the service of the weak, of their team or organisation, and for the empowerment of others. Real weakness, such as lack of opportunity to exert any real influence or being mentally challenged, inspires a protective urge in Type 8. Thus someone told me that he could not bear it when a boss mistreated a worker, and that he had attacked him impulsively. By contrast, people who pretend to be weak while they are not weak in objective terms, and who choose the role of victim when they could (and should) do otherwise – well, Type 8 wants to clean the floor with them.

Type 8 is goal- and action-oriented. Wants to make decisions quickly. Has great will-power and perseverance. Can shoot straight for the goal. Gives the impression of being motivated and self-assured. He has a natural tendency either to take the lead or to have this thrust upon him. Many Type 8s say that one way or another, without them really intending it, they always end up in a position of leadership ('I became a member of the tennis club to play tennis but after three weeks I was already on the management committee').

Type 8 is always clear about things himself, and expects a partner in discussion to be clear, direct and firm also. Type 8 hates people who are evasive and prevaricate. As a worker he expects clear rules and strong, honest, just leadership. Managers who are inconsistent are regarded as incompetent.

Type 8s think in black and white rather than in shades of grey; nuances are wasted on them. They have an 'all or nothing' attitude, and clear ideas about what is right and wrong.

There is a tendency towards excessive behaviour. This can express itself, for instance, in working very long and hard, fanatical participation in sports, partying till late at night, acquiring still more companies, or eating and drinking. Everything can be taken to excess, in fact. Limits are not seen or not respected, something which can be damaging both to themselves and to others. Type 8s can work longer hours than is good for their own health, insist that something be done in a certain manner, or hurt people by saying to their faces whatever they feel inside. Their courage arises partly from the fact that they do not see danger. There is a feeling that rules are not made for them, and therefore that they do not need to be kept.

When staff depart from a rule or hold back information, however, this inspires distrust and can be like a red rag to a bull. Type 8 wants people to be predictable, but not blindly submissive. Lack of loyalty is unforgivable. Type 8's own people are protected but may also be tyrannised. Consistency is of no value to him – he makes rules and does not keep them himself. At one moment Type 8 is flexible with their application; at another the rules must be followed to the letter. At one moment he delegates power and then he changes his mind. He keeps control, is on the alert for being manipulated, and in general is watchful for people with hidden intentions. Loss of face to others is not something that bothers him or that he tries to prevent.

Truth and justice are very important for Type 8s. With the average type there may be confusion between self-interest and objective truth, and between justice and revenge. These people make no distinction between the work in hand and personal relationships: a professional difference of opinion means a personal enemy. They can react disproportionately to a (supposed) threat. They blame others before examining themselves. Feedback may be regarded as an attack demanding a counter-attack. Thus a manager with Type 8 once exploded when a staff member wanted to order a certain item: 'Do you think I'm crazy enough to spend money on something that's still lying in the cupboard?' When his attention was drawn to the fact that this was not the item in question he was quiet for five seconds. Then he became even angrier: 'Aha, so you have misinformed me!'

Type 8 can burst into a rage, but afterwards the air is clear for him and he can forget it. If he is later accused of inappropriate behaviour, he may genuinely believe that the incident never took place. The impact of these explosions on others is much greater than Type 8 actually realises – other people remember them all too well.

In general others fail to notice gentleness, tenderness and sensitivity in this type, although Type 8 himself often does not realise this. Thus someone with Type 8 said: 'What do you mean "not sensitive"? I'm extremely sensitive. If I'm hurt I curse and swear and kick doors and throw things at the wall.' He did not see that others did not interpret this behaviour as gentle and sensitive. One's own weaknesses, fear and vulnerability can be denied, just like problematic information.

In his own eyes Type 8 has almost limitless energy; in the eyes of others this can be an intrusive energy.

Basic patterns of Type 8

The *attention* goes to control, domination and power, and the prevention of vulnerability. The *basic motivation* is obtaining respect and protection, and hiding vulnerability by being strong, powerful and confrontational. Type 8 *perceives the world* through the 'spectacles' of strength or weakness. He calculates others' strengths, and is attentive to whether others are sufficiently respectful, how he can bring things under his personal control, and who might help or hinder him in this. The truly weak arouse his protective instinct. The *emotional programming* is an over-sensitivity to injustice, lack of loyalty and possible vulnerability. This means that personal feelings and the work in hand are not kept separate. The *basic assumption* is that this is a hard and unjust world, in which you can survive by will power, by being hard and confrontational, and by hiding one's own vulnerability. The *basic fear* is of being hurt. The *survival strategy* is therefore to avoid being hurt by being strong, powerful, confrontational and in control, by imposing one's own will and truth, and by denying one's own vulnerability. The *paradox* then is that the exercise of power stimulates opposing forces, and thus one's own vulnerability is actually increased. The reed bends, the oak breaks. The *temptation* is one's own concept of justice. What is *avoided* is one's own vulnerability. The *ideal self-image* is: 'I am powerful, strong, invulnerable, able to do everything; I am responsible and I serve the truth.' The *driving emotional energy* of Type 8 is lust for life, desire. The *mental preoccupation* is the need to take revenge on those who (apparently) thwart this driving emotional energy. The *defence mechanism* of Type 8 is denial.

Variants and manifestations of Type 8

Different variants and manifestations of Type 8 arise from (among other things):

- sub-types
- stress and relaxation
- development stages or states of consciousness
- higher virtue and idea.

Sub-types

The basic patterns of Type 8, the inner mechanisms, express themselves via the sub-types. The sub-type themes of Type 8 are the following:

- *Self-preservation – satisfactory survival*. This sub-type translates the fondness of excess common to all Type 8s into physical survival and material safety. There must always be supplies of everything that is considered necessary – often including mundane needs. Preferably these are stored in an impregnable bunker, with everything that is comfortable (food, books, cat) within easy reach; failing that, they must be easily obtainable in the immediate surroundings. This sub-type does not have such a need to show himself – until someone treads on his territory, when all hell breaks loose. He is afraid of being considered inferior. The need for privacy is like Type 5's. There is a preoccupation with surviving in a 'Type 8' manner: people are dominated and intimidated to instill fighting spirit in them; departure from rules cannot be tolerated, otherwise 'the whole business will collapse immediately'.
- *One-to-one – possession and surrender*. This sub-type tends to exercise power over his or her partner and other important people and to control them. This sub-type wants to know everything: all secrets must be shared. There is a battle for power, but winning is the end of the game. The relationship then becomes less interesting, because the struggle gives

those involved vital energy and is also a way of testing partners. When the other person has proved to be trustworthy and loyal, and able to take the 8 on, then this sub-type can surrender and also be vulnerable and small. There is a need for trustworthy allies in a dangerous world. If this safety is not attained, however, this sub-type is a competitor who never gives up.

- Social – friendship. People of this sub-type are always looking for friendship. Their time is occupied with sports activities, discussions, long drinking sessions, and so on. They can give of themselves amongst their comrades. This sub-type fights powerlessness and injustice by being a member of a group, mostly in a leading role, and putting its anger and aggression at the service of a common cause. The world in divided into friends and enemies. Friends and the cause can be more important than personal feelings and needs; he wants everybody to feel good and co-operate. This sub-type can be like Type 2. He says that restraining himself within a group is an unpleasant experience.

Stress and relaxation

Type 8 goes under stress to 5. On the positive side, he then has space to think things over and absorb them. On the negative side, this can lead to withdrawal from what has to be done. In relaxation Type 8 goes to 2. On the positive side he acquires more of an eye for the needs and feelings of others. On the negative side he can become manipulative in order to obtain recognition.

Development stages or states of consciousness

The development stages or states of consciousness are:

- *Developed:* frank, truly just, magnanimous, constructive.
- *Average:* enthusiasm, intensity, need for stimuli, direct, goal-/action-oriented, feeling of justice, taking the law into one's own hands, dominating, does not respect boundaries, black-and-white thinking, tendency towards excess.
- *Pathological:* quick-tempered, aggressive, intimidating, tyrannical, revengeful, sadistic, disciplinary and hostile, finds pleasure in denigrating others, pitiless, tends towards projection (others are untrustworthy, aggressive, controlling), megalomania.

Higher virtue and idea

The *higher virtue* of Type 8 is innocence and frankness, just as a child without inhibitions can take life as it comes and experience every situation anew without having to keep control of anything. The *higher idea* is sensitivity for real truth instead of associating this with self-interest – the ultimate truth of the universe, the truth shared by everyone and everything instead of the personal truth.

How to proceed

For the reader making first acquaintance with the enneagram:

If you think this is your type, then check also Types 1, 4, 5, 7 and 9. (Many people see this type as sociably desirable, hence this large number of types that are also fairly likely.) See if you recognise the stress Type 5 in stress situations and the relaxation Type 2 in situations in which you feel emotionally secure. Find out also if you recognise anything of the wings, Type 7 and Type 9.

The 'self-developer' and the professional will find detailed information in Part IV. Here are a few very brief tips:

- For the 'self-developer': bridle your impulsive tendency towards action a little more, use no more strength than is necessary, make a conscious effort to give others more space, admit your own feelings of vulnerability.
- For the professional with Type 8 the personal pitfall is a wish to steer and control too much. In working with others with Type 8 it is important to provide him with feedback about the effect he can have on others. The professional must visibly occupy space himself; if he does not do so, Type 8 will not respect him.

Type 9

In Chapter 6 we dealt with all the concepts that occur in this type description. Here we discuss:

- The world of a Type 9: this is an exercise to let you experience the inner dialogue of this type.
- Qualities, pitfalls, and characteristics of an average Type 9.
- Basic patterns of Type 9; these are shared by everyone with Type 9.
- Variants and manifestations of Type 9; these show how people with type 9 can differ from one another.

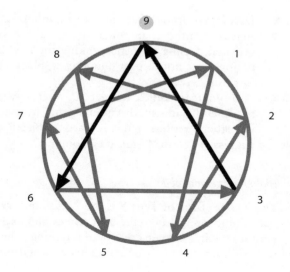

The world of a Type 9

You have the feeling that your boss doesn't take you very seriously. You've already said a number of times that the amount of work you have can't be done by one person. But then he just grins and says you know perfectly well that extension is not the company policy. You suspect he doesn't appreciate the importance of your work for the company, and you feel wronged. You let it filter out that you don't agree, and now and then you drop a hint.

This morning the two of you had a meeting with the whole staff about the move. Not so pleasant. The management had come up with a room allocation that satisfied no one, under the principle 'it's impossible to please everyone'. Now, that was right at least! Everybody was dissatisfied and made no bones about it. With such an attitude on the management's part that was only to be expected. You offered to draw up an alternative plan, in consultation with everyone, which everybody would be satisfied with, for that is perfectly possible.

You are in a task group with a number of colleagues. This afternoon the group is meeting for the second time. You hope it isn't like the last time. Two colleagues hogged the discussion and others (including yourself) couldn't get a word in edgeways. They had different standpoints, but you felt there was something to be said for both. You don't understand why people fight over these things: those standpoints can be reconciled quite well. When they asked at the end what you wanted yourself, you didn't know what to say because you had actually been occupied solely with their standpoints. Once you were home, you thought again and found there was a far better approach. You'll bring that up today. You just hope there will be room for it and that those two colleagues won't use up all the time again.

Actually it's annoying that you have to sit in this group yet again. You're already in so many groups, and that way you can't get on with your own work at all. Ah well, on the other hand it's actually important to be involved everywhere, otherwise nobody thinks of taking your work into account. It'll end up with you taking work home with you again. But there's so much to do there as well that you never get around to. What's more, your partner wants some attention too. A person ought to have nine lives.

Qualities, pitfalls and other characteristics of an average Type 9

Qualities of Type 9 are being able to see different points of view and finding acceptable solutions, being able to listen well, productivity, and trustworthiness. A Type 9 can come across as a laconic, friendly, level-headed individual, but also as an obstinate, straightforward one.

The attentions of Type 9s are automatically directed to their environment – or, as they feel, drawn to it. This makes it more troublesome to know what they want personally. They can identify well with various viewpoints; they want to know what everyone thinks, and can combine those viewpoints in solutions that all those involved find acceptable. It is important that everyone is in agreement. If this is not the case then this causes tension, a tension that they prefer to disperse as quickly as possible. Type 9 is a true seeker of harmony. He does not like competition with colleagues and needs comradeship and co-operation. He prefers to avoid conflicts and differences of opinion, or to resolve them as quickly as possible. He finds practical solutions for troublesome problems. He can create a neutral and safe atmosphere. He is considerate and sensitive, and can listen well. He often puts into words what is being felt within a group. He can set up networks and promote them.

Because Type 9 can identify with many standpoints, he can sometimes find it hard to adopt a personal stance. After all, there is something to be said for everything. Decisions take time. Goals change with differing circumstances. There can be a tendency to postpone decisions, and not to take risks.

If this type has agreed to something, however, you can count on him. He can be extremely productive if there is a clear plan, and in situations where he feels accepted. Because he has difficulty saying 'no', he tends to take on too much work. The fact that he has many different interests and does not want to choose between them can also lead to him being overburdened. Sometimes Type 9 has trouble taking a personal standpoint, and would rather hear first what everyone thinks. Type 9 has difficulty guarding his own boundaries. As a consequence he tends to be aware of his own ideas only when out of range of other people. When others are present he orients himself towards their views. He has, therefore, a great need for personal space, both literally and figuratively. He tends to let someone else talk on even if he does not agree. This can lead to misunderstanding – others think Type 9 agrees with them when he is only keeping quiet. He agrees to compromises quickly and can regret it later. Sometimes he is too late to claim a position: he does not come forward easily but feels hurt nonetheless if people have not taken him into consideration.

A Type 9 with a viewpoint can be very stubborn, however, and not give in. In particular, this stubbornness emerges under pressure, when a Type 9 may actually be a bad negotiator. He quickly feels threatened and soon thinks that others do not notice him. He wants to be involved, and wants respect and recognition as a matter of course, without having to ask for them or having to take trouble to obtain them.

Type 9 finds everything he does quite normal; others have to point out to him that this is actually not the case, that there are very few others who do something his way or who have achieved the same results. Conversely, Type 9 is surprised at the way others can profile themselves. What they do he also perceives as normal, and he actually finds it embarrassing if people make a big thing of it. Complimenting others is therefore something that Type 9 has to learn.

If this person does not agree with something, he does not always feel in a position to say so, but can then exercise control by keeping silent and delaying things. Anger and energy are held back, and feelings of resentment remain unexpressed. This can be converted to passive aggression: A Type 9 will not quickly say that he is angry but will let anger filter through. If someone picks up this signal and accuses him of these feelings he may, in turn, deny being angry ('Something wrong? ... Not at all! What do you mean?'). Type 9 can also be very angry with someone, but finds this anger dissipates as soon as the person comes in: the rage disappears like snow in the sunshine ('Oh, it wasn't that important ...'), only to return when its object has left. Type 9 tends to find everything of equal importance and to let his life be ruled by the pressures of the environment. Because he pays just as much attention to unimportant as to important matters, he often does not get around to dealing with matters that are essential for him. Everything can contribute to not coming around to essential matters: eating, watching television and hobbies, but also hard work or diligence in matching up to the expectations of others.

In general Type 9 makes a restful impression. He sometimes holds back energy.

Basic patterns of Type 9

The *attention* goes to claims by others, to what they might possibly expect or think, to approval or rejection. The attention is diffuse: that is to say, it is not focused on one specific point but is widely spread. Just as a mother always hears that her baby is crying, irrespective of what she is doing, so the attention of a Type 9 goes to others, irrespective of what he is doing. The *basic motivation* is harmony, belonging, and comfort, created by forgetting oneself and by paying diffuse attention to others. The *world* is *perceived* as a whole range of possible conflicts which have to be prevented or avoided. The possibility of rejection is magnified. The *emotional programming* is an over-sensitivity regarding not being seen, and for people who present themselves (too) ostentatiously. The *basic assumption* of Type 9 is that if he complies with others, they will not notice how worthless he is. The *basic fear* is of being ostracised, not being seen, not being accepted, indeed not being at all. The *survival strategy* is therefore to seek affiliation with others and to create harmony by forgetting oneself and satisfying the supposed expectations of others. This is seen also in not noticing possible conflicts or avoiding them, and not wanting to be seen oneself. The *paradox* is that someone who tries to establish an affiliation by giving oneself up is actually trying to be accepted for someone he is not. This is not real harmony. The *temptation* is making oneself small and refusing to recognise possible conflicts ('We never quarrel – that is to say, we never discuss things about which we think differently – thus we have a good relationship'). The *things avoided*, therefore, are conflict, confrontation, discomfort. The *ideal self-image* is: 'I am peaceful, satisfied with what I have; I am not difficult; I adapt easily; nothing is important enough to make me angry.' The *driving emotional energy* is inertia: that is, inertia in choosing what is really important for oneself. The associated *mental preoccupation* is forgetting oneself, making oneself unimportant. The *defence mechanism* of Type 9 is numbing out, narcotisation or addiction, which expresses itself in spending all one's time on things of lesser importance. Deflection is also a defence mechanism of Type 9. This is a way of making affiliation more secure by avoiding real contact: for instance by indirectness with others, by putting oneself in perspective and mocking oneself, by using stereotypical language, or by replacing deep emotions with superficial ones.

Variants and manifestations of Type 9

Different variants and manifestations of Type 9 arise from (among other things):

- sub-types
- stress and relaxation
- development stages or states of consciousness
- higher virtue and idea.

Sub-types

The basic patterns of Type 9, the inner mechanisms, express themselves via the sub-types. The sub-type themes of Type 9 are the following:

- *Self-preservation – appetite.* This sub-type excels at creating a practical infrastructure and a daily rhythm, and can substitute material goods for essential aims. Not just food but everything can be hoarded: not because it is needed, but in case it becomes necessary. This sub-type can flee from essential things that have to be tackled to cosy activities such as reading magazines, doing crossword puzzles, eating crisps in front of the TV or shopping. However, gardening, reading philosophy or visiting museums can also serve as flight activities. This sub-type does not view these activities as procrastination at all. Instead, they feel like 'looking after myself', and are actually perceived as stimuli. This sub-type says 'yes' if another person wants something else, but afterwards makes sure that he gets what he wants himself, usually in an indirect manner.
- *One-to-one – union.* This sub-type wishes to be bound up with a partner, with nature, or with God. Has problems in guarding his personal boundaries. Is carried away by the enthusiasm of others. Lets another person give direction to his work and life. Is first bound up with the other person, whereby the feeling of not being noticed disappears; only afterwards begins to distinguish what belongs to himself and what belongs to the other, and what he actually want himself.

- *Social – participation.* This sub-type adapts easily to the style and agenda of friends and social groups – sometimes as leader and contributor to the general good, sometimes (in self-forgetfulness) in a comfortable social role or in activities. Often does not enter into real connection. Is regularly present and wants, on one hand, to participate in a group yet also, on the other, has doubts after he has joined as to whether he wishes to belong. A certain ambivalence persists.

Stress and relaxation

Type 9 goes under stress to 6. On the positive side he can then analyse risks better and he develops loyalty to people and causes. On the negative side he begins to suspect others of bad intentions and to think of 'worst-case' scenarios. In relaxation Type 9 goes to 3. On the positive side he then develops an image towards the outside world and can be very productive. On the negative side he can worry himself too much about the impression he makes on others.

Development stages or states of consciousness

The development stages or states of consciousness are:

- *Developed:* self-esteem, decisiveness in things that are really important, quiet and soundly based, receptive, a supportive peacemaker.
- *Average:* can identify with other viewpoints, has many interests, is sensitive, can be productive and does what he is told, has difficulty protecting his personal boundaries and saying 'no', adapts well, sometimes finds it difficult to take a personal standpoint, has difficulty in setting priorities, can be passively aggressive, is friendly, unpretentious and easily distracted.
- *Pathological:* exaggeratedly adjusted to the surrounding environment, dependent, passive, lacks initiative, subordinates himself, makes great efforts to avoid being alone, is over-sensitive to criticism and rejection, claims to experience few emotions, is afraid of being let down, tends towards symbiotic relationships, is excessively attached to routine and tradition, applies deflection to avoid being blamed for holding particular viewpoints and being criticised personally.

Higher virtue and idea

Type 9 is the central type in the enneagram. In some ways Type 9 represents all types and his themes are relevant for everyone, irrespective of type. The *higher virtue* of Type 9 is the development of love and personal worth. In this way the feeling of not being good enough is overcome. The *higher idea* is decisiveness or right action: the decisiveness to choose what is essential for one's own development.

How to proceed

For the reader making first acquaintance with the enneagram:

If you think this is your type, then check also Types 1, 2, 6 and 7. See if you recognise the stress Type 6 in stress situations and the relaxation Type 3 in situations in which you feel emotionally secure. Find out also if you recognise anything of the wings, Type 8 and Type 1.

The 'self-developer' and the professional will find detailed information in Part IV. Here are a few very brief tips:

- For the 'self-developer': direct attention to your own needs; establish priorities; bring possible conflicts into the open and discuss them.
- For the professional with Type 9 the personal pitfall is that he is too accommodating, that he attaches himself too closely to another person. In working with others with Type 6 it is important that the professional gives them room to discover and to express what they think, not to put them under pressure, and to respect their boundaries.

Type 1

In Chapter 6 we dealt with all the concepts that occur in this type description. Here we discuss:

- The world of a Type 1: this is an exercise to let you experience the inner dialogue of this type.
- Qualities, pitfalls, and characteristics of an average Type 1.
- Basic patterns of Type 1; these are shared by everyone with Type 1.
- Variants and manifestations of Type 1; these show how people with type 1 can differ from one another.

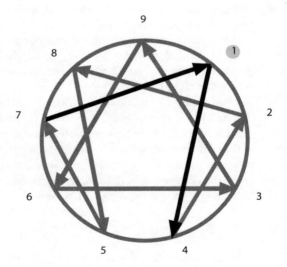

The world of a Type 1

It is a shambles again today at the office. The secretary had not quite finished the slides for your presentation, although you had been quite specific that you needed them today. Moreover, in the part she did finish there were two mistakes. Good job you saw them! You would die of embarrassment if you stood in front of the meeting with wrong slides. You were irritated beyond belief, but tried in as friendly a manner as possible to make clear to her what had to be corrected before 10 o'clock. 'Do you think I work just for you?' she had responded testily. The problem is you don't know how to use PowerPoint yourself, otherwise you would have done it yourself.

And then the meeting itself. In the first place they had pushed your part back in the schedule. What do you have an agenda for then, you wonder? Half of them hadn't prepared properly and asked questions they could have answered themselves if they had read the documentation. You did your very best to remain friendly but you're afraid they still noticed your disapproval. You hadn't been looking forward to this meeting because it dealt with a subject you were not yet completely familiar with. But your boss didn't think that reason enough for a postponement. You always know five times as much as anyone else, he said, and there are decisions to be made. You find that a totally wrong mentality: the company wants quality management, doesn't it? After the meeting he wanted to evaluate it with you. He thinks that you should deal more flexibly with questions. Now, I ask you! You know far than most about it, and you have worked hard to come up with the best proposal possible. Most of the questions were of poor quality, and a number of those present hadn't even taken the trouble to prepare themselves, and then you have to be flexible?! That's unacceptable! Ah well, you spluttered a bit with your boss but finally said you would watch out the next time. When you got home, it turned out the table wasn't laid, although the agreement was that the children should take turns doing it. You were furious and fell out with the first child you saw. Now you regret it terribly, letting yourself go off the deep end like that. You feel guilty: you're not even a good parent.

Qualities, pitfalls and other characteristics of an average Type 1

The qualities of Type 1 are striving for high quality and/or high morality, dedication, sense of responsibility, independence, pleasure in a task well done.

Type 1 has an acute awareness of high quality and standards and strives to attain them. This type always wants to improve himself and others. He feels himself responsible, is painstaking, pays great attention to ethics, and sets his own standards. His standards are so high that other people's are always lower, in his experience. Incidentally, this applies only to matters that a Type 1 regards as important. Thus, for instance, a trainer with Type 1 can prepare his courses to perfection but disregard the administration. This sometimes makes it difficult to recognise a Type 1. Indeed, his norms can be quite different from those of the people in his environment, so that others can get the impression that he is not such a perfectionist after all. On the contrary, in their eyes a Type 1 can be extremely negligent. His behaviour is therefore independent of the norms of others. But although he regards his own norms as the highest and really does not wish to adapt himself to the expectations of others, he still needs approval and reward.

He is sometimes a slow starter because he wants to perfect something before he puts it into practice. For the same reasons he can have difficulty finishing something off. Because he is afraid of making mistakes he can postpone decisions. He tends to compare himself with others, which makes him even more insecure.

The reverse side of the fact that Type 1 sets his own standards – and usually concludes that there is one solution that works best – is that there is a certain arrogance, or sometimes maladjustment, and sometimes he has problems with co-operation. In a team this type often wants to be right and have his own way, just as in conflicts. This person is oriented more towards the task than towards co-operation, and enjoys doing something well. He commits himself willingly to a good cause. If he has thought out a perfect plan, he is often not very open to others suggesting changes, or to new information. As a result, others can feel themselves under control or limited in their creativity. He is sensitive to criticism, however, in the sense that this can re-kindle the internal question 'Am I really good enough?' He can be a passionate speaker who can make people enthusiastic, but can also be off-putting because he allows no room for other opinions.

This type does not like it if another person profits from his efforts. He does not feel like contributing to the work of others, and easily feels 'robbed' or 'exploited'. Thus, someone with this type did not want to put material he had developed into the network computer because then everyone could use it. This type does not like ambiguity. He thinks in black and white: a project is perfect or worthless, a relationship good or bad. He wants to know exactly what his responsibilities are. Correctness is important, both in work itself and in dealing with people.

A typical pitfall is that Type 1 is too self-critical and never feels able to do anything well enough. However, there are also people with this type who are convinced that they do the right thing while others do not. These people are not troubled much by self-criticism, but are all the more critical of others.

Anger is not easily expressed. Rather, this type is exaggeratedly polite. Only if Type 1 can justify his anger – can see it as legitimate – can he give expression to it.

Type 1 often has trouble recognising what he himself wants and fighting for it. He tends to repress his own needs and emotions. This costs a great deal of energy. No one can sit on the safety valve forever, though. Thus, when someone with Type 1 has repressed his own needs and emotions too long, he can suddenly burst into a rage. This fury can frighten him, because it does not accord with his ideal self-image. This aggression can be redirected: someone is angry with his boss but is cross instead with his partner or children, or releases his anger by digging the garden. This outburst then leads once more to feelings of guilt.

Type 1 is afraid of losing control and does not relax easily. But the pressure can become too great. Some people with this type lead a double life. For instance, someone may be conservative, controlling and correct at work but quite different away from it: relaxed, jolly, throwing themselves into everything.

Type 1 has intense energy which can be directed inward and/or outward.

Basic patterns of Type 1

The *attention* goes to what is right and wrong, particularly what can be improved and corrected. The *basic motivation* is generating love and acceptance by being good and doing the right thing, correcting mistakes and attaining one's own high standards. The *world* is therefore *perceived* through the 'spectacles' of what can and must be improved and corrected. The *emotional programming* is an over-sensitivity to not being treated properly, and to errors. The *basic assumption* of Type 1 is that he or she can earn personal worth and love by being good and perfect. The *basic fear* of Type 1 is of being judged and condemned for not being good enough: not perfect. To prevent this the *survival strategy* involves noticing everything that is not good, that is not perfect. Type 1 compares himself with others. Anger and impulses are repressed – after all, these are not good. The *paradox* is that noticing everything that is not perfect increases the continual frustration that nothing is ever good enough. This leads to a negative judgement of one's self. In the real world there is not just one good answer but several; furthermore, Type 1's 'good' is not necessarily the best. The *temptation*, therefore, is to strive for perfection. What is *avoided* is making mistakes, and what is bad. Bad things, for example, include one's own impulses and anger. Loss of control in these things is also avoided. The *ideal self-image* is: 'I am correct and good: industrious, reliable, responsible, efficient, loyal, painstaking, tactful. I am self-disciplined; I can organise things.' The *driving emotional energy* of Type 1 is anger. This type is furious that the world and people are not perfect, and that he himself cannot be good and perfect. The associated *mental preoccupation* is resentment. Type 1 resents imperfection in whatever form. The *defence mechanism* of Type 1 is 'reaction formation', that is to say, doing the opposite from the actual impulse (for instance, someone who feels miserly then acts very generously). Type 1 can compensate for fury about the mistakes of others by being correct, (over)friendly, (extra) helpful, by evading confrontation, and so on. He can overrule what he sees as his own bad impulses by being a real 'do-gooder'.

Variants and manifestations of Type 1

Variants and manifestation forms arise from (among other things):

- sub-types
- stress and relaxation
- development stages or states of consciousness
- higher virtue and idea.

Sub-types

The basic patterns of Type 1, the inner mechanisms, express themselves via the sub-types. The sub-type themes of Type 1 are the following:

- *Self-preservation – anxiety, fear.* This sub-type is either excessively anxious or excessively self-controlled. In the first place there is anxiety about things in the field of survival, such as food, house and family. This anxiety is translated into material achievement as a way of being good and doing the right thing. There are fantasies about what can go wrong in the survival field. Being prepared is a prerequisite. This sub-type can be like Type 6. It is every man for himself: one must hold on to what one has. This sub-type looks after himself and worries if he has to look after others. There is resentment of people who do not have to worry about their material livelihood: that is simply not fair.
- *One-to-one – jealousy, zealotry.* Self-control through clear-cut rules and standards governing correct behaviour, which are sometimes applied with excessive zeal. This sub-type behaves in an angry and possessive manner; the partner's attention is of vital importance. This sub-type has a strong likeness to Type 4: he wants the perfect partner and an idealised relationship. When anything diverges from this, this sub-type gets in a sweat from humiliation and despair. There is also jealousy towards people who have more scope for self-expression, who subject themselves less to rules laid down by others, who get themselves promoted, who are popular, and whose ideas are taken seriously. Of the three sub-types this one expresses anger most easily.
- *Social – non-conformity.* This sub-type is generally friendly and at ease in groups, but nonetheless can limit himself from fear of making mistakes. There is a strong tendency to want to lay down rules for the group. Wanting to do things well according to his own or to other accepted rules makes it hard for him to adapt to new situations or to absorb new information. Only one decision can be the right one. Anger can also be expressed by taking up good causes, social ideals, or political or religious convictions, whereby his own conviction is seen as the only true way.

Stress and relaxation

Type 1 goes under stress to 4. On the positive side he can get rid of his stress by being busy artistically, and can make contact with his own feelings. On the negative side he can become depressive. In relaxation Type 1 goes to 7. On the positive side he begins to see many attractive possibilities, have pleasure, and view everything in a much less serious light. On the negative side he can back out of responsibilities he has taken upon himself.

Development stages or states of consciousness

The development stages or states of consciousness are:

- *Developed:* wise, tolerant, an objective teacher, idealistic without losing touch with reality, high moral sense.
- *Average:* reformer, does good, structure, order, judging, perfectionist, conscientious, responsible, correct personal relationships, dominant, strongly self-critical, repression of impulses, emphasis on personal standards, anger is repressed.
- *Pathological:* hard to please, intolerant, relentless, obsessive, rigid, moralising, emotional expression under strict control, reaction formation, sways between obedience and rebellion, angry, critical, dominant, perfectionist, excessively self-critical.

Higher virtue and idea

The *higher virtue* of Type 1 is serenity and the *higher idea* actual perfection. Serenity involves Type 1 accepting that reality is what exists at any given moment. Wishes, needs, impulses and instincts simply form part of human life. Life is perfect as long as nature is perfect. A person cannot make a sunset more beautiful than it is. There are a great many ways towards actual perfection, and not just a single ideal one.

How to proceed

For the reader making first acquaintance with the enneagram:

If you think this is your type, then check also Types 2, 4, 6 and 9. See if you recognise the stress Type 4 in stress situations and the relaxation Type 7 in situations in which you feel emotionally secure. Find out also if you recognise anything of the wings, Type 9 and Type 2.

The 'self-developer' and the professional will find detailed information in Part IV. Here are a few very brief tips:

- For the 'self-developer': accept that there is more than one 'right' way, direct the attention to what is good, accept imperfection in others and in yourself.
- For the professional with Type 1 the personal pitfall is excessive perfectionism. In working with others with Type 1 it is important to accept them as people, even when they fail, encourage them to apply the '80/20' rule (80 per cent of the result is attained with 20 per cent of the effort; the remaining 20 per cent costs 80 per cent of the effort – for many purposes an 80 per cent result is good enough), and to discuss subjects without making judgements.

Part

III

Philosophical Background for Working with the Enneagram

In Chapter 1 we have already sketched very briefly the various levels of consciousness that are important in working with the enneagram. In this part of the book the different levels of consciousness are worked out further. Chapter 10 discusses the nature of consciousness itself and why self-guidance without higher consciousness levels is unthinkable. Most of the knowledge we possess about these consciousness levels does not come from psychology but from philosophy and spiritual traditions. The question of which parts of these traditions are relevant, and which are not, is considered briefly. Chapter 11 discusses how various enneagram experts regard consciousness levels. A chart of the levels concerned is borrowed from the Kabbalist tradition. Possible similarities to other traditions and to transpersonal psychology are also covered. Integrated in this chart are the interpretations of various enneagram experts. In Chapter 12 its meaning for working with the enneagram is explained further, both in the sense of various tendencies that exist in one and the same person, and in the sense of being a 'ladder' upon which one can develop more self-guidance and greater personal mastery.

CHAPTER 10

The Nature of Consciousness

The enneagram of fixations and the enneagram of higher virtues and ideas imply different levels of consciousness. In this chapter the concept of consciousness is explained first of all. For some people this concept has somewhat vague, or even psychedelic, connotations. What are involved, however, are completely ordinary, everyday phenomena which everyone experiences. Everyone is acquainted with different states of consciousness; no one needs drugs to access them. Sleeping is a state of consciousness different from being awake. Driving automatically to work while one's fancies take wing is a different state of consciousness to concentrated writing. Most people know the experience of 'waking up' suddenly behind the wheel of a car with the thought 'Where am I, and where was it I was going?' When someone lets himself go in an automatic, emotional 'type' reaction, that is a different state of consciousness than that experienced when the same person looks consciously at his automatic type reaction and does not surrender to it. Most people know the experience of clear-sighted moments, and the experience of 'I can't see it at the moment.' In other words, everyone knows different states of consciousness. Associations with flower power, fungal-derived hallucinogens and other drugs – 'smart' or not – are understandable but cover only a very limited part of the 'states of consciousness' concept.

Self-management requires development of consciousness

States of consciousness can be divided into more or less conscious states. Identification with the enneagram of fixations is a less conscious state. Condon gave one of his articles about the enneagram the title 'In a deep trance'.[1] Wolinsky, another enneagram expert, also spoke of 'Trances people live'.[2] People at this level are, in fact, driven by the mechanisms of the enneagram of fixations, such as perception of the world, focus of attention, basic motivation and the other basic patterns, without having control over them.

Self-management demands a certain degree of consciousness. The individual steps, as it were, out of the automatic experience of reality of his own type, in which he saw only a ninth part of reality, and out of his unconscious automatic reactions (Gurdjieff's 'robot people'). As soon as he begins to reflect on his type reactions he breaks through their automatic character. He becomes more aware. When he becomes even more aware he not only reflects but also begins to act differently. Now he starts to make conscious choices about the way he acts, and thus how he manages himself. In so doing he creates personal mastery. The enneagram of higher virtues and ideas is a still higher level of consciousness. Here there is a real 360 degree view. In addition, we talk here of a trans-personal level. More about this in the next chapter.

Form and consciousness in philosophical and spiritual traditions

Countless systems of thought have differentiated various levels of consciousness. Thus Professor Karlfried Graf van Dürckheim, a transcendental psychologist, distinguishes five levels,[3] and the doctor and practitioner of transcendental meditation (TM) Anthony Campbell seven.[4] Transpersonal psychologist Ken Wilber described the similarities between the 12 levels of consciousness of the neo-Platonist philosopher Plotinus, from the third century AD, and the 12 levels of the Hindu spiritual teacher Sri Aurobindo (1872–1950).[5] The concept of different states of consciousness is more important than their precise number. What matters is that one can work with them in practice.

Knowledge about different states of consciousness can be found in present-day transpersonal psychology and in many philosophical and spiritual traditions. What is concerned is the mystic branch – the experiential side – of those traditions.

All religions have a formal side and an experiential side. The formal side consists of dogmas, basic principles, church laws, commandments and prohibitions, and the interpretation of holy scriptures in a manner seen as desirable or truthful by the church authorities. When I visited the holy places of various religions in Israel, to avoid giving offence anywhere I carried around a big bag of props: cover the arms here, take your shoes off there, further on no bare legs, then something on your head again, but in the next house of God the head-covering off again. Thus every religion has its own rules for expressing the concept 'respect'.

The formal side divides. The Jewish-Christian-Islamic tradition has a common origin. Judaism and Islam both claim descent from the Patriarch Abraham; Christendom stems from Judaism. In the Bible and the Koran we encounter the same stories related as history, although the same people play different roles. Thus Abraham goes to sacrifice Isaac in the Bible and Ishmael in the Koran. However, the division did not stop with the development of these three religions. In the course of history each of the three has divided itself further into all sorts of movements which conflicted with one another, often literally, by fire and by sword. Church schisms, excommunications and the burning of heretics are always concerned with the formal side. On the formal side there is always a church hierarchy which places itself between the faithful and God. This hierarchy, in its own judgement, is pre-eminently well informed about the rules, and on this basis tells the faithful what they must do and what not. It has power because it can impose sanctions when the rules are transgressed. These processes are similar in all religions.

The mystic, experiential or consciousness side of a religion or philosophy is connected with the direct relationship of a person with God, or with his being part of the (mystic) unity, the universe. When someone has that direct relationship, to some extent it is irrelevant what a church institution has to say about it. This person has, after all, a direct experience. In general, formal churches of whatever faith have not been very appreciative of these direct relationships in the past. What remains, after all, for the church establishment when people begin to arrange their relationship with God themselves? That impairs the power of the church. Many mystics in various religions have been excommunicated or murdered. I certainly do not wish to assert that a sincere faith experience would not be possible within the regular churches. What I am saying is that a church establishment wishes to determine the form of such experiences.

The similarities between the mystic sides of various religions and philosophies are noticeable. Mystics of different paths describe similar experiences. In all sorts of mystic movements and schools for consciousness development, one encounters the same kinds of exercises. Apparently people in diverse cultures and in various eras have had similar experiences, and have used similar practices in order to create these experiences or to participate in them. When we speak of knowledge from the various traditions which can help us in the development of greater consciousness, then we are talking of the mystic, experiential or consciousness side of those traditions.

In Chapter 11 we will now go further into the various levels of consciousness and their meaning for working with the enneagram.

CHAPTER 11

Anatomy of Consciousness

In general terms, people are agreed that one can speak of different levels of consciousness. However, various enneagram experts hold different opinions on the precise nature of those levels. Some say that all people have the level of higher virtues and ideas within themselves and that everyone is acquainted with it. In their view, one does not have to take any further trouble in this respect. Others say that this higher level is another level of consciousness at which only very few people can arrive after many years of intensive spiritual practice. Some argue that one should simply not occupy oneself with the lower level if one wishes to function on a higher one. Others think, on the contrary, that only by working through the problems of the lower level does one ever gain the chance of attaining the higher level. Others again believe that there is no question of levels which one attains successively, but rather of states of consciousness which one can access at will. Who is right?

There is a universal model in which all these different views fit in a coherent, logical and understandable manner. This model offers, as it were, a map of the landscape of consciousness levels with which we must deal in working with the enneagram. Additionally, it marks out a clear route for coming from the lower to the higher level via a number of intermediary levels. Furthermore, this model makes it clear that no single level is better or worse than another, but that one needs them all equally.

That universal model is the concept of the *tree of life*, a symbolic representation of reality derived from the Jewish mystic tradition, the Kaballah. In the Kabbalistic tree of life a number of enneagram elements may be found: the 'law of 3', nine qualities, 'fixations' and 'higher ideas', and the educational routes of heart, head and body, in which the three centres are recognisable. Levels or states of consciousness, and how people can work with them, are worked out much further in the model of the tree of life than in the enneagram.

The concept of the tree of life makes the whole system of thought round the enneagram crystal clear, and integrates the views of different authors and teachers. In addition this concept appeals to working people because it does not require several years' withdrawal to a monastery or the desert. One can simply put it into practice while working.

This chapter describes the tree of life and the various levels of consciousness that are relevant for working with the enneagram. The next chapter, Chapter 12, goes into its meaning for working with the enneagram. Successively, we shall deal with:

- the tree of life
- the various levels of consciousness in the tree of life.

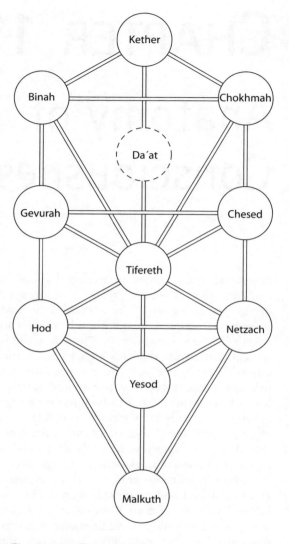

Figure 11.1 The tree of life

The tree of life

The Kabbalist tradition describes reality with the help of the symbolism of the tree of life.[1] This is illustrated in Figure 11.1.

Manifestations of unity

The spheres in the model are called *sefiroth* (the plural of sefirah). There are different views on the correct translation of the word sefirah which are not relevant to the purpose of this section – considering how can one work with different consciousness levels. The topmost sefirah stands for undivided unity and can be compared with the circle round the enneagram symbol, which also represents undivided unity. The nine subsequent sefiroth (*Da'at* is not a sefirah) are all different manifestations of the first. It is as if the pure white light of the undivided unity shines through a prism and is thus divided into many colours. These colours all arise from the original white light and together can form white light again. The different sefiroth stand for different qualities such as wisdom, understanding, love, strength and solid grounding. Here a similarity can be seen to the 'Facets of Unity' described by A.H. Almaas in his book about the enneagram of higher virtues and ideas.[2] One might imagine a diamond with many facets. These facets are all sides of the same diamond; every facet represents a higher quality. In the same way every higher virtue and idea represents a quality of Unity. Almaas called his method of working 'the diamond approach'.

The nine sefiroth also represent the nine names of God which we encountered with Ramon Llull in Chapter 4. Ichazo based the development of his enneagram system on Llull, among others.

Various attempts have been made to identify the sefiroth with the enneagram types.[3] Probably these cannot be made to correspond with each other one-on-one, but a common origin is very likely (see also the reference to projections in Chapter 1).

The tree of life, from top to bottom, symbolises the process of creation. We cannot discuss this area of significance within the framework of this book. The path from the bottom to the top is the path of the development of consciousness. On this upward path are distinguished the levels necessary for being able to work with the enneagram.

The search for balance

The 'law of 3' can be recognised in the three columns of the tree of life. The right-hand column is the *pillar of expansion*, of active forces. The left-hand column is the *pillar of limitation*, of passive forces. The middle column is the *pillar of equilibrium* between both forces, and also representing consciousness (Figure 11.1). An excess of the qualities in the right or the left column leads to problems. Development involves, among other things, establishing a balance between active and passive forces.

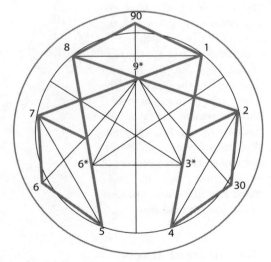

Figure 11.2 The Sufi enneagram

In fact, this is also what the Sufi enneagram tells us (Figure 11.2). The Sufis see the enneagram not as a system of personality types but as illustrating tendencies in humankind that one must overcome in order to attain moral goodness. Points 8, 1, 2, 4, 5, 7 in the Sufi enneagram all represent too much or too little of a certain quality. Points 3, 6 and 9 represent those qualities. The point 0 – the centre of the enneagram – is the perfected balance. This is the goal of development. Someone who has attained 'point 0' can, via the middle point of the enneagram, enter the world of intuition (see also the framework of 'The four worlds', later in this chapter).

Three paths of development

The three triangles at the bottom of the tree of life represent three paths of development: action, study and devotion. In this we recognise the three centres: belly/body, head and heart. We can also speak of the path of the body, the path of the head and the path of the heart (Figure 11.3). Other traditions – Hinduism, for instance – describe these paths as well, and they correspond to the paths Ouspensky described and which we have already mentioned in Chapter 5. These are the way of the yogi (i.e. the path of the spirit), the way of the monk (the path of the heart) and the way of the fakir (the path of the body). Ouspensky's fourth way – the development of all three centres in equilibrium and in daily work and life – was not new to the Jewish tradition.

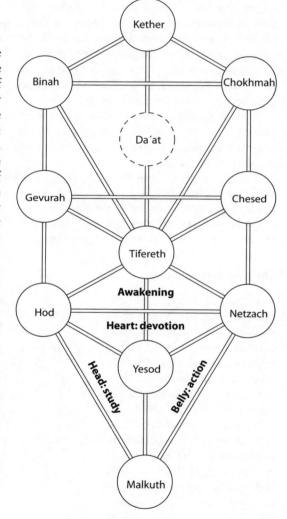

Figure 11.3 Three paths of development

The different levels of consciousness

The tree of life symbolises different levels of consciousness. The path of development of consciousness goes from bottom to top in the model.

Roberto Assagioli, the pioneer of psychosynthesis, spoke of 'psychological mountaineering'.[4] Assagioli thought that psychoanalysis did not do justice to human nature, and developed a psychology in which both the lower and the higher capacities of people had their say. Different levels of consciousness also had their place in this rationale. These correspond to a large extent with those of the tree of life.

The levels of consciousness form, on the one hand, the path to ever greater personal mastery. On the other hand, they are all present simultaneously but one is not always aware of this. But everyone knows the experience of simultaneously wanting several things that seem incompatible with one another. For instance, someone can be dying for a beer but at the same time wants to reduce weight because that is better for his health. Someone may want to score at work, but in so doing have doubts about the extent to which he can put aside ethical considerations, or interpret them in a way that lets him do what he wants nonetheless. Someone can want to give in to the motivation of his enneagram type because he thinks he can become better that way, but at the same time does not wish to because of a fear of undesirable effects. Insight into the levels helps when making choices in this kind of situation.

Anyone who wants to improve self-management and attain personal mastery has to consider the following levels (Figure 11.4):

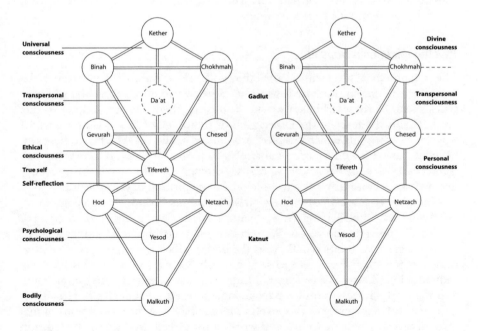

Figure 11.4 Levels of consciousness

- bodily consciousness
- psychological consciousness (the enneagram of fixations)
- self-reflection
- the true self
- ethical consciousness
- transpersonal consciousness (the enneagram of higher virtues and ideas)
- universal consciousness

Bodily consciousness

To bodily consciousness belongs the will to survive physically. At this level people are oriented towards the three Ss: sustenance, (physical) safety and sex (propagation). The American humanistic psychologist Abraham Maslow has said that all this must be provided first before someone has the energy for higher levels.[5] On this level of consciousness people do the same as plants and animals: survive as well as they can in a literal, physical sense. Vitality belongs to this level.

What Assagioli calls the 'strong will' belongs to this level.[6] The strong will knows only 'now', wants immediate fulfilment of wishes and pursues this with great vitality. One of the goals in bringing up children is teaching them to postpone the fulfilment of needs. This is an absolutely sound educational aim, provided it is pursued with wisdom. Parents of an older generation sometimes used to say 'the will has to be broken'. Without the strong will, however, one cannot begin anything.

Psychological consciousness

The psychological level – also called the ego level – is the world of imagery, the world of the unreal, false or lower self. When various religions and philosophies speak of the world as a world of illusion, then they are talking of this level. This is the level of the enneagram of fixations, of false assumptions, of 'spectacles' through which one sees a coloured reality in which one believes, of mental models and the survival strategies based on them. But a strong ego is also necessary for being able to realise something in the world. Moreover, it is a necessary condition for psychological and spiritual development.

This level is associated with ego-wishes such as 'belonging', 'recognition', 'appreciation', 'performing well', 'being envied', 'being better than others', 'winning', 'power', and so on. We recognise in them the basic motivations of the enneagram of fixations. There is the desire, albeit unintentional, to realise things in the short term, and to secure psychological safety. At this level the individual wants to live out an enneagram fixation pattern. In people's life and work the same patterns keep recurring; there is a great degree of repetition.

The positive meaning of this level is that people need the motivations of this level in order to be able to live and work in the world. In the Jewish tradition there is the story of a village which begs its rabbi to pray to the Eternal One to take away the evil from the world. The rabbi does just that. The next day no bread is baked and no rubbish removed, no work is done in the fields and the cows are not milked. No work is done at all that day, nor the next day, nor the day after that. The moral of the story is that people need a healthy dose of self-interest in order to be able to live in the world. There is nothing inherently wrong with self-interest. It 'goes wrong' when someone is not aware of it, is ruled by it, or uses that self-interest for the wrong ends. In other words, it goes wrong if this level is not directed from higher levels.

To this level belongs what Assagioli called the 'skilful will'. People acquire skills in order to realise in concrete terms all the things they want to attain, and they use those skills. Assagioli uses the analogy of people who do not want to follow a straight line from A to B in a town (which may involve swimming across a canal, climbing over a block of flats, and so on) but choose a clever route which brings them as quickly as possible and with minimum effort to their destination.

At this level people do everything in order to survive in a psychological sense – that is to say, to belong, to obtain recognition, and so on.

Level of self-reflection

Without self-reflection people remain unaware of their automatisms. Examining those automatisms is the first step in development. In the tree of life this stage is called 'the path of honesty'. It involves beginning to free oneself, through de-identification with the ideal self-image, the defence mechanisms and the typical view of the world. It also involves examining objectively both the positive and the negative sides of how one functions, the typical qualities, and also the basic patterns of one's type which are described in Chapter 6 and worked out in Chapters 7–9.

Level of the true self

This level has a key position in the tree of life and has three functions. All those functions have to do with people's self-management capacities.

The first function is directed at self-reflection. Here this level represents the part within ourselves that can study our type: the *inner observer*.

The second function is knowing what we really and most deeply want, and also what is good for us in the longer term. If people use expressions such as 'being more myself' or 'being in touch with my real self', then they are often referring to this level. We can call this the *inner guide*.

Third in this level is the cross-over point from the psychological to the transpersonal world (see 'The four worlds', below). It forms the link between lower and higher levels. The part of the tree of life below this point is called *katnut*, the area of little awareness (katan is the Hebrew word for small). The area above this point is called *gadlut*, the great awareness (gadol is the Hebrew word for great).

The four worlds

The true self as cross-over point can be seen clearly if we look at 'Jacob's ladder', so called because the Patriarch Jacob once had a dream in which a ladder extended to heaven. In the Kabbalist philosophy four worlds exist which are represented as four overlapping trees of life. Together they form a ladder along which one can reach higher forms of consciousness (Figure 11.5).

The four worlds, in order of creation and from top to bottom in the illustration, are the divine world, the spiritual world, the psychological world and the material world. Steven Fisdel[7], when describing the four worlds, uses for the analogy of providing energy. The divine world is the public service company, the spiritual world the power generator, the psychological world represents the transformers and the material world the consumers. It would not do us much good to plug our lamp directly into the generator – in fact, not much of it would be left after our attempt. The transformers are needed to enable us to plug the lamp in safely in the power socket at home.

The *divine world* is a perfect world. This is why that world is unchangeable. It corresponds to the formless world of Buddhism.

The *spiritual world* is the world of ideas, of the essences of everything that exists and of the driving forces of macro processes such as the development of humankind. We encounter here the primordial concepts of what is realised and materialises in the lower worlds. We must not imagine a primordial concept as a concrete image but as an essence: for instance what it is that all different roses have in common that makes them roses, rather than some other flower. This world corresponds with Plato's world of ideas, with the Buddhist world of the pure form and with the enneagram's world of higher virtues and ideas.

The *psychological world* is the world of forms, of images, of 'spectacles' through which we look at reality, of subjectivity. It corresponds with the Buddhist world of sensual desire, of Plato's sensorily perceptible world and with the world of the enneagram of fixations. In the psychological world we form images of the higher virtues and ideas; we make for ourselves an imaginary picture of them, and different people make different pictures. There is nothing wrong with this as long as we remain aware that they are pictures and do not take them to be reality. The thirteenth-century Sufi poet and mystic Rumi once compared the difference between the world of reason (the psychological world in the ladder) and the world of intuition (the spiritual world on the ladder) with the difference between the light of a candle and that of the sun at midday in the desert.[8]

Finally, the fourth world is the *material world* and the world of action.

We see that the level of the true self, *Tifereth*, forms the heart of the psychological world, and is at the same time the bottom of the spiritual world. The true self is thus the place where we can go from the psychological world to the world of higher virtues and ideas. This is sometimes also referred to as the 'eye of the

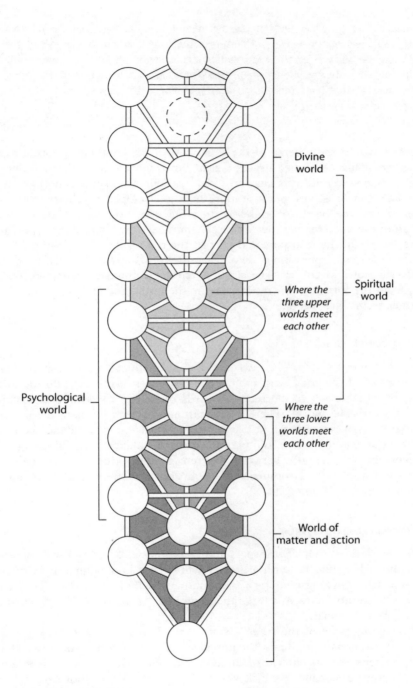

Figure 11.5 Jacob's ladder

needle' through which we can go from the one world to the other. The nil from the Sufi enneagram which we described above is also called the 'eye of the needle'. We see very clearly in this symbolic representation that we cannot come in contact with the higher virtues and ideas from enneagram of fixations, because at that level there is no overlap between the psychological and the spiritual worlds.

If one looks at the scheme of the four worlds, the common question as to whether higher developed psychological functioning is actually the same as higher virtues and ideas is answered clearly – but the answer is both yes and no. The answer is 'yes' because more highly developed psychological functioning and the world of higher virtues and ideas overlap. Then one can speak of the same themes, just as we saw in the descriptions of the types, and here we are in the transpersonal part of the tree of life. The answer is 'no' because there is a question of two different worlds and consequently of two different states of consciousness: the psychological and the spiritual. Looking from the former one cannot imagine the latter. Seen from the latter the former seems like 'sleeping'.

Ethical consciousness

Back to the tree of life. The next level is that of ethical consciousness. Assagioli spoke of the good will. Ethical consciousness has to do with the question of whether we act correctly towards ourselves, towards other people and towards the world. There is a continuous search for balance: balance between task-orientation and orientation towards people, balance between looking after oneself and looking after others, balance between mercy and judgement, and balance between different interests (for instance, between transport and the environment). Without ethical consciousness we cannot lead our lives with integrity.

Transpersonal consciousness

The next level is that of transpersonal consciousness. At this level someone feels himself bound up with a greater whole, and knows himself to be one with it. He is aware of having a function in this whole. Intuitively he knows things he cannot know as a separate individual. At the same time this person is still an individual.

Assagioli spoke of the *transpersonal will*. This level has less to do with what we want as individuals (the unreal self, the level of fixations). We abandon ourselves to the current of the universe, while we react to it as individuals at the same time. As Erik van Praag wrote: 'We cannot do anything about the storm, but we can learn to sail.'[9] Not wanting there to be a storm has absolutely no effect. Nonetheless, in practice we invest a great deal of energy in trying to stop a storm. And because a storm *does* eventually stop, we also come to think that those endeavours are effective. But accepting that things come as they come can be much more effective, and costs much less energy. 'If you can't beat them, join them' is a expression from the management world that expresses this. Then we accept things with equanimity when we suffer a setback or things go well with us: we do not excite ourselves about it, and act appropriately. At this level people should say things like 'this is apparently (not) how it was meant to be', or 'apparently the universe thinks differently'.

Universal consciousness

At the highest level we find a universal consciousness where individuality has disappeared completely. One sometimes comes there in deep meditation. People have told me that they have had similar experiences in overwhelmingly beautiful scenery, at the birth of a child or at a deathbed (in both cases a door is opened briefly to another world), or in experiencing beauty.

The number of people who believe in an anthropomorphic image of God (the old man with the beard in the paintings of medieval artists) is rapidly dwindling. But many people do believe 'that there is something to it' despite this, that there is a unity of existence, that the universe is an animated whole, and so on. The reality is that every conception we can have of this level falls short by definition. Indeed, as soon as we add a qualification as to what it would be in factual terms it would not be anything other, and thus no longer a unity of everything any more.

If we ascend the ladder from bottom to top this level seems practically unattainable. Possibly only very holy people come there. But, at the same time, everything that exists is a part of this level. We could also say it permeates all that is, and in that way we interact with it every day. Christendom speaks of the transcendental, practically unreachable God and the immanent God, who is present in everything. The Jewish tradition distinguishes Ayn Sof, the Eternal and Unknowable, and the Shechinah, the recognisable presence of the Eternal on Earth.

Does this level have any relationship with daily practice in an organisation? It does continually, in fact, but usually we are not aware of this.

Integrating the various interpretations

The tree of life is not reality itself but a symbolic representation of reality. It is a map of a country, but not the country itself. As we see, a number of steps lie between the enneagram of fixations and the enneagram of higher virtues and ideas. The tree of life provides a map of the road from the one enneagram to the other.

We see now that all the interpretations which were described at the beginning of this chapter have a place in the system. The teachers who say that we have the higher level within us, and that we already know it, lay the accent on immanence. Those who say that the higher level is another level of consciousness, where only a very few can come after many years of intensive spiritual practice, are looking from the level of fixations and lay the emphasis on transcendence. The authors who say that we simply should not have anything to do with the 'lower level' if we want to function on a 'higher level' are looking from a transcendental level. From that level, in fact, they are right, but in practice we have dealings with all levels. Those who think that only by being occupied with the 'lower level' can we ever have a chance of reaching the 'higher level' lay the emphasis on the development routes. Those of the opinion that there is no question of levels that one reaches successively, but rather of states of consciousness that one can access at will, assume that all levels are equally accessible to our consciousness: an assumption which, I fear, is not always tenable although it is theoretically correct. This assumption, however, concerns only highly developed individuals.

In the following chapter we shall consider working with these levels. In doing so the various levels are seen in two ways: as different tendencies in one and the same person, and as a ladder up which one can climb in order to gain more effective self-management and greater personal mastery.

CHAPTER 12

Working with the Levels of Consciousness

In this chapter two ways of working with the consciousness levels are discussed. The consciousness levels can be seen as different tendencies in one person. They can also be seen as a ladder up which one can climb in order to gain more self-management and a greater personal mastery. We shall now deal in succession with:

- The levels of consciousness as different tendencies in the same person.
- The levels of consciousness as a way to more effective self-management and greater personal mastery.

The levels of consciousness as different tendencies in one person

The various levels of consciousness can be regarded as different tendencies in the same person. These tendencies do not always wish to go in the same direction. People can experience them as different inner voices that say different things.[1]

It is not true that a higher consciousness level is 'better' than a lower. All levels are necessary. Without physical will there is no life. We would stop eating, and there would be no more children born. Equally, one cannot function without ego. We need a well-developed ego to be able to realise things in the world. It is also a prerequisite for further development. For example, someone who has developed himself well ethically but has a weak ego function will be naive, unable to look after himself and will not be able to bring his good ideas to fruition in the world. This person remains a moral crusader, a voice in the wilderness. It is precisely when someone wants to develop their higher levels that it is essential to keep both feet firmly on the ground. Otherwise he will be unable to do anything with the higher levels that is of any significance in practical work. What is true, however, is that the lower consciousness levels need the guidance of the higher levels. Otherwise we would live like animals.

All the consciousness levels are active at the same time, although we are not always aware of this. There is then an inner dialogue between the various voices within us. Sometimes it seems like a whole meeting.

This inner dialogue explains why people sometimes do not act effectively when they know perfectly well what they ought to do, and at other moments they do something that they actually do not want to do because they think it is correct. I regularly encounter both cases. People in training sometimes refuse to do what they ought to do in order to be more effective: for instance, attuning to the personality type of another may hurt their ego too much. 'No, the other person is wrong, and he has to change!' But the other does not do this, and so a stalemate ensues. It is not effective. In this example, the will to be effective (minimal at the level of self-reflection) is weaker than the will of the ego level which seeks recognition and justification, and compensation for past suffering.

There are countless examples of the second case (someone doing something he does not wish to do because he thinks it to be right). People put their own (ego) needs aside: for ethical reasons, for instance; or because they find that they have a contribution to make to a greater whole, such as the maintenance of a family or advising in an organisation; or because they feel that the path of their lives is different. Everyone who brings up children knows the experience of sometimes setting aside what one wants oneself for the good of the child.

Thus someone with Type 3 can hanker after prestige, and want most of all to destroy all competition, yet still give a colleague the credit due to him by putting him in the limelight. In that way he conquers himself; we can also say his higher self conquers his lower self. Someone with Type 9 can come to the conclusion that his path of life necessitates him presenting himself positively to the outside world and go to work on that systematically. Someone with Type 6 can feel intuitively a need to take a certain risk and find the courage to follow this inspiration, in spite of the inner voice saying that that is far too dangerous.

Even if someone is not aware of his different inner voices, they still have influence subconsciously. We do not have control over what we do not know or deny: it has power over us. Someone can surprise himself. 'He was always such a respectable man: how can he now suddenly let himself go like that on sports day?'

Sometimes a voice is not in accord with the path someone has sketched out for themselves. He silences it; only later does he realise that he has always known what the voice was saying. Thus someone can realise that he actually knew for years that an employer did not suit him personally, but only at the moment did he finally decide to start a business himself. Or someone can realise in old age that he has actually wanted something throughout life but had always found that it was unattainable: because it would not be accepted by those around, because it did not seem realistic, or because it was incompatible with the person's own norms.

If someone is aware of his different inner voices and listens to them, he can weigh them up consciously. A person who does so is then in charge of them. He acquires personal mastery.

The levels of consciousness as a road to more self-management and greater personal mastery

The levels of consciousness can play a role in someone's development in different ways. Here we consider:

- The consciousness levels as a path for life.
- The relationship between the levels of consciousness and first-, second- and third-order learning.
- Intentions one can work on with the various levels of consciousness.

The levels of consciousness as a path of life

One recognises the path of life in the levels of consciousness. In the first instance, the small child is occupied with physical survival. It wants food, the right temperature, and clean nappies.

In the adolescent phase someone is occupied a great deal with self-image. He compares himself with others, and this continues in young adulthood. Energy is devoted to becoming 'someone', to developing a career. Levinson calls this the *establishment period*.[2] All this belongs to the ego level. From this, it is apparent once again that we cannot do without a healthy ego. An individual begins to discover the qualities and pitfalls which belong to his type, and to learn compensating skills.

A little later someone begins to ask himself what work really suits him, irrespective of image or the income it would bring. Then he becomes aware of the level of the true self.

In middle age, many people begin to ask themselves 'Is this is all there is?' They now have everything they originally wanted: a house, a car, a family or another mode of life or living together, their own social life, a career, a good income. How are they going to fill in the second half of their lives? With a second house, a bigger car, a new family, earning still more? For many people these aspirations now have less appeal. The higher levels of consciousness come into the picture.

We speak here in terms of statistics once again. There are people who never come to the higher levels at all, and there are people who concern themselves with these levels at a much earlier age. Thus there is a rule in the Jewish mystic tradition that people may not begin with the Kabbalah before they are forty, because they must first earn their bread and have a family. Some great Kabbalists, however, died long before that age, so involvement by younger people is not impossible. But many people have no interest in these things when they are younger: they are too busy living, or simply surviving. In fact, here again we find Maslow's hierarchy of needs: first of all comes the physical level of food and safety. If these needs are provided for, then there are the social needs of belonging and recognition; only after that comes self-realisation.

After a possible mid-life crisis, many people's interest shifts towards passing on what they have learned, rather than wanting to continue achieving themselves. The older one becomes the more an interest in material things tends to diminish (we are talking here of people in relatively affluent countries), in statistical terms, while interest in spiritual values increases. One climbs the ladder.

Relationship of the levels of consciousness to first-, second- and third-order learning

In climbing the ladder of consciousness levels on the way to more self-management and greater personal mastery, we encounter other lessons on every rung. This the same as in learning a language or a sport: lessons and exercises for beginners are followed by those for more advanced learners.

In Chapter 1 we spoke briefly of the different levels of learning with the enneagram. First-order learning – broadening the repertoire of behaviour – lies on the ego level. Second-order learning – investigating the type pattern and opening it to discussion – lies on the level of self-reflection and the true self. Third-order learning – transcendence of the type fixation – lies on the level of the true self and higher levels. Many exercises at these three levels of learning are described in Part IV.

Intent at various levels of consciousness

The lower levels function optimally only under guidance from the higher levels.

The intent with which one works on one's own development is itself subject to the levels. If the intent behind developing arises from the enneagram of fixations – the ego level – one continues to play out one's patterns, but now with a different content. Someone with Type 3, for instance, may be competitive about who learns the most, who can distance themselves best from their fixations, or who is highest on the ladder of consciousness development. Someone with Type 5 perhaps wants to know everything about background theories and how they all fit together, without relating them to his own experience and feelings. Or this person can become a 'feedback junkie', collecting ever more information without really doing anything with it. And a Type 9 can become absorbed in more and more interesting books on the subject without actually beginning on any development.

If the intention behind the development arises from the true self, we are really concerned with learning about ourselves, and thereby with the path to personal mastery and social intelligence.

How to follow this path is the subject of Part IV of this book.

Part

IV

Working With the Enneagram

In Part I we discussed the principles, background and application possibilities of the enneagram. In Part II the types were discussed. In Part III we considered the philosophical background that is necessary for understanding the enneagram properly and for being able to work with it as it is intended: as an instrument for personal development. Here in Part IV, the central subject is working with the enneagram in practice.

In order to be able to work with the enneagram, one must first of all be able to determine one's own type as well as that of a client, colleague, or other person. Chapter 13 deals with different ways of determining the type. The first part is of interest to everyone. The chapter is closed with a section that is particularly relevant for professionals who want to work with the enneagram. Chapter 14 goes into working professionally with the enneagram. In this one's own type plays a role. The professional ought to be aware of his or her own qualities and pitfalls and be able to deal with them in a professional manner. Also involved are the phenomena of transference and counter-transference – the projection of one's own subjective personal experiences on to another person – as well as how to deal with these phenomena. This chapter is relevant for everyone who works with people, not just the professional enneagram expert but also the manager, colleague or executive, because everyone has to deal with the same phenomena. Chapter 15 discusses how to deal with people with different types, according to the stage of their development. Chapter 16 deals with the principles of development intervention. It is meant for the person who wants to develop himself further and for the professional who supports other people in their development as part of their work. Here we go into the different phases that can be distinguished in working with the enneagram, and into the different levels of learning with the enneagram. Subsequently, Chapter 17 discusses general development interventions that are suitable for every type, while Chapter 18 considers type-specific development interventions.

Chapter 13

Determining the Type

The enneagram only becomes an instrument for practical use when the person who uses it has determined his or her own enneagram type, and can determine that of others if he or she wishes to work with them.

The ethical code of the International Enneagram Association emphasises that one does not stick numbers on people, but lets them discover themselves which types they have.[1] The reason for this is as follows. The discovery of one's own type is a development path in itself, which involves growing self-insight. In an expedition it is not just the destination that is interesting. The road towards it can also reveal all kinds of things. Thus the programme to put the first man on the moon yielded all kinds of technological innovations that were applicable elsewhere (for example Teflon is now used, among other things, for pans). The professional therefore strives to help others by letting them discover their types themselves, instead of pulling these out of a hat.

There are various ways of determining the type:

- the naked eye
- questionnaires
- self-study
- panels
- the typing interview.

Not all of these methods are equally effective, for reasons that are discussed below. The last three methods are particularly relevant for someone who wants to determine his or her own type. For professionals who want to determine the type of a client the typing interview is of first importance; some questionnaires may provide assistance too, but most are not suitable for this purpose.

The naked eye

This method is not recommended. In the first place, the enneagram is not about outwardly perceptible behaviour but about underlying basic patterns. Often these cannot be discerned from outward behaviour.

Broadly speaking, we can say that that the correspondence between type and behaviour becomes weaker the further someone develops himself. And nearly everyone develops in the course of their life.

Certainly a typing based on outward perception may be correct. Some people are simply so prototypical that it is almost impossible they do not have Type X. However, it also happens frequently that such judgements fail the test of the professional critic. It appears that the rule is that people cannot be typed on the basis of outward behaviour, with the exception that some can.

This (among other things) is apparent from the following example. In the *Enneagram Monthly*, the leading international professional journal about the enneagram, three famous and very experienced enneagram teachers were asked which type the former American President Bill Clinton had. Their separate answers were Type 9, Type 3 and Type 8.[2] Yet all three answers were well argued. Statements about the types of famous people, living or dead artists, current international politicians or Roman emperors from the year dot must therefore be taken with a large pinch of salt – unless these assessments are based on professional research.

A hypothesis about someone's type can indeed be formed on the basis of outward behaviour, but that hypothesis must be tested professionally. Professional testing involves more than just asking a few questions about the conjectured type. I myself, for instance, have Type 9, but because I sometimes show perfectionist traits on those grounds someone might conclude that I have Type 1. If a few questions about Type 1 were to be asked, the following exchange could result:

> *Question:* Are you critical of yourself and others?
> *Answer:* You could say that. Less than before, and I try to control myself, but certainly I was in earlier life. [The type is often clearer in younger people.]
> *Question:* Do you have a strong sense of responsibility?
> *Answer:* You bet! If I take something on, it gets done as well as everything else, even if it kills me.
> *Question:* Do you express your anger easily?
> *Answer:* No. Better than before but not easily – although I can sometimes be very angry.

This brief extract seems to confirm the hypothesis that I have Type 1. After all, I was once apparently critical of myself and others; I have a strong sense of responsibility; I hold back my anger, although there is an outburst now and then. These are all characteristics of Type 1. So it looks as if the Type 1 hypothesis is confirmed, yet I do not have Type 1. Another person once imagined I had Type 4.

> *Question:* Does longing have an important place in your life?
> *Answer:* Certainly. I long very much for a better world and a deeper link with my origins, and I have always had that.
> *Question:* Would you like to be different?
> *Answer:* I become more ordinary the older I get, but earlier on I certainly found it very important to be different. I not only thought that, I also felt myself to be quite different from others.

So this looks like Type 4: longing is a theme, as is being different in earlier life. Over the years people have told me that I seemed very much like a Type 8, or a Type 5, or that I was seen as a Type 7, while within myself I recognise strong tendencies that seem to belong to Type 3 and Type 6.

Exactly, say enneagram experts, but that comes from the fact that you have Type 9, which recognises itself in all types. That is true. But all the other types also have wings, stress and relaxation points, and so forth, and all types can look like one another in certain respects. Everyone who does typing interviews in a professional manner knows that in practice it is sometimes very difficult to distinguish between the remaining possibilities after several types have been considered and eliminated.

Beware, therefore, of people who already know your type as soon as you come in. Sometimes they are right and sometimes not. Also be sceptical about articles in the weekly and monthly press about the types of famous people. Usually they have no foundation in research, and the person concerned has been typed with the naked eye.

In short, the naked eye alone is not a reliable method.

Questionnaires

If the naked eye cannot be relied upon, how then should we proceed? It would be very useful if there were some kind of handy instrument with which one could establish one's own type and that of others. So one thinks of questionnaires. All kinds of questionnaires can be found on the Internet. Alas, many do not suffice if one wants to determine one's own type.

I have tried out all sorts of questionnaires on myself, but hardly ever did Type 9 emerge as the only possibility. Sometimes the scores for four or five options were almost equally high, with Type 9 among them, and sometimes another type came out at the top on the basis of my answers to a certain questionnaire.

This section first lists the reasons why many questionnaires are not suitable for type determination. Thereafter it discusses an instrument developed at the University of Stanford which can be used as an aid in determining someone's enneagram type.

Why are many questionnaires unreliable?

There are various reasons why questionnaires do not generally provide a good picture:

- The enneagram is concerned with someone's underlying basic patterns and not his behaviour or skills.
- An individual's self-insight can be insufficient for filling in a questionnaire reliably.
- Someone may have grown up with a false personality type.
- Some answers are given on the basis of social desirability.
- People may be passing through different phases of their development.
- If someone experiences a great deal of stress or is usually very relaxed, he can display long-term characteristics of his stress or relaxation type.
- Someone can have a strong tendency towards one or both wings, and thus respond positively to questions concerning both these types
- Nearly all types can be like each other in certain respects, a phenomenon that is strengthened further by the similarities among the sub-types.

Basic patterns, not behaviour or skills

The essence of the enneagram is concerned with basic patterns and not behaviour or skills. People can develop skills which belong to every type and display similar behaviour. Their basic patterns, however, remain the same. As people develop themselves further their behaviour may diverge further from their type pattern. In addition, people have free will. They do not have to behave according to their types if they do not want to (although that can require an effort).

The same motivation can lead to different kinds of behaviour; the same behaviour can arise from different motivations. Thus the basic motivation 'search for harmony' (Type 9) leads to avoidance of conflict or to greater efforts to resolve conflicts. Once someone phoned me about a certain article and said: 'I read your article. I'm busy with that subject as well and would like to talk to you.' A telephone call like this can arise from very different motives: for instance, wanting to point out things for improvement (Type 1), looking for an excuse to establish a link with this supposed authority (Type 2), wanting to prevent competition (Type 3), wanting more knowledge (Type 5), or out of interest in the subject (Type 7).

Questionnaires oriented to this level of behaviour or skill instead of to the basic motivation do not focus on the proper level of the enneagram. Many questionnaires are concerned far too much with behaviour. Here is a small selection of statements I have encountered in enneagram questionnaires:

- 'What is more true: "I avoid conflicts" or "I tackle conflicts"?'
- 'In general do you take the lead? Yes/No.'
- 'Indicate whether each of these concepts applies to you very often, often, regularly, little, or not at all: performing well, many projects, compliment ...'
- 'I often buy things that are actually too expensive for me: not true (0), true (6).'

These are all examples in which someone is asked about what he does, not about his impulse, tendency or motivation for doing something.

Measure of self-insight

Apart from a few individuals who are well advanced on the road of self-realisation, everyone has a part of himself that he knows and a part he does not know, the so-called 'shadow'. I once interviewed someone with Type 2, a type with a tendency towards manipulation. His first statement about himself was 'I do not manipulate.' It is interesting in itself that someone asked to describe himself in a few key words mentions something that, according to him, he does *not* do. Why should he do this? Clearly the subject concerns him, otherwise he would not mention it at all. Perhaps someone has once suggested that he did this. Be that as it may, in a questionnaire this person would answer 'no' to the question 'Do you occasionally manipulate people?', although he actually has Type 2.

Many people are more familiar with their positive qualities than with their pitfalls. There are also people, however, who recognise every negative quality in themselves but do not notice the positive sides. In the better questionnaires both sides are covered. Often respondents answer the questions referring to their shadows negatively.

And what should one think of questionnaires with statements like 'I accept myself as I am and am honest about my limitations and talents' (this is supposed to indicate Type 3), or 'I am almost never wrong if I follow my intuition' (according to this questionnaire this should indicate Type 5)? In fact, the question posed here is how well someone knows himself – a question that is impossible to answer since, after all, one does not know what one does not know.

False personality type

People who are verbally, emotionally, physically or sexually abused sometimes take on the aggressor's behaviour via the defence mechanism of identification. This is then a false personality type. It can be resolved with the help of psychotherapy, so that the real personality type comes forward once more. Before that point, however, someone may answer a questionnaire on the basis of his false personality type.

People can also be *brought up* as another type. The perfectionist father (Type 1) can try to make perfectionists of all his children. A mother with Type 5 will probably try to impress upon her children that one must always think first and only then act. The father with Type 8 may feel that he can best prepare his children for modern society by making them able to fight for themselves – they shouldn't be ninnies. When children take on the norms of their parents, their real types sometimes come to the surface only later in their development. Before that point is reached they can, in questionnaires, fill in the types of the people who have brought them up. After all, that is their norm: how they ought to be. And this leads onto a further category.

Answers on the basis of social desirability

In some environments some types are considered more attractive than others. Thus nearly half of a group of young entrepreneurs thought they had Type 7. The image that Type 7 conjures up is pro-active, enterprising, positive, never throwing in the towel and always seeing new chances. Nowadays we teach managers just these kind of qualities in management training: seizing chances, seeing opportunities, turning threats into possibilities, and so on. This group had learned the lessons well: Type 7 was their favourite self-image. In a group of newly graduated trainees Type 7 and Type 3 were popular (Type 3 gets things done, is result-oriented, creates prestige and presents himself as a winner). Managers sometimes find Type 8 attractive: invulnerable, taking control, bending things to their will. In a group of company welfare workers it was Type 2 that was seen as desirable: helpful, supportive, supporting people in developing their capacities. People can have a tendency to interpret questionnaires on the basis of social desirability, not on the basis of objective reality.

Which types are regarded as socially desirable is determined partly by individual conceptualisation and partly by culture. In one organisation everyone must work towards results; in another one must understand very well what other people mean; in a third one must be pro-active, enterprising and flexible in seizing chances; and in a fourth one must be scientifically analytical. Even so these workplaces are not wholly populated by (respectively) result-oriented Type 3s, empathic Type 2s and 9s, opportunity-spotting Type 7s and analytical Type 5s. People can think they fulfil such a desirable image culturally speaking, however, and fill in a questionnaire on that basis.

Differences between people with the same type

No questionnaire does justice to the possible differences between people with the same type. We discussed these differences in Chapter 6 and worked them out in Chapters 7, 8 and 9. They concerned sub-types, wings, stress and relaxation, stages of development, gender difference, how type mechanisms can have different contents, and going with or against the type theme. Where questionnaires are aimed at an average type, people often recognise themselves less in the questions that ought to deal with their own type.

Good and bad questionnaires

Some questionnaires, on the basis of the criteria above, are quite simply bad because they focus too much on outward behaviour. Within the proper context, something can be done with other questionnaires which are aimed at the right level, that of basic patterns. There can be reasons for wanting to work with questionnaires, even though they do not always lead to the irrefutable determination of a type. At least they eliminate the less probable types. For instance, I myself use a questionnaire when I want to get something about the enneagram across to a large group in a short time, and give the participants a first idea of the direction in which they should look for their type. My preference in this context is for the questionnaire that follows.

David Daniels and Virginia Price developed the SEDIG (Stanford Enneagram Discovery Inventory and Guide).[3] The question section of the instrument consists of short descriptions of the nine types, comparable to the summarised descriptions in Chapter 1. Thus every type is given 'form', be it ever so condensed. Step 1 in working with this questionnaire is to find out which of these descriptions are more or less applicable. Some are eliminated immediately; a few options are left over.

Daniels and Price investigated the probability of someone selecting a certain type as his own on the basis of these short descriptions and actually having that type. That probability turned out to vary from 37 per cent (those who name Type 8 as first choice have a 37 per cent chance of having Type 8) to 68 per cent (those who name Type 9 as first choice have a 68 per cent chance of actually having Type 9). The other types had probability percentages between these. In the instrument, it is indicated which other types should be considered if someone has selected a certain type. Thereafter the most important differences between each two types are given. When the respondent has, for instance, Types 2 and 4 left over as possible types, the similarities between Types 2 and 4 are described (sensitivity, orientation towards relationships, and so forth), and thereafter the differences (for instance that Type 2 is oriented more towards others and Type 4 more towards himself). These descriptions help in making a final choice. The claim that everyone can establish their type irrefutably with the help of this instrument is not borne out in my experience. However, it offers a good 'leg-up' in a workshop, for instance, where the type is investigated further; many questionnaires are unsuitable here, for the reasons mentioned above.

All in all, we have to conclude that no single questionnaire leads in all cases to the incontrovertible determination of a type, but that some questionnaires come closer than others. For someone who wants to determine his own type it is important to take the result of many questionnaires with a pinch of salt, and certainly not to regard them as the last word. Professionals who want to help determine the type of someone else can use a questionnaire – naturally one of the better ones – as an aid. They may stimulate someone to think about himself and thus be a step towards establishing the type.

Self-study

It may well be possible to reach a conclusion about one's type by reading books. Because many books describe an 'average' type, recognition of one's type becomes easier the more one represents a more or less average type. The further someone diverges from that 'average', however, the less descriptions in books apply. In Chapter 6 we described the different variants and manifestation forms of the types which were worked out subsequently by type in Chapters 7, 8 and 9.

It is a warning signal if a book emphasises behaviour rather than basic patterns. For instance, it is certainly not true that every Type 4 goes around in black or purple, that every Type 5 has a very sparsely furnished house where he eats simply and to which no one else is ever admitted, or that no Type 9 can make decisions.

The number of variants of a type is far greater than can be described in a book. Someone who wants to determine his type (or that of another) principally on the basis of a book about the enneagram would do well not to depend on one book but to read several, preferably written from different viewpoints and by writers with different types. The Appendix (page 281) lists books by authors of different types. It is crucial not to get stuck at the level of the behaviour descriptions but to look for what the author has to say about basic patterns.

While reading books, an image arises of how the mechanism of the various types works. It is recommended that the image one forms of a type through reading is tested in practice. This can be done, for instance, by looking at *panels*.

Panels

A panel consists of people with the same type who are interviewed about the basic patterns of their type, as manifested in them individually. Naturally the members of a panel must know their type, but this is not required of spectators. One of the aims of observing a panel, after all, is the discovery of one's own type. When panels are used for that purpose one sees nine panels, each of a different type.

Helen Palmer and David Daniels, who developed the panel method, called their way of working 'the narrative tradition'. In a more restricted sense, this term refers to the panel method developed by them. In a broader sense it covers every method based on factual investigation involving representatives of a given type, who themselves provide information about their own type. The oral transfer of information from one expert to another is not understood under 'narrative tradition' in this sense, however.

Some enneagram training courses consist exclusively of panels. Panels can also form part of a training course or work conference in which other work methods are also used.

When a panel is interviewed, the interviewer deals with the qualities and pitfalls of the type, the basic patterns of the type and how these manifest themselves in the work and private lives of the people concerned. Depending on the time available and the setting in which the panel is held, there can be further investigation of stress and relaxation, sub-types, development within the type, and other aspects.

A panel can be used in various contexts. For instance, it may form part of a basic training course in the enneagram in which the primary aim is to delineate the types more clearly, with the aim of the participants being able to determine their own types. However, it can also form part of a work conference or seminar dealing with a particular theme. Themes could be (for example) leadership, dealing with conflicts, negotiation, co-operation, time management, education and training, or any other subject that was discussed in Chapter 2, dealing with application areas in organisations. Panels are then interviewed about the way in which their type works out the themes. Thus we hear about nine styles of leadership, nine qualities and pitfalls in dealing with conflicts and in negotiation, nine kinds of conditions laid down for co-operation, nine qualities and pitfalls in time management, nine teaching and study styles, and so on. Whatever theme is under discussion, the typical basic patterns always come out.

A panel interview provides another kind of information from that a book can offer, just as seeing a play performed is different from reading it. It provides direct experience of a type. In a panel with Type 8s, we feel the energy level in the room rise. If a panel with Type 5s has its turn next, then the energy level drops again. If a panel with Type 2s is interviewed, then their tendency to flatter or seduce is perceptible. During a panel with Type 7s one can observe how they provide positive explanations for painful things. In a panel with Type 1s one can feel them radiating criticism. All these insights are also to be found in books, but seeing, experiencing and feeling them offer an extra dimension.

At the same time a panel session makes clear how much people with one and the same type can differ in behaviour. Thus a woman in a Type 9 panel went so far in her tendency towards symbiosis that she actually wore her partner's clothes; another woman in the same panel actually rebelled against her natural tendency to surrender herself, trying to shut herself off from the influence of others. Yet this divergent behaviour actually arose from the same basic pattern: a tendency to go along with others in order to preserve harmony. In another panel, for instance, one Type 1 was highly critical of the others while another Type 1 did his best not to pass judgement. Here, too, the basic pattern was the same although these individuals dealt with it in different ways.

By observing panels, someone can get the feeling 'This is still different from the way I am', or 'This feels very much like the way it works with me'. Looking at panels is therefore a good way of obtaining greater clarity about one's own type. The question of whether one feels good about – or feels attracted to – a certain type is a good criterion for determining one's type. Some people have an intense dislike for their own type and can only with difficulty admit to themselves that the type concerned is really theirs, while types an individual finds very attractive are often precisely those that he is not.

The panel method offers an outstanding way to obtain a clear under-standing of the various types and so to discover one's own type. It has a few practical limitations for use in organisations. If we say that a panel of a certain type has to consist of at least three people, already one needs nine times three representatives of a type, and thus 27 people who know their type and are willing to talk about it. This is not a realistic expectation if one is working with a management team consisting of only five people, or if a staff department wants to work more with the enneagram but consists of eight people. The 'full' panel method is applied primarily in seminars with many participants. With smaller groups a specially adapted method is applied in practice: people talk about their own type in the group sessions, but in order to be able to do this the type must be determined before the session. The typing interview is used for this.

The typing interview

The aim of the typing interview is to help people determine their own type. This is done by eliminating less probable types. Often one type is left over. Sometimes two or three possible types will remain for the person interviewed to consider a little longer, for instance using the above-mentioned methods of self-study, by observing panels of the types concerned, by participating in a workshop, or by discussing the matter with people who know him well. Here, 'knowing well' means being aware of what drives someone. Sometimes people know each other their whole lives and yet only know each other on the level that they like playing tennis and do not like spinach.

The added value of the typing interview over the questionnaire, for instance, lies in the fact that the interviewer has more possibilities for acquiring information on basic patterns. The interviewer can adapt his manner of asking about these patterns to the person being interviewed, for example, because he receives immediate feedback on which questions are understood and which not. Further he does not pay attention only to the literal text of the person being questioned, but also to whether the questions are answered decisively or hesitantly, and whether the answers are 'black and white' or nuanced. The interviewer pays attention to which questions the interviewee answers with emotion, to their general attitude (for instance rational, evasive, emotional), to which questions the interviewee find easier or more difficult to answer, to the way he deals with the interviewer himself and the feeling the person inspires in him. Counter-transference, or the feeling that the interviewee calls up in the interviewer (see Chapter 14 for a detailed discussion) can contribute to the diagnosis. This means that the interviewer must have insight into his own counter-transference patterns. In this way more information is acquired than might be gained from a questionnaire; what is more, this information is at the proper level. It also becomes much clearer where the interviewee's blind spots might lie.

The interview is participative to a certain degree. Together with the interviewee, the interviewer discusses what suits him better or less well. It should be clear that a trained interviewer is an absolute necessity.

The typing interview demands a good interview system and technique. It also requires a thorough knowledge of the enneagram. This knowledge is not only needed for asking the right questions, since these could be read out by an interviewer. Interpreting the answers correctly is a much more difficult matter. Furthermore it is important to keep different possible types 'in the frame' for as long as necessary, instead of wanting to fix a type as quickly as possible.

The section that follows deals with type interviewing. It is of particular interest for readers who want to work professionally with the enneagram. The system, however, also has something to offer those who want to determine their own type.

In succession, we shall deal with:

- the nature of the typing interview
- the system of the typing interview
- the interview technique
- pitfalls in type interviewing.

The nature of the typing interview

The nature of the typing interview is diagnostic. This has consequences for the way in which questions are asked. The typing interview can take place within the framework of coaching, counselling, consulting or training. However, a (too) helpful attitude during the interview is a handicap to typing. For example, when the interviewee speaks of something that arouses unpleasant memories, the interviewer, prompted by this event, can tend to begin coaching, consulting, or other such behaviours. He might, for instance, pay attention to the way the interviewee has interpreted this event and discuss other possible interpretations. Or he could discuss how the interviewee could have acted more effectively in this situation, and also practise this. Or he could consider how to prevent the interviewee becoming regularly caught up in this sort of situation. These are all perfectly useful, justifiable and legitimate interventions within the framework of coaching, counselling, consulting, and so on, but they do not lead to the determination of someone's type.

During the typing interview one searches for the basic patterns of someone's type by means of asking questions, and if necessary by asking follow-up questions should an answer require this. Not only what the interviewees say but also how it is said, their interpretation of the questions, their non-verbal behaviour – all of this is regarded as information.

System of the typing interview

The typing interview demands good preparation. There are a number of phases in the interview itself:

1. General questions.
2. First round: questions aimed at eliminating the less probable types.
3. Mid-interview review: a number of types fall away; a few are left over.
4. Second round: questions which discriminate between the remaining types.
5. The rounding-off and concluding discussion.

Preparation for holding typing interviews

The interviewer can make a list of questions that may be drawn upon during the forthcoming interviews. This consists of the following parts:

- General questions such as 'How do other people describe you?' or 'What do you find important in your life?'
- Core questions regarding each type.
- Discriminating questions for each pair of types, including questions related to stress and relaxation points and questions about the sub-types.

Often the questions are not used literally in the typing interview. The special value of the interview, after all, is that the interviewer can take the interviewee into account as a person and the way in which the interview progresses. Why go to all this trouble, then, to formulate questions? The most important aim of this exercise is to practise posing questions at the right level: that of the basic patterns, and not at the level of behaviour. In practice this is more difficult than it might at first seem. In the first instance, by using a list of self-formulated questions as a point of departure, one can systematically control which sort of questions work and which do not, and so become increasingly skilful in posing questions that are relevant.

The practised interviewer works mostly with a short list of themes that play a role with the various types. The way in which questions are posed about these themes then depends on the interviewee and the course of the interview. The principle 'not behaviour but basic patterns' remains valid.

Themes which could come up for consideration per type are as follows:

Type 1
- Wanting to be good and do the right things, striving for perfection.
- Tendency to judge and compare, strong inner critic, also criticism of others.
- Strong feeling of responsibility; work comes before pleasure.
- Self-set standards which are independent of others', nonetheless very sensitive to praise and criticism.
- Tendency to repress impulses and needs; sometimes an impulse breaks through in uncharacteristic behaviour.
- Anger held back, repressed anger, legitimate anger (legitimate according to self-set norms).

Type 2
- Attention to needs of others who are seen as important (in the sense of status, or because someone can give something in return).
- Tendency to display different sides of oneself, according to what the other needs.
- Central importance of relationships; dependence on relationships for identity.
- Expressive and tending to take the initiative in making contacts.
- Tendency to repress personal needs or express these indirectly.
- Proud to be able to give, to be indispensable, to know what others need.

Type 3
- Wanting appreciation for performing well.
- Task- and result-oriented.
- Need for recognition, prestige, image.
- Wanting to be the best, competition, winning.
- Tendency to pay no attention to personal feelings and those of others.

Type 4
- Attention to the feeling that something important is missing from life.
- Envy of people who appear to have what is lacking in one's own life; competitive behaviour or shame arising from this deficiency.

- Tendency to overvalue the absent, the distant, the unattainable; undervaluation of the here and now; idealism.
- Striving for genuineness and authenticity in relationships.
- Intensity of emotions; attracted to extremes.
- Empathy, especially with the suffering of others.

Type 5
- Observation and collection of information before (or instead of) acting.
- Conceptual orientation.
- Sensitive to the expectations of the world; protecting oneself from them; keeping them under observation and control by separating territories in life (work, private life, sport, etc.).
- Ungenerous, economical with time, space, energy and knowledge.
- Dealing with people costs energy; privacy needed to recharge batteries.
- Strives for independence, for instance by minimising needs and emotions.

Type 6
- Wishing to create safety by watchfulness.
- Tendency to fear, doubt or worry; preparation for what might go wrong.
- Thinking in terms of 'worst-case' scenarios.
- Loyal.
- Ambivalent attitude to figures of authority: love–hate, obedience–rebellion.
- Tendency towards distrust.
- Preference for a difficult project with setbacks; difficulty with success.

Type 7
- Looking for pleasure and avoiding pain; life is an adventure; re-labelling unpleasant experiences as positive.
- Paying attention to many attractive future possibilities.
- Does not want limitations; losing options inspires fear; therefore also levelling with authority.
- Many interests; experience of a process/task more interesting than the result (but result is sometimes found important); tendency to take on too many projects at once; fascination.
- Narcissism, the feeling of having a right to the good things in life, gaining the attention of others.
- Charming and disarming.

Type 8
- Power, domination and control in order to win respect and mask personal vulnerability; little room for others.
- Tendency to all or nothing, black-and-white thinking, excess; always wants action.

- Direct and confrontational; expresses anger easily and is then rid of it.
- Standing up for the weaker; empowering them.
- Searching for truth; just; sense of justice also confused with self-interest, then becomes vengeful
- Tendency to deny personal vulnerability and weakness and not to respect personal boundaries, either own or others'.

Type 9
- Striving for harmony, comfort and belonging; avoidance of conflict.
- Diffuse attention, directed at others.
- Ability to identify with different standpoints, to see all sides of a subject.
- Tendency to automatically go along with the opinions of others; difficulty in taking a position; has difficulty in saying no, or holds on obstinately to a personal standpoint
- Indirect anger; under pressure stubborn, passive aggression.
- Does not choose, everything is equally important.

First round

This is meant to exclude the least probable types. To begin with, the interviewer asks some general questions, such as 'How would you describe yourself in a few key words?', 'How do other people describe you?', or 'What have been the most important development themes in your life?' The answers to these questions can already point in the direction of certain types. Later in the interview – in the mid-interview review, for instance, or in the final conclusions – the interviewer can call on these again. (For example: 'We have now two types left over, x and y. What you said about yourself in the beginning fits y more.')

Thereafter the interviewer poses some core questions regarding each type, for which the previously mentioned themes serve as a connecting link. A question about the theme of one type, however, can produce an answer which indicates another. The interviewer keeps notes about this. Questions about a theme for a Type 1 are, for example: 'How do you deal with anger?', 'Do you get angry easily?', 'Do you express anger easily?' An answer such as 'I am highly explosive, but when I have said it then I am rid of it' is certainly not an answer typical of Type 1, but sounds more like Type 8. The interviewer can then fall back on this when coming to questions related to type 8.

There are a number of themes where nearly every type has a characteristic answer. Anger is such a theme, and the question of what inspires fear is another (see 'Basic fear' in the type descriptions in Part II). Every type also has a characteristic answer to a question such as 'What causes stress in you?'

The first questions are about the themes associated with the internal triangle of the enneagram, Types 3, 6 and 9. These are the core types of each of the three centres. The reason for beginning with these three types is that an idea can arise about the centre in which the type should be sought: for instance 'it is certainly not a head type', or 'it would really surprise me if it wasn't a head type'. In my experience, however, that picture is not always formed by this stage. In general we can scrap a type as a possibility if there is no positive response to two or three of the themes mentioned. Thereafter all the other types are investigated: the other heart types 2 and 4, the other head types 5 and 7, and the other belly types 8 and 1. The best order is the order of the arrows: 1–4–2–8–5–7. In some cases one covers the head, heart and belly types in succession, thus 5–7, 2–4, 8–1. In all cases it is important to check all types. As an interviewer one can be taken by surprise. Thus I once interviewed a lady of non-European extraction who presented herself as friendly, modest, forthcoming and empathic. From the interview it turned out that she had Type 8 – just about the last type I would have thought of at first. The way she presented herself was determined more by the culture from which she came than by her type.

Mid-interview review

After the first-round questions an interim evaluation takes place, in which interviewer and interviewee discuss their conclusions about the types that are rejected. The interviewer presents his or her preliminary conclusions; the interviewee comments on them. If the interviewee has doubts, then the type concerned is not excluded for the time being.

Second round

There are many aspects in which the types or their sub-types can resemble each other strongly. Thus both Type 8 and Type 3 are result- and action-oriented. A Type 9 with self-preservation as sub-type can closely resemble a Type 5 in their need for privacy. The one-to-one sub-types of Type 4 and Type 1 both display jealousy and envy. A contraphobic Type 6 can seem very like a Type 8 in displaying single-mindedness and a virtually irrepressible tendency to take action. The self-preservation sub-type of Type 6 with the theme of warmth can be like Type 2 in the way in which relationships are important. Type 6 and Type 1 are sometimes difficult to distinguish because both hesitate and procrastinate. Each type can seem like another in certain respects.

The types left over after the mid-interview review display certain similarities; otherwise they would not have been left over together. In the second round, therefore, the interviewer asks questions aimed at distinguishing between the remaining types, according to the model 'what fits better, x or y?' Examples of discriminating questions are:

- *Between Type 2 and Type 9*. If you come to a party where no one knows you, which impulse fits more: make contact (Type 2) or wait until someone comes to you (Type 9).

- *Between Type 3 and Type 1.* Naturally everyone wants to be appreciated, but if you really had to choose, what do you prefer: a project in which, with a reasonable performance and not too much effort, you can still score and win a great deal of praise (Type 3); or a project in which, with considerable effort, you can actually achieve fully what you had in mind but which is noticed by few other people (Type 1).
- *Between Type 4 and Type 7.* When someone around you is in difficulty, do you tend to solve his problems quickly and cheer him up (Type 7) or do you tend to discuss his problems in depth (Type 4)?

The interviewer can use stress and relaxation points for posing discriminating questions, for instance:

- *Between Type 3 and Type 9.* What is more like you if you are under a great deal of stress: withdrawing and postponing difficult matters (Type 3 goes under stress to 9) or imagining calamities and attributing bad intentions to others (Type 9 goes under stress to 6)?
- *Between Type 4 and Type 7.* What is more like you if you find yourself in a very stressful situation: directing your attention to the needs of others, orientation on relationships (Type 2 is the stress point of Type 4), or doing your very best to do things faultlessly (Type 1 is the stress point of type 7)?
- *Between Type 7 and Type 8.* If you feel completely safe emotionally and at your ease, what is more like you: creating private space and withdrawing (Type 7 in relaxation goes to 5) or directing yourself more to what others need (Type 8 goes in relaxation to 2)?

In the same way, the sub-types can be used for posing discriminating questions:

- *Between Type 4 and Type 3.* What fits more: recklessness (sub-type of Type 4) or security (sub-type of Type 3)?
- *Between Type 8 and Type 9.* What fits more: wanting to possess another (sub-type of Type 8) or wanting to unite with another (sub-type of Type 9)?

The rounding-off and concluding discussion

Finally the interviewer decides together with the interviewee which type has incontrovertibly come to the front, or which types are left over for further investigation. As mentioned earlier, the interviewer ought to leave someone the freedom to find out for himself which type he is. In this the typing interview is an aid. The interviewer will therefore also conduct this part of the discussion participatively, sharing their ideas with the interviewee. For instance: 'From your answers there does not seem to be any relationship orientation; that shuts out Types 2, 3 and 4.' At the same time the interviewer invites the partner in

the discussion to offer their own comments if he wishes. Thereafter the interviewer provides a more detailed description of the types that remain. Sometimes it will have already become clear from this discussion which type remains
as the only one. When more than one type is left over, the interviewer gives
material to the interviewee – a reading list, for instance, or an exercise in self-
observation – so he can think further about his own type. The interviewer can
also suggest that the interviewee should talk sometimes with people who know
him well.

Sometimes an interviewer will be convinced that the interviewee has a
certain type, while the interviewee disagrees. There can be different reasons
for this. It is possible that the interviewee does not find the type concerned
attractive and will not or cannot yet recognise that this is really his type.
Forcing the issue is not the right way; offering material to help further
consideration is more appropriate. It is possible that the interviewee has a
wrong or incomplete picture of the type concerned. Information can help
here. The interviewee's self-knowledge may be poor, and the answers given
during the interview might not represent their true type. In this situation, a
process is needed to help strengthen self-knowledge. Finally, it is possible
that the interviewer has interpreted answers wrongly.

Interpreting answers

Posing questions is one thing; interpreting the answers is quite another. In my
own experience supervising typing interviews, I have often noticed that
someone can have sufficient knowledge to ask perfect questions yet, at the
same time, insufficient knowledge to be able to interpret the answers
correctly. An interviewer can prepare for asking questions with the available
printed matter about the enneagram. In order to be able to interpret the
answers, however, a thorough ready knowledge of the types is needed. The
interviewer must have encountered the types in practice and observed them.
This will ensure he has had contact with many variants of the same type. He
will have observed, for instance, how Type 4 and Type 7 can seem like each
other while on paper they are each other's opposite poles; how Type 1 and
Type 6 are sometimes difficult to distinguish, how Type 5 and Type 9 can
display similarities, and so forth. The interviewer will have felt the types'
energies, such as the room-filling energy of Type 8 and the 'withdrawn'
energy of Type 5. Only someone who has acquired extensive 'live' experience
with the various types in the enneagram is able to interpret the answers to
questions correctly.

Interview technique

Apart from knowledge of the enneagram, someone conducting a typing
interview requires a good interview technique. This consists of a series of
rules which apply to every interview, in which one really wants to know

what is going on inside the interviewee. (This makes them quite unlike the kinds of interview often seen on television in which the interviewer either tries to draw 'amusing' responses from the interviewee, or aims to catch the interviewee on the wrong foot politically.) These rules are as follows.

Open questions

To an open question any answer is possible; a closed question can only be answered with 'yes' or 'no'. An example of an open question is: 'What disturbs you most?' An example of a closed question is: 'Does it disturb you if people push themselves to the foreground?' A mnemonic aid here is that open questions begin with W or H (where, when, what, how, how much, and so on) and closed questions with a verb.

Neutral questions

It is important not to ask leading or normative questions. Thus the interviewer can, for instance, allow a choice to be made between positions instead of going to one extreme in his questions. He can then ask, for example: 'Do you tend more to have people around you always, or do you prefer more to be alone?' – instead of: 'Do you always have people around you?' Or 'How easy or difficult is it to ...?' instead of 'Is it difficult to ...?'

It is essential that the interviewer gives no indication of any judgement about what is asked, but is seen to be open to every possible answer. The intonation of the question contributes a lot to this. For instance, when an interviewer (on the basis of their own type) is repelled by Type 3's tendency to seek to make an impression on others, he must be doubly careful that this feeling is not echoed in the tone of questioning.

Sometimes interviewers find it difficult to ask certain questions. Thus I found it difficult as a less experienced interviewer to ask about Type 8's tendency to excess, or about Type 4's lack of fulfilment. 'One just doesn't ask these things', I thought as the tension-evading Type 9. It turned out, however, that my discussion partners were not at all put out by such questions. On the contrary, they reacted enthusiastically. Every type, after all, has a different conception of what is acceptable and what is desirable behaviour.

Follow-up questions

These are questions like 'What do you mean by that?', questions seeking concrete examples and also requests for information about the concepts the interviewee uses, such as 'When do you regard something as a conflict?' Thus a couple of Type 5s once said they found conviviality very important. When asked what they understood by conviviality, one answered 'Being on my own running the marathon' and the other 'Reading the newspaper in a café without talking to the others who are there.' It is always important not to fill in one's own definition of a concept used by the interviewee, but to ask for his own interpretation.

Inner process

These are questions for learning about the inner process instead of the outward behaviour. For example:

- 'How do you feel if this or that happens?'
- 'How do you reach decisions?'
- 'If you have done something wrong, what goes on inside you?'

Cohesion of the interview

The interviewer can refer to answers given earlier. For instance: 'You said earlier that you do not like conflict; how do you deal with conflicts in general?' If necessary, the interviewer asks for clarification if contradictions become apparent. For instance: 'You said earlier that you were clear, and now that you are indirect. What do you mean exactly?'

Non-verbal

The interviewer pays attention not only to the verbal content of the answers but also, and particularly, to the prevailing atmosphere, and to the interviewee's emotional response and manner of answering. Hesitant or forthright? Immediate or delayed? Evasive or direct? How does the person being interviewed react to the interviewer? And so on.

The following points for attention apply specially to the typing interview:

Type-specific questions

The interviewer asks questions which are as type-specific and discriminating as possible: that is to say questions which help in the exclusion or admission of types. Examples of type-specific questions include: 'Are you a real searcher for harmony?' (Type 9); or 'Is competition something that drives you?' (Type 3). Many questions do apply to a type but are not discriminating. Thus every type can be a workaholic, no one likes failure, everyone hates it if the road to his goal is cut off, everyone thinks good relationships are important, and so on. I have never heard someone say that he does best with bad relationships. Discriminating questions are questions like 'What is a good relationship for you?', because every type demands something different in relationships, or 'Why do you work so many hours?', because this is a question about motivation and reaction patterns.

Asking type-specific questions which nevertheless remain open is quite an art. Questions about type themes, after all, soon become closed ones: 'Is competition a motive?' (Type 3); 'Do you tend to imagine the worst?' (Type 6); 'Do you have an impulse to explain negative things in positive terms?' (Type 7). This dilemma can be solved by bringing up the (closed) type theme as openly as possible. This can be done by providing further possible answers oneself. For example: 'Is competition a motive, or do you find being first unimportant?'; or 'Some people are always full of positive possibilities; others have more of a tendency to consider what can go wrong. What is the case with you?'

Motivation and attention

The interviewer asks about underlying basic patterns, impulses and motives, not about external behaviour. Questions are not about what someone does but what his first tendency is, why he does something, and what he thinks and feels in doing it.

Earlier life

Often the type is clearer when one is young and has not yet developed as an individual. The flowering of the type is sometimes fixed around the age of 20. The criterion, however, is development, not age. Some people begin to develop much earlier; others flower late or do not develop at all. Often the interviewee indicates this personally: 'Nowadays I find that attractive', 'I don't have difficulty with that any more', and so on. The interviewer then continues by asking how things were previously, when the interviewee had not yet developed. If the interviewee provides no indication the interviewer can pose such questions as 'Has that always been the case?', 'Do you do that naturally or have you learned it?', or 'How was it when you were younger?'

As we have seen earlier in this chapter, there are exceptions to the rule that the type is clearer when one is young. Some people first imitate the type of those who brought them up, or other influential people. They may follow the pattern of cultural expectation, they may do what they have been taught, or take over the pattern of an aggressor. These people only come to their real type later in life. We mentioned earlier the example of a female Type 8 who was brought up as a 'lady' – that is to say, in a classic female role pattern – and only discovered later that this did not suit her at all. Or a Type 9 may be brought up as Type 1 and only discover later that he himself does not actually strive for the highest that is attainable.

Pitfalls in type-interviewing

There are a number of pitfalls I have noticed with inexperienced interviewers, and which I wish to specify here. If one watches out for these, then the first battle in determining the right type has been won.

Thinking too quickly that one already knows the type

This is the biggest pitfall. Certainly the interviewer must take care when the thought arises at the beginning of the interview that the type is 'quite clear'. In all cases it is important to go through the whole protocol – in other words, the whole procedure of the typing interview – and to remain open for contradictory information. I often see interviewers who have already formed an opinion interpreting all the subsequent answers in that spirit, while the answers themselves are open to very different interpretations. From my earlier experience of conducting typing interviews, I remember that I would be delighted if I thought I had recognised a type but would also become very unhappy if contradictory information emerged.

Asking questions for too long at too early a stage

It is not necessary to ask many follow-up questions about every type in the first round of the interview. After all, the aim at this stage is to exclude types, not to establish one type. For excluding a type three questions are usually sufficient, provided the questions deal with different themes of the type. In the second round the remaining types can be considered in more depth. The interviewer can run out of time by asking too many follow-up questions in the first round.

Interpretation

It may seem obvious that the interviewer should not try to tell an interviewee what he means by his own answers, but should ask this of the interviewee. Nonetheless, interviewers still make this mistake occasionally. Instead, the interviewer's own interpretations should be tested by asking the interviewee to explain his answers further.

Projection

The interviewer ascribes his own experience to the interviewee. The interviewee is no longer in the picture: the interviewer creates his or her own picture.

Verbal and non-verbal behaviour

Verbal and non-verbal behaviours may conflict. The interviewer takes both kinds of information into consideration. Just as in all communication, so too in the typing interview: much of the message is communicated non-verbally. It has even been said that 70 per cent of meaning is communicated non-verbally. If interviewers react only to the literal 'text' and do not take non-verbal information into account, they can reach a wrong conclusion. For example, someone may insist he has absolutely no problems with something while tears come to his eyes.

Stereotyping

Not all people answer to the stereotypes of the types – far from it, in fact. The gestalt – the total picture – is what matters. If interviewers use stereotypical descriptions of type as stepping-stones, they can end up in trouble. In practice, for instance, not every Type 4 admits to melancholy; there are Type 9s who do make sound decisions; some Type 2s regularly like to be alone. None of these traits would be predicted working from the basis of stereotypes.

Profiling as expert or guru

Everyone likes to come across as a professional. The interviewer who indulges in this can be tempted to conjure a type up out of a top hat at the end of an interview. It is an important part of the process, however, for the person being interviewed to reach a conclusion himself. It is more professional to guide him in this than to want to show off one's own knowledge.

Counter-transference

This is a negative attitude or a counter-productive reaction arising from one's own personal experience with a type. This phenomenon is examined further in Chapter 14. The interviewer has probably had bad experiences with a certain type and the person being interviewing (who has the type concerned) arouses the same feeling. The interviewer must be prepared for this. If he is not, then the relationship with the interviewee can be influenced negatively. On the contrary, awareness of this can help the interviewer to use this feeling as a diagnostic aid. If someone inspires in him the same feeling as someone from the past, then this could indicate that the interviewee has the same type as the person from the previous experience. Naturally such a feeling is never sufficient in itself for establishing someone's type; it is only one of several possible indicators.

In the following chapters we shall discuss how to proceed once the type is determined.

Chapter 14

Working Professionally with Others

If people want to work professionally with the enneagram, for example in the role of coach, educator, trainer, consultant, manager or facilitator (henceforth we shall simply call all these 'professionals' – thus managers are included), then they must first do so with their own type. If they are not aware of their own type qualities and development points, they run the risk of projecting these personal characteristics on clients, colleagues or fellow-workers.

Furthermore their personal experience with other types plays a role. They can tend to think positively or negatively about types with which they have had positive or negative experiences in the past. The only thing is that another person was then involved. In the same way, clients, colleagues or fellow workers can project their experiences onto the professional.

In working with others various kinds of intervention are possible. In this chapter the various possibilities are discussed. These are worked out further in Chapters 15–18. The subjects for discussion in this chapter are:

- Working with the enneagram in a professional manner.
- The role of one's own type in working with others.
- Differentiating various kinds of interventions and their aims.

Working professionally with the enneagram

Some people say that only the person of the counsellor is important. Research into psychotherapeutic treatment has indicated that the greatest success factor was the person of the psychotherapist. But here one therapist was compared with others. In terms of their personal development people can owe more to friends, family and neighbours than to professional assistance. However, a professional assistant (in the broad sense of the word, thus including trainer, coach or consultant) offers a development 'toolkit' which is generally not available to friends, family and neighbours. It is therefore important to be clear from the beginning what someone wants. Is the question 'I want to know my enneagram type and gain insight into the mechanisms which play a role in that'? If so, everyone who has been professionally trained in the enneagram can be of help here.

If the question is 'I want to develop myself in my type', then the more obvious thing is to embrace someone who is not only professionally trained in the enneagram but, in addition, is also a professional developer.

People who want to apply the enneagram in working with others must begin by studying the enneagram in depth. They must also know themselves so well that they have seen through their own enneagram mechanisms, and in principle can distance themselves from them. This prevents projection onto the client and makes unavoidable phenomena such as 'transference' and 'counter-transference' (emotional reactions to a type – see later in this chapter) manageable. People who identify completely with their type and have no insight into this had better not go to work with other people yet.

Professionalism also means review by fellow professionals. Those who go their professional way alone – with whatever good intentions – run the risk of growing accustomed to wrong interpretations which are then not corrected. Professional review – for instance, in the form of certification, supervision or intervision (mutual supervision) or inter-collegiate consultation – prevents this. Advanced training also keeps the professional level up to the mark. A professional's development is never finished. After all, an important characteristic of professionals is that they keep on learning.

One's own role in working with others

People who want to work professionally with the enneagram must do so, paradoxically enough, with their own type in the first place because when someone works with others, his or her own type plays a not insignificant role, as has been pointed out already. It is also important to take into account one's own various emotional reactions with regard to specific types. Both these aspects are now discussed in sequence.

The role of one's own type

Everyone has his own 'typical' qualities, pitfalls and development points. These also manifest themselves when one works with others as a professional. Qualities and pitfalls of the different types when working with others can be, for instance (with the average type):

- *Type 1*. This type can be respectful, offer structure and possibilities for improvement. But he can also want to be too perfect as a professional. Then he tries to create a perfect process or to find a perfect solution for problems, and attempts to impose his own values too much with regard to what has to be achieved and how it should be attained.
- *Type 2*. A Type 2 can usually understand very well what his client (in the broad sense of the word) needs, assessing his potential well and helping to realise it. But he can also want to be his client's best friend, and need the relationship with the client in order to feel good. He can impose his help on the other, want to be indispensable, want to create dependence, and be too concerned with receiving something in return.
- *Type 3*. A Type 3 can work purposefully with his client, judge well what he wants and apply himself to the task. But he can also be too keen to create an image as the model professional. He can yield too much to the expectations of those with whom he works, whereby his own contribution is lost. He can want to achieve results, if necessary at the expense of clients or fellow-workers, because he can score with that elsewhere. And he can pay too little attention to the feelings of the other or himself. This is illustrated by the example 'A coach with Type 3'.

A coach with Type 3

Lydia, with Type 3, has a number of rules which she follows if she has a new client for coaching. Goals must be set; an approach is planned and a time schedule agreed; the number of sessions is fixed. The client must do homework in order to attain the goals. It all looks very professional, and with many clients this is a very successful approach.

But now she had John as a client. John has Type 9 and has done little about his development yet. John thinks it is a very good approach, so it should work, he says. But ... John does not manage to do his homework. And he begins to feel pushed; he wants more time. Furthermore, he keeps coming back each time with the same problems. On top of that, he begins to wonder if Lydia really understands how serious his problems are. Surely you can't solve problems like that in three months? Lydia becomes impatient. This way she will never achieve the stated goals in time.

Lydia can now do one of two things. If she is not aware of the influence of her Type 3 she will let herself be ruled by her impatience and put John under more pressure. That will result in John becoming even slower, for Type 9 reacts to pressure with resistance. And the relationship will deteriorate. If she does happen to be aware of the influence of her Type 3, she will be able to realise that her method of coaching is not the way Type 9 learns. The less pressure the better.

- *Type 4*. This type can sense well how painful processes can be for people and can act supportively. He can realise an ideal and make a unique contribution. But he may also want to be special in his professional role and expect from others more emotion, suffering from a situation and authenticity than he is prepared, or in a position, to give. This person may want a more personal relationship than the other wishes.
- *Type 5*. Characteristic of this type is a good analytical ability, an ability to come up with an objectively good solution, and knowledge of how to remain calm in crisis situations. But he can also analyse without feeling for the emotions of the other, and try to exclude the emotions of the other and himself. See also the example 'A consultant with Type 5'.

A consultant with Type 5

Marcel is a consultant with Type 5. He is asked to advise in a difficult situation. The management teams of two organisations forced to merge by the government have failed to agree. Actually they do not want to talk to each other any longer. Harsh words have been exchanged and quite a few times a meeting has been broken off because one of the parties had left the room and not closed the door quietly behind him. But, they have to – and salvation must now come from the consultant.

Marcel goes firmly forward to work. He inventories interests and standpoints, does comparative research into mergers of the same kind of organisation, and writes a thorough report in which he proposes a solution. Looked at objectively this is the best approach in these situations. Alas, the report is judged very negatively. Various people feel that they have not been taken seriously, that no account at all has been taken of their feelings. Marcel would have had more success if, in his personal talks, he had not just inventoried business interests but had also examined in detail the sensitivities of the various people involved.

- *Type 6*. In general Type 6 can analyse risks well and give an impression of loyalty. But he can also be worried about what can go wrong, attribute hidden agendas to others, and display doubt and ambivalence.
- *Type 7*. Type 7 is good at pointing out the many possible routes that can be taken and at finding positive explanations for events experienced as unpleasant. But he can also focus primarily on having a good time, see too many possible ways of working, fail to focus his attention properly, and disregard his own painful experiences or those of others.
- *Type 8*. Type 8 can take things on vigorously, introduce active work methods, and protect or stimulate those who are weaker into using their initiative and taking responsibility. But he can also want to be too commanding, too much in control, want to call up too much energy

where this does not suit the other person, become involved in a power struggle, be too confrontational, or want to record results too quickly.

- *Type 9*. Type 9 can listen well, identify with many standpoints and go along with the themes clients put forward. But he can also be too accommodating, attach himself too much to the other person, provide too little counterbalance (by being very empathic but not confronting), let himself be led too much by the expectations he ascribes to the other, or offer too little structure.

Transference and counter-transference

When someone sees another person as the cause of feelings and emotions that actually were elicited in the past by someone else – for instance a parent or grandparent – then this is called (after Freud) *transference*. The person in question then projects feelings and emotions associated with the father or grandmother on to the person with whom he is dealing at that moment and therefore identifies this person with people from his personal life history. Usually this is connected with matters which for someone have negative (but also sometimes positive) associations. Transference is usually unpleasant for the person onto whom feelings and emotions are transferred. The person is seen as someone else, more or less, and is also treated as such. Irritating or not it does happen, however, and is thus something to be reckoned with in working with the enneagram. A professional with the same type as the mother or uncle of a client who has negative experiences of either runs the risk of being saddled with those feelings and images.

In this context, posing then a question such as 'Do I sometimes make you think of your mother?' is often not an effective approach. Particularly with people who think themselves justifiably angry, this is adding fuel to the flames. However, what works better is asking questions about the way in which the professional has apparently summoned up those images and feelings in the client. The professional asks for feedback from the client, who then feels himself to be taken seriously, so that the relationship is improved. Sometimes a professional will realise anyway that these images and feelings do not really fit into the actual situation.

Counter-transference is the negative attitude the professional can have vis-à-vis a client or fellow-worker as a result of associations which that individual summons up in the professional through association with someone in the professional's own life history. The only difference between this and transference is that transference is something the client does and counter-transference something the professional does. The latter concept had not yet entered Freud's view of the world. The psychoanalyst, after all, sat behind the couch and remained out of the picture as a person.

As Charles Truax and Robert Carkhuv put it so well, counter-transference is a negative attitude or counter-productive reaction arising from subconscious feelings that have their origin in irrational projections, identifications and other defence mechanisms.[1] If, for instance, a professional has had a father with Type 1 and suffered greatly from his continuous criticism when young (and then had not yet realised that this is precisely the way in which a Type 1 shows love), and has dealings with a little-developed (in terms of his type) Type 1 in his consulting-room or conference hall, then that person with Type 1 can inspire a negative feeling in the professional concerned. This person, after all, will unleash perfectionism on the trainer or coach who will then feel the rejection of the other, and that inspires in him the old resistance that his father also always called up in him. Truax and Carkhuv continue: 'The therapist must not permit his own unconscious feelings and attitudes aroused during phases of treatment to intrude in his relation toward the patient.'[2] That is nicely put, but it is an illusion to think that someone would be able to see to it that these feelings did not arise. Those feelings are evoked. What the therapist can ensure is that he or she is aware of those feelings and their origin. This is why all therapists in training receive therapy themselves. Actually anyone who works with people should receive this, since one can then recognise what belongs to one's own self and what belongs to the other. If, for example, a trainer or consultant once suffered greatly under the toe-curling efforts of his mother to encourage him to be different (because he himself did not want to be noticeable at all), and someone with Type 4 now joins a group with this professional and makes tremendous efforts to be noticed, then he feels the opposition rising that he always felt earlier. But if he is aware that his mother had Type 4, then he can put that feeling in its place and distance himself from it thereafter. Then he no longer sees his mother but the person who is with him in the group at that moment. This person displays similarities to his mother but also differences. (See also the example 'The student who does not learn'.)

Professionals can also use this phenomenon as a diagnostic tool. Someone with an as yet unknown type kindles a certain feeling in the discussion leader. This individual could very well be the type that most often arouses that same feeling. Naturally this hypothesis must be tested further (see Chapter 13 for determination of the type).

The student who does not learn

Carla provides training. She always has great success with a role-playing approach in which she mirrors, with slight exaggeration, the behaviour of the course member. In her experience humour works well: students see themselves in proportion and space is created for experimenting with other behaviour.

But in this training course she encounters a student with whom that does not work. He maintains fairly emotionally that he did *not* act like that. She almost ends up in a battle over who is right. She feels herself getting angry;

the student has to see that he definitely did not perform effectively. In the interval he comes to her. He is furious and says he thinks it extremely unprofessional that she has made him ridiculous in front of the whole group. 'That is simply not done', he repeats again and again.

When Carla comes home she wonders why she became so angry herself. Why was it so important that this student realised his faults? Usually she is not so insistent. She comes to the conclusion that he only wanted to hear how wonderful he was and did not want to learn. But why did that make her so angry? Often there are students who are less eager to learn and then she does not get wound up at all – she always regards that as their own responsibility. Then it dawns on her. Her mother, who has Type 2, had the same need for admiration, and became furious in the same way if she felt that that admiration was being withheld. There is nothing worse for a Type 2 than looking foolish in public. With her mother she always had the feeling that she was merely a side-role in her play, and she has always resisted this. Just as with the student.

Kinds of interventions

In working with the enneagram someone can intervene in various ways. True, interventions cannot always be separated so strictly in practice, but to obtain good insight they can certainly be distinguished according to their aims and their degree of specificity. Specificity can vary from 'always good for everyone' to 'only suitable for this specific person at this moment and in this place'. These two points of view will now be sketched briefly (see also Figure 14.1); in Chapters 15–18 which follow, the various kinds of intervention are worked out further.

Aim of the intervention

The first question with an intervention is: What for? As far as this is concerned there are two kinds of intervention to be distinguished: interventions on the basis of someone's type and where he is in terms of his development (thus the *status quo*, with as aim, for instance, lessening or preventing resistance), and interventions which are meant to help someone to develop within his or her type.

	Attuning and complementing	*Developing*
General		
Type-specific		
Person-specific		

Figure 14.1 Matrix of interventions

Interventions on the basis of the status quo: attuning and complementing

These are interventions whereby one accepts that someone has the type he or she has, and have reached a particular stage in terms of type development. The intervention can be intended to lessen or prevent resistance, to motivate someone, to resolve conflicts, to allow a team to function better, to let someone benefit more from training, and so forth. In all these kinds of cases the intervening party accepts that the person has his type, and is where he is in his own development. The professional takes this into account. This is known as *attuning*. Sometimes, however, the professional actually wants to act in a compensatory manner, for instance to counsel a Type 8 to be patient or to encourage someone with Type 1 to take things a little easier. This is termed *complementing*. Attuning and complementing interventions are discussed in Chapter 15.

Interventions aimed at development

One can also intervene in order to support someone in his or her further development. In this case the one who intervenes has a different role from that in the previous kind of intervention. Naturally there can only be any question of development interventions when explicit agreements have been reached about them. These interventions are suitable for roles such as coach, personal development consultant or trainer, or spiritual director. Development interventions are discussed in Chapters 16–18.

The same person can fulfil different roles. A manager, a consultant or a trainer can both attune to their employees or clients and pay attention to their development. The latter, however, will not suit every worker or client. A staff member will be willing to talk about his or her personal development with their manager only if there is a good mutual relationship. A client may first want to see what that consultant or trainer has to offer, or if a good working relationship arises and the person is to be trusted. Sometimes this situation arises only over a period of time. A professional begins with attuning; if, in doing so, a good relationship is achieved, he or she can shift to development interventions.

Attuning and complementing are interventions one makes with others. Many of the development interventions discussed in Chapters 16–18 can be applied to one's self and also used when working with others.

How specific is the intervention?

The second distinction between interventions concerns the degree to which an intervention is a specific one. To be distinguished are *general*, *type-specific* and *person-specific* interventions.

■ *General interventions.* These are interventions which, within the framework of the enneagram, are good for everyone irrespective of type. They include broadening the behaviour repertoire, stimulating self-observation, interrupting type automatisms, opening discussion about type assumptions, de-identification from the type, the training of willpower, the development of intuition. In Chapter 17 general development interventions are discussed at three levels of learning.

- *Type-specific interventions.* These are interventions which form the proper path for one specific type. It speaks for itself that a type-specific intervention is possible only when one can determine or help determine the type accurately. Chapter 15 discusses type-specific attuning and complementing interventions for each type, and Chapter 18 deals with type-specific development interventions for each type.
- *Person-specific interventions.* People do not differ merely according to their types but in other ways as well. They have their own personal life histories, and these can be very different for people of the same type. Each type can be introvert or extrovert, auditive, visual, or kinaesthetic, relatively conservative or innovative, more or less intelligent, and so forth. The intervening professional can attune to all these aspects.

Person-specific interventions are not dealt with in this book, but naturally they are important in working in practice. No two people are exactly the same.

In Chapter 15, type-specific attuning and complementing interventions are now discussed, whereby the status quo is assumed. In Chapter 16 development principles in connection with the enneagram are dealt with, as well as three levels of learning with the enneagram. Chapter 17 describes general development interventions at three levels of learning. In Chapter 18 type-specific development interventions are discussed, also at three learning levels. Person-specific development interventions fall outside the framework of this book about working with the enneagram, as do general attuning and complementing interventions.[3]

CHAPTER 15

Working with
Others: Attuning
and Supplementing
Interventions

With the interventions to be discussed in this chapter, one assumes that someone has the type that he has, and that he is where he is in terms of his development. We discuss:

- the principles of attuning and supplementing
- type-specific attuning and supplementing interventions.

The principles of attuning and supplementing

Attuning

By attuning, it is meant that professionals speak the type-language of a discussion partner, thus putting both people on a common wavelength. For example, with someone with Type 3 he will speak, in a result-oriented way, about things that the person involved wants to achieve and with which he can score. With Type 6 he can talk about the good cause being fought for without self-interest. This helps Type 6 to take risks – it is worth it, after all. With Type 8 he is direct, open and clear, and does not evade confrontation. He gives Type 9s plenty of space and time to form their own judgements.

With attuning the professional wins the trust of his discussion partner(s). They can talk with the professional because he 'speaks their language'.

Apart from that it is important when attuning to pay attention not just to the type but also to the whole person. A professional can also attune to someone's concern about the environment, desire to climb higher, political interest, pleasure in running things, enthusiasm for childcare, or fanatical interest in preserving the nation's castles. Or to his educational, professional or intellectual level, certain skills he does or does not possess, or his knowledge of the subject under discussion. Or to his opinions, convictions, suppositions and paradigms. These are all things which are not bound to types (see 'Attuning', below).

Attuning

Manager Roderick has an employee Daniel with Type 2. If he attunes to Type 2 Roderick places feedback within a positive framework, certainly does not criticise him in the presence of others, and thinks more than many other people would about expressing appreciation and paying attention to the relationship.

But he knows more about Daniel than just his type. Daniel is an impassioned amateur genealogist and has already gone back as far as the fifteenth century in the search for his ancestors. He is more than averagely intelligent. He is convinced that every little contribution towards improving the environment counts. He is decidedly auditive.

If Roderick attunes to these things he can, for instance, use a genealogical analogy if he wants to make something clear. Because Daniel is auditive it will not be enough for Roderick to send him a plan on paper – that is more for visual people. Instead he will discuss the design with him. But because Daniel is of greater than average intelligence he will not need to provide endless explanations. Roderick can stop as soon as Daniel indicates that he has understood the core of the matter (and that will be much faster than Roderick's average staff member). And Roderick can take into account that Daniel will be enthusiastic about a plan sooner if it also makes a contribution to environment improvement.

Often the person who makes the intervention is not in the position to undertake first a typing interview with the person concerned. One cannot trust the naked eye, however, as we have already seen (for both forms of type determination, see Chapter 13). How, then, can one attune to someone else's type? Strictly speaking it is not possible if the other's type is not known. With an intervention, however, someone can keep the enneagram at the back of his mind as a series of possible hypotheses and pay careful attention to what the discussion partner says precisely – and, above all, to how he says it. That helps the professional to understand or to sense what makes the person opposite tick. With his knowledge of the enneagram, the professional does not assume that the other person shares his make-up. Often, one can exclude some types on the basis of what the person says about himself or on the basis of preoccupations and motivations that come to the surface during the discussion. Such signals, however, principally form indications of type in people who have not developed themselves in their types. With them there is still a fairly direct relationship between type and the way they express themselves. Fortunately, for people who have developed themselves further, it is less important for another person to attune to his type; they are more open to a variety of approaches and one need not be so precise.

When one deals regularly with the same people it is a good investment to acquire knowledge of each other's enneagram type. One has then a handle for optimising the co-operation (see the example 'Management team', below).

Management team

Members of a management team realise that the same discussions are repeated regularly and that the same people regularly react to each other in the same way. The others are left feeling 'Yawn ... here we go again!' With the next subject they are at it once more. It is not that people are so dissatisfied with the course of events, but they wonder nonetheless if co-operation might be better. A suitable consultant is sought.

The consultant first does a typing interview with each of the team members. Then in a session together the whole group mutually exchanges views on what everyone's strong points are, what their motives are, and which points each individual wants to develop. In a second round, mutual interaction is on the agenda. What is the best way to infuriate the individual members of the management team (the emotional programming)? How can someone best be spoken to if you want his co-operation (attuning)? How can colleagues help someone in his development?

Thereafter there is discussion of how the management team can assemble the pieces of this puzzle, because what the one asks for is not always what the other wants or is able to provide. Thus the team member with Type 1 wants a high degree of perfection while the colleague with Type 7 primarily wants a great deal of renewal and very soon becomes bored with projects once these reach the practical phase. The team members negotiate with each other about solutions with which everyone can live. Agreements are reached and resolutions made.

These are evaluated after every management team meeting. Much less energy is now spent on old, rusty patterns of interaction. People hold each other to the agreements and resolutions made. There is more creativity and productivity in the team, and the team members take more pleasure in the meetings.

Supplementing

Supplementing is 'compensatory' behaviour. Supplementing is sometimes needed to reach a result. Even if the client has Type 9, decisions have to be made; even with Type 7, routine work must also be done; even with Type 6, a risk has to be taken occasionally, and so forth. Supplementing is thus stimulating a greater aptitude for decision-making in Type 9, encouraging Type 7 to finish a job and telling Type 6 that some degree of risk is necessary and even healthy.

Our natural tendency is often to supplement sooner than to attune. This, however, continually stirs up resistance which (if we ignore small numbers of exceptional cases) is less effective. The most effective sequence in working with others is therefore to attune first – since trust is built up in this way – and only then to supplement, whereby a change is brought about.

A coach with a client with Type 3 will agree what results have to be obtained in the first session with him. With a Type 7 the coach will discuss sooner what attractive methods he could use. With a Type 4 the coach will invest in the relationship, and this will certainly involve some degree of self-revelation. All of this is attuning. In this the problem arises once more that a coach must do the attuning in the first session without much knowledge of the client; after all, no typing interview will have been possible at this stage. Fortunately clients often ask literally for approaches that suit their type:

- 'What results can I expect?'
- 'I would appreciate it if you told me something about yourself?'
- 'I would like to keep it flexible.'

These are remarks which might suit Types 3, 4 and 7 respectively. Supplementary to these examples could be the following:

- With Type 3, emphasising the process character: 'We don't know how long a process will last nor precisely where we shall end up.'
- With Type 7, push on with 'What don't you like in your work at the moment? What has to change?'
- With Type 4 observe that only the client's own process is involved and that the coach is of no interest.

The dissatisfied manager

A consultant visits a new client, Tom, for the first time. He wants some training courses set up in the consultant's professional field. For this, the consultant has to work with the head of IT. In confidence Tom tells the consultant during the preliminary briefing that he is dissatisfied with the IT chief, Carl.

According to Tom, Carl shows too little initiative, does not take a firm enough line, and is too evasive. He is not strong in negotiations with external consultants, and makes too many blunders. The consultant notices in this talk that Tom sees a lot of faults in others, but in this first discussion he emphasises the importance of quality (attuning).

Carl turns out to be a pleasant, hard-working man who likes to be friends with everyone and to oblige people. The co-operation between the consultant and Carl is fine. Suddenly Carl disappears: first he is at home suffering from stress; then he is given another job in the company. In the courses the consultant runs he hears that this is happening to people more often. Other people in direct contact with Tom also disappear, first to recuperate from stress but then permanently, and whenever the consultant talks with Tom the finger is always pointed at someone else who deserves criticism.

Once he has worked for the company for some time and has built up a good relationship of trust with Tom, the consultant brings the subject up in a talk with him. It seems as if a pattern is involved. Could it be that Tom makes demands that people cannot fulfil (supplementing)? The consultant proposes an enneagram typing interview.

Tom turns out to have Type 1. The consultant can now discuss the fact that there is nothing wrong with Tom's desire for top-level performance. He explains, however, that there are very few people who can fulfil his demands. For instance, the new head of IT, who has been sought for so long, fulfils only 80 per cent of the job profile. The consultant suggests that this new IT chief will also come unstuck if Tom demands 100 per cent of him. His failure can therefore be predicted. Tom will have to accept that the new head of IT can do only 80 per cent of what Tom demands and not 100 per cent. Tom has to realise that he made this choice when he employed that person. He will have to find the missing 20 per cent somewhere else. Tom, indeed, follows this advice.

In attuning and supplementing the professional accepts the status quo although, from the example of 'The dissatisfied manager', supplementing goes in the direction of development. At least, that is usually the motivation of the professional who decides to supplement. However, woe betide the professional who is troubled by an uncontrollable urge to educate. The risk is great that this person will disturb the contact with his client(s). There is an anecdote about the usual course of a relationship. One falls for someone with another type because the difference is attractive. Once one 'has' him or her, one then tries to make him or her be like one's own type as much as possible – after all, people ought to be like that. If that works then the people separate because then there is no longer any interest left.

It is important to respect someone else's type, because it does the other person justice and because it is effective.

Type-specific attuning and supplementing interventions

A number of attuning and supplementing interventions are now described with reference to each type. Here we are dealing once again with the notorious 'average' type. This check list, which is not exhaustive, can be used by professionals for inspiration in making their interventions.

Type 1

Attuning

- Attune to the need for correctness: a clear structure, a proper division of labour, correct procedures, respect.
- Divide up educational material or consulting process into sections, each of which has a (learning) result.
- No open situations but an agenda, a task, homework.
- Plan in time and leave time for decision-making.
- Appeal to expertise and skills in his/her specific field.
- Where possible allow him/her to work independently.
- Admit your own faults; this makes it easier for Type 1 to do this also.
- Don't judge (well, that will not always be possible, but the professional can always watch how he formulates something); instead discuss a goal to be attained.
- Let acceptance of the person be apparent, also if someone isn't perfect (which is always the case, in fact).
- Prevent Type 1 feeling being used for someone else's purpose.
- Leave room for anger; clarify the causes of the dissatisfaction by asking questions.
- Don't enter into discussion about who is right.
- Don't play down Type 1's contribution.

Supplementing

- Emphasise that mistakes are the best way to learn.
- Emphasise that many roads lead to Rome.
- Discuss common frames of reference and standards.
- Correct.
- Insist on a decision.
- Introduce the 80/20 rule: 20 per cent of the effort leads to 80 per cent of the result. The remaining 20 per cent of the result costs 80 per cent of the effort.
- Say that 'good is good enough'.
- Teach to ask questions.
- Ask about Type 1's personal needs.
- Let him/her list what is actually good.

- Ask someone to appreciate the effect of his/her performance; appeal to their sense of compassion.
- Be clear yourself.

Type 2

Attuning

- Person-directed attention and recognition: this type works for people not tasks.
- A good atmosphere, personal contact.
- Be clear about what is expected.
- Be reassuring if something goes wrong.
- Emphasise acceptance as a person, because this type is (over)sensitive to criticism.
- Package criticism positively.
- If Type 2 becomes emotional or is angry ask where this emotion, this anger, comes from.
- Talk from the standpoint of your own emotions.
- Let proposed changes be introduced by an important person.

Supplementing

- Say that everyone is the same and that no one has special privileges.
- Say that you don't want any indispensable people in your organisation; everyone must be replaceable.
- Direct the attention to the task.
- Don't let yourself be seduced but hold on to your own line.
- Don't accept help but ask what Type 2 needs.
- Be direct.
- Bring up manipulation and vindictiveness (initially in private).
- Find out or ask if Type 2 can really do everything that he takes on.
- Set objective conditions for promotion, well-defined rules and clear job descriptions, to prevent favouritism, competition, and old-school-tie politics.

Type 3

Attuning

- Give public recognition.
- Stimulate with bonuses and promotion.
- Make projects exciting and bring scoring chances within view.
- Learn from experience.
- Provide concrete positive feedback.
- Prevent loss of status.

- Provide a personal area of responsibility.
- Present threats as opportunities to solve problems and bring a more effective strategy into view.
- Clarity (hints and subtle indications do not help).
- Accept and be involved with the person, independently of his performances.
- Don't be misled by superficial self-confidence: Type 3 cannot bear criticism and being under attack.
- Good presentation.

Supplementing

- Discuss your own and his feelings.
- Let him know he is allowed to fail.
- Link status to the functioning of the whole team; value co-operation over rivalry.
- Weaken competition.
- Have a clear authority structure.
- Let it be known what you really find important.

Type 4

Attuning

- Provide attention and a feeling of belonging.
- Provide special treatment.
- Recognise unusual or controversial contributions.
- Talk about there and then, the ideals we are working towards.
- Ensure a good emotional atmosphere: leave room for his feelings, talk about your own feelings, value authenticity.
- Provide his own territory.
- Don't cheer him up but sympathise; don't solve his problems for him but empathise; return to them if necessary.
- Hold on, remain balanced if Type 4 seems to make efforts to end the relationship.
- Stay steady, single-minded, consistent, trustworthy if Type 4 is emotional.
- In adversity don't let go and appeal to his image.
- Individual contact.

Supplementing

- Emphasise the here and now.
- Expect that ordinary routine jobs must also be done.
- Pass on the message that everyone is equally special in his own way.
- Provide a clear structure, order, clear directions and deadlines.
- Direct the attention to positive affairs and the present.

Type 5

Attuning

- Link up at a mental, cognitive level, not at an emotional one: support ideas with information, strive for objective solutions, think together, provide a complete overview instead of one opinion.
- Concentrate on the task, not on private life.
- Respect the need for privacy and personal space; don't ask for spontaneous reactions; don't disturb Type 5 unexpectedly; don't break into the agenda without announcing this well beforehand; don't push yourself.
- Make no claims; draw a clear distinction between demands and requests.
- Provide time for preparation and also set deadlines.
- Make expectations clear, give well-defined instructions, maintain transparency.

Supplementing

- Stimulate the exchange of ideas.
- Put his ideas up for discussion.
- Talk about your own feelings and his feelings, ask him to express himself, confront him with emotions.
- Ask for participation, being part of a team.
- Provide feedback about the effect of his performance.
- Invite him to empathise with someone else.

Type 6

Attuning

- Provide security; be consistent, serious and trustworthy.
- Answer questions directly.
- Keep contact; lack of contact leaves room for fantasies about calamity.
- Transparency: don't censor information, be open about what you yourself have in mind, what you think and feel; be clear about aims and procedures.
- Provide time for orientation.
- Provide recognition (otherwise you are untrustworthy or oppressive).
- Don't play down fears and worries, discuss bad scenarios.
- Give time for investigating doubts (but not endlessly).
- Ask for feedback.
- Don't spread rumours.

Supplementing

- Provide feedback on the extent to which Type 6's thoughts are realistic.

- Combat doubt by thinking and asking questions.
- Analyse negative scenarios.
- Ask also for positive scenarios; encourage him to undertake positive actions.
- Encourage faith in the future.
- Discuss with an eye on the future how to avert the catastrophe.
- Deadlines.
- Grant permission for him to express himself.
- Humour.

Type 7

Attuning

- Make sure things stay energetic, pleasant, stimulating, varied.
- Create a flexible structure in which Type 7 can come and go according to his needs.
- Let him work on more than one project at a time.
- Let him join in at the start of a project but not in the execution.
- Turn problems into exciting new challenges and learning experiences; make a clear distinction between feedback and criticism.
- Don't expect a consistent learning curve.
- Remain focused without controlling too much.
- Give him space if something he has done needs correction; don't give precise instructions.
- Approach commitment rationally.

Supplementing

- Raise re-labelling and rationalising as topics for discussion.
- Make clear that tasks must be finished; set unequivocal deadlines and supervise the last phase of a project directly; make him accountable for results.
- Ask how he thinks he can realise something.
- Prevent so much being taken on that nothing is finished.
- Hold the attention in the here and now.
- Help to direct the attention outside himself.
- Bring forward clearly his own needs and feelings as important.
- Don't be led astray by charm.

Type 8

Attuning

- Don't evade Type 8: be direct and confrontational yourself.
- Indicate clearly your own limits; occupy space yourself.

- Work interactively and in a participative manner, but hold on to the controls yourself.
- Address Type 8 personally.
- Create clarity but not competition.
- Be trustworthy, honest, firm and flexible.
- Make the goal clear with sufficient degrees of freedom for attaining it.
- Base evaluation on results, not on how they are achieved.
- Careful and honest feedback.
- Encourage instead of saying what is wrong.
- Share in Type 8's enthusiasm and energy.
- Show appreciation, but ration it.

Supplementing

- Provide feedback on the effect of Type 8's actions on others (such as saying hurtful or intimidating things, taking up space).
- Force him to listen.
- Provide insight into the fact that Type 8's truth is a personal truth, and not the whole or the objective truth.
- Let him see the value of receiving.
- Discuss vulnerability.

Type 9

Attuning

- Co-operation, participation, no competition and not imposing on him.
- Provide encouragement, support, respect, recognition.
- Ask about his needs, help him to find his own standpoint by exploring out what he does *not* want.
- Provide room for expression of anger and stimulate this; be alert for dissatisfaction and listen to him about it.
- Don't place under pressure; leave time for decision-making; give him the feeling of deciding for himself, by presenting more alternatives for instance.
- No sudden changes; first announce any intention clearly; give time to become accustomed to the idea; only after this come with further development, preferably in co-operation with him.
- Provide clear directions and structure.
- Learn from experience, confirm positively, provide feedback on strong points.
- Express trust.

Supplementing

- Distinguish primary from secondary matters; set details in the context of a greater whole.

- Don't wait for initiative from Type 9 but take the initiative yourself.
- Help to establish priorities; stimulate him to make decisions; help to establish boundaries.
- A clear plan and deadlines keep up the tempo and the energy level.
- Hold the attention.
- Make Type 9 the centre of attention; he does not do that himself.
- Stimulate him to make a rational analysis if he is offended by something.

Once again: regard these notes as a source of inspiration, not as an exhaustive summary. Where someone is in his development makes a difference when deciding how best to attune to him. Not every Type 2 needs to be reassured if something goes wrong; not every Type 9 has to be helped in making decisions. Knowledge of people's types does not relieve us of the need to keep observing them acutely as individuals.

Attuning to the centres

One can attune to the types, but also to the centres.

If a professional notices that someone talks about ideas, concepts, schemes and models (head), then 'attuning' means that the professional will do that also, while 'supplementing' in that case can mean, for instance, that he asks how the other reacts emotionally, what he thinks about certain situations (belly), or how he sees the mutual relationships of people involved (heart).

If a professional sees that his partner in discussion is very sensitive to recognition by others (heart), then he attunes, for example, by clearly granting recognition for the other's contribution or by thinking with him about the question of how one can score in the project in hand. Supplementing means in this case that the professional deals primarily, for instance, with what someone actually feels intuitively himself from within (belly), or notes that he proposes a rational analysis (head).

Should it transpire that the other person needs control and depends on how he feels something (belly), then the professional attunes to this, for instance by demonstratively leaving the decision to the other and taking seriously what he feels. Supplementing could be (for example) a theoretical discussion (head) or confirmation of the health of the relationship (heart).

CHAPTER 16

Self-Management and Working with Others: Principles of Development Interventions

Development interventions take place, in principle, when another person asks for them. By an intervention we understand everything the professional undertakes with the aim of supporting his client, advising him, providing him with insight, changing his behaviour, teaching him something, helping him to develop, and so forth. The questioner might wish, for example, to solve a problem, or to learn how to function more effectively in future.

A development question can arise from a complementing intervention. The previous chapter described how a consultant decides, at a given moment, to talk with top manager Tom about his overstressed workers. He tells Tom on this occasion that all those problems could well have had something to do with the way he behaves (complementary intervention). It is conceivable that Tom then asks how he should behave. Then the consultant in this example can begin with his development interventions.

If someone develops himself with the enneagram and if a professional offers support to other people, the following phases can be distinguished:

- Phase 1: Finding out what the type is.
- Phase 2: Owning the aspects of the type, that is to say recognising in one's self both the positive and the less appealing sides of one's own type and assuming responsibility.
- Phase 3: Working at development.

Phase 1 – finding out what the type is – is dealt with in Chapter 13. This and the following chapters are concerned with Phases 2 and 3. To be dealt with successively in this chapter are:

- Owning all aspects of the type.
- Developing: Three levels of learning.

Thereafter general development interventions are discussed in Chapter 17 and type-specific development interventions in Chapter 18.

Owning all aspects of the type

Phase 2 is an extremely important phase in someone's personal development. It leads in general to greater self-acceptance, through this to a lessening of feelings of guilt, shame and inferiority, and through this to a greater feeling of well-being. Furthermore acceptance is a prerequisite for developing. Someone cannot develop something which he denies in himself.

Sometimes people see their enneagram type as a justification for the way in which they function. At last they can be themselves without feeling guilty about it, without being ashamed and without feeling inferior. Everyone, after all, has a type, and apparently everyone lacks something. So why should anyone then want to develop?

Everyone occasionally has days when they want to 'act out' their own type unashamedly. Regularly I hear people say things like 'Can't I ever be impulsive any more, then?', 'May I never then let myself go completely?', or 'All that being conscious all the time is not nice at all; give me a nice neurosis – that makes people interesting!' The wish to develop oneself within one's type is not to be taken for granted.

That does not mean there is not enough to do in Phase 2. This phase demands honesty with oneself, and that is not always easy. As regards the positive qualities of one's own type it is not so difficult. Here the enneagram can even contribute knowledge if someone has always seen primarily the negative side of his type. Thus someone with Type 1 can always have had great trouble with his exaggeratedly critical attitude and never have realised his capacity for doing things really well. Someone with Type 5 can have been disturbed by his own inadequacy in getting the feeling of something, and not have realised that he is the one who knows how to keep a cool head in a crisis situation.

It is usually more difficult to be confronted with negative tendencies. Everyone has things he would rather not know about himself, or would rather not have other people know. Only by taking possession of these 'nasty' tendencies, by regarding them as facts, can one develop personal mastery. One has no power over things one denies. One is, however, influenced by them. What is denied holds the strings, in fact. The ancient Greeks used to say all gods must be served. A god who was not served was in the habit of taking revenge. So is it too within people. A person encounters trouble from the parts of himself that he denies. It is the same with a change process in an organisation. If some departments or people are ignored, if they are not asked for their opinions and decisions are made over their heads, then the organisation creates resistance, certainly if the top management listens openly to others.

Someone who can admit to himself that he is, for instance, vengeful, sarcastic or niggling, that he has the tendency to attract power to himself, not to take people into account, or to hurt them, creates the capacity to have these tendencies but not to put them into practice. As long as one denies those tendencies they are continually converted into deeds, mostly accompanied by a justification: 'I had to because ...' The reasons for the behaviour are then simply attributed to another. After all, one does not experience the tendency as part of oneself.

Essentially there are three kinds of denial:

- Denials whereby one does injustice to one's self. For example: 'I actually feel fine if I'm not noticed'; 'Emotions usually lead to trouble.'
- Denials whereby one does injustice to others. For example: 'He has to feel it', 'Then he ought not take such a position'; 'I don't have to consider someone like that.'
- Denials whereby one does injustice to the environment. For example: 'What do you mean "work climate"? It doesn't bother me at all.'

Anyway, everyone has the tendencies of all types within himself, although those of his own type are predominant. It is therefore worthwhile not only to take possession of one's own type but also to examine oneself from the aspects of the other types which can be recognised in oneself. After all, it is ultimately not about the type but about one's own person.

In practice Phases 2 and 3 overlap. It can be a whole process in itself to find out which forms of manifestation of the type are applicable and which are not, and also to examine the less pleasant sides of one's own type. The person who develops himself will gradually find it easier to examine parts of himself and focus more sharply on his real driving motives. Development interventions help in this. Phases 2 and 3 must therefore actually be regarded as an iterative process.

Furthermore, this is a lifelong journey of discovery. As soon as someone thinks he has made a great deal of progress something happens whereby he thinks that he has learnt nothing in the past 30 years. Naturally that is not so. But the themes of the types keep coming back, albeit in an ever-more subtle fashion.

Development: levels of learning

In Phase 3 there are, as we have seen in Chapter 1, three levels of learning to be distinguished:

- *First-order learning:* learning new skills in step-by-step improvement, broadening of the behaviour repertoire.
- *Second-order learning:* clarifying the underlying patterns, studying the 'software', reframing.
- *Third-order learning:* transformation learning, transcendence of the type fixation.

We now deal with these in succession. After that, some observations are made about the application of these three learning levels.

First-order learning: changing outward behaviour and developing skills

In this form of learning someone solves the problems which are the consequence of his or her type.

Someone with Type 9, for instance, can have trouble with the fact that conflicts are not resolved because he avoids them. He will now learn to tackle conflicts and resolve them. He can, for example, take part in a course on assertiveness, a workshop on handling conflicts or a seminar on personal presentation in order to learn this.

Someone with Type 6 may be shunned by his colleagues because he always sees the black side of a proposal and never joins in with enthusiasm. He will learn to present his contribution in such a way that people also do something with it. He could follow, for instance, training in influential skills. There he learns to stop saying things like 'Nothing will come of it', or 'No one wants to pay for that', and learns to formulate his contributions more constructively. For instance: 'How can we make it work?'; or 'That is an interesting option – but if we do that, how do we see to it that we get paid?'

Someone with Type 4 perhaps went through life unique but misunderstood, lonely in his superior emotional life. Now he learns to attune to the 'not particularly exceptional' level at which others function. He can, for example, take part in discussion training.

At this level of learning people remain within their types. They change their behaviour and broaden their behaviour repertoire. This can be very useful. The underlying type pattern, however, does not change. The behaviour changes, the basic motivation does not. Under stress people tend to fall back into their old patterns. Under more favourable circumstances, however, one certainly has an advantage with a more extensive behaviour repertoire.

In principle everyone can learn the skills of all types: that is to say, the skills for which someone of a certain type has a natural aptitude. Thus a Type 8 is usually good at being confrontational, a Type 9 at really listening, a Type 5 at rational analysis, a Type 7 at seeing chances and possibilities, and a Type 3 at self-presentation. People with some other types do that less by nature. They can learn these skills if they take the trouble to do so.

Second-order learning: clarifying the underlying thought pattern, studying the 'software', redrawing frames of reference

This level of learning involves recognising and seeing through the basic patterns of focusing attention, the motivation and the manner of interpreting the world. Reframing is always possible. One can, for instance, look through the 'spectacles' of another type. How does the world look then? It is an interesting exercise to look at a certain situation through each of the nine pairs of spectacles and to set the nine interpretations alongside one another.

At this level of learning, for example, someone with Type 9 studies his underlying pattern. Why actually does he avoid conflicts? When does he do so, and when not? When is something really a conflict? How serious is it actually to differ in opinion from someone? Does adapting oneself to others really produce desirable results? This person can discover that rows can be very liberating – they can even produce desirable results – and that the relationship thereafter simply remains as it was. Perhaps he notices that he keeps resenting the fact that he must get angry first before he is taken seriously. And so on.

Someone with Type 6 will notice that he actually never thinks about what could turn out well. He begins to wonder why that is. He catches himself out with his first tendency to distrust people. Perhaps he notices on occasion that with certain people his suspicions are not borne out. Perhaps someone points out to him that his mistrust can make him seem inconsistent to others: he goes back on decisions, what is given with one hand is taken back with the other, he expresses doubts about people which are not based on facts. And so forth.

Someone with Type 4 starts to think about how his uniqueness serves him. Why is that actually so important? He notices that if people remark on his uniqueness this calls up a feeling of embarrassment. Strange, it was always so important. And then that pattern of attraction and rejection. 'Possession is the end of the pleasure' is an aphorism that would suit the situation. Why do people and things lose their lustre as soon as they are available? What would it be like to enjoy what there actually is? And so forth.

In second-order learning one therefore looks at the basic patterns of one's own type under the magnifying glass. Here the real level of the enneagram of fixations is studied: basic motivations, focus of attention, the way in which one sees and interprets the world, and all those other aspects we discussed in Part II. The basic assumptions are opened to discussion. Through a growing consciousness of the underlying type patterns one begins to react less automatically and thus one becomes better able to choose effective behaviour suitable to the situation.

Third-order learning: transformation learning, transcendence of the type fixation

In this form of learning, the 'spectacles' of one's own type are laid aside and a mental and emotional openness arises whereby one can view one's environment objectively. At this level someone can co-operate with others without adopting the prejudiced position of his type.

For someone with Type 9 a transformation would involve developing the conviction that he as a person – as himself – is worthwhile, and also presenting himself as such. He also learns to choose the right action instead of dividing attention between a thousand and one activities which all seem equally important. Someone with Type 6 develops the courage to go his way in spite of risks. He learns to trust in what are, in principle, the good intentions of others. Someone with Type 4 develops equanimity and a feeling of attachment.

Peter Senge regards third-order learning as the essential level of the learning organisation and talks of 'metanoia', a shift of mind.[1] Third-order learning actually is a shift of mind. One leaves the prison of the enneagram of fixations and looks at the world with a free mind. With third-order learning one comes in contact with one's real self and with the enneagram of higher virtues and ideas.

Attachment to their own type fixations continually hinders people from reaching this level of consciousness. Indeed the type fixation also offers supposed psychological safety. The false basic assumption is that one needs one's type in order to survive.

Dealing in practice with the three levels of learning one has to be careful with these learning levels. Attuning is important here also. The professional must make sure for himself that his client understands his interventions at the right level. Someone with Type 3 once told me that she had trouble getting her new business off the ground because her coach had told her 'not to profile herself'. The coach probably did not mean that she should not undertake the necessary marketing activities, but had advised her to examine critically her automatism for profiling and to stop when this was not an appropriate (re)action. This businesswoman had interpreted a second-order intervention as first-order advice.

The questions most often put to a professional by people in the context of an organisation are of the first and second orders. An organisation can make first-and second-order demands on personnel. Third-order learning, however, cannot be imposed from without; that can only come from within.

These forms of learning can be distinguished but not separated. It will be clear that first-order learning can be absorbed better if someone brings along second-order learning also. Second-order learning will often result in first-order learning. Third-order learning is unthinkable without learning of the second order.

On each of these three levels interventions can be made. The exercises described in the two following chapters can be used to this end.

CHAPTER 17

General Development Interventions

In this chapter all sorts of exercises are described. Many of them can be done by someone alone. With others guidance is needed. Although some can be done alone, they yield more benefit if they are done under guidance. The process can be compared to learning football. Everyone can kick a ball around, but most footballers will perform better with a trainer.

The exercises described in this chapter are suitable for every type. Type-specific interventions are dealt with in Chapter 18. In both chapters exercises are divided into learning of the first, second and third orders.

Naturally the selection of exercises is not exhaustive: thousands of exercises are possible. Those I have chosen have proved to work in my practice. The aim is to provide insight into which sorts of exercise are possible.

The chapter is ordered as follows. There is a main division into first-, second- and third-order learning. At every learning level development action is specified, for instance self-observation or interruption of type automatism. For every development action a number of work methods and exercises are provided. Most of those dealt with, however, can be used for more than one action. Regard them, therefore, as examples.

One development action can lead to another. Thus disidentification can lead to new self-observation. The interruption of type automatism can give rise to the wish to develop new skills.

Trying to do all the exercises is not recommended. Not only would it be physically impossible, but it would also make little sense. People can absorb only a limited amount of learning material at once, certainly where their own person is involved. You can best choose a few exercises that appeal to you at the moment and carry these out for a longer period. You can carry on with some exercises – for instance, self-observation – for the rest of your life. With others you are finished at a given moment.

There are a great many good work methods.[1] But not every method is good for everything and everyone at every point in their development. For me there is only one criterion: does this method work for this person at this moment or not? If it does not work it can still be a good method, but the person concerned needs another method at that moment. This can change in the course of time. It is true of all methods that the benefit becomes greater if one applies them regularly over a longer period.

The exercises are described from the perspective of the enneagram. If you wish to apply the exercises described as a professional, I assume that you are a professional already. This chapter therefore contains no instructions regarding behavioural training, cognitive restructuring, personal guidance, psychotherapy or other professional skills.

General development interventions of the first order: changing behaviour and broadening the behaviour repertoire

In this section the following development actions are considered:

- Building further on the strong sides of the type.
- Developing skills suited to the type, other than those which are natural, and exercising other behaviour.

Building further on the strong sides of the type

In order to build further on the strong sides of one's own type, someone must first know what those strong sides are.

Making notes

In this exercise you write down everything you find strong about your own type. Thereafter you also write down your weaker sides. You then consider what is good about every weaker side. A few examples may illustrate this.

The strong sides of Type 6 include loyalty, sensitivity for hidden agendas and calculation of risks. Weak sides are imagining threats which are not there, endless doubt and a tendency to postpone decisions constantly as a result. This last weak side, however, has a positive aspect in the form of great trustworthiness. After all, if a Type 6 actually makes a decision for once, then from a human standpoint one can hardly consider anything going wrong, because everything that might be foreseen has been foreseen. Type 9 is not very assertive by nature. The counterbalance to this is that he is continually aware of precisely what someone else has in view. Type 1 tends by nature to find fault with everything. The positive side of this is that the end result is of high quality. People with Type 8 often have little patience. The reverse side of this is that they have a great capacity for getting things done.

Core quadrants

Another means of finding the strong sides is the core quadrant of Ofman.[2] Too much of a good quality becomes a bad quality. Thus concern can become fussiness, assertiveness can degenerate into 'me, me and to hell with the rest', and flexibility can dissolve to spinelessness. The bad quality is the pitfall. Sometimes people are blamed for the pitfall, but it is also a pointer to someone's good qualities.

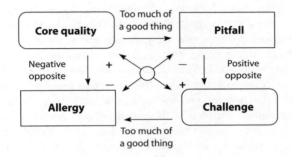

Figure 17.1 The core-quadrant model of Ofman

Facing a good quality there is often an opposite good quality which is developed to a lesser degree, or not at all. This development is required in order to be a more complete person and to have a fuller packet of skills available. This is then the challenge. For instance, Type 8 has among his core qualities directness, clearness, self-presentation. The exaggeration here can be bluntness or lack of tact and being emphatically present – Type 8's pitfalls, indeed. What Type 8 has to develop in himself, his challenges, include his diplomacy and ability to grant space to others. Type 8 can encounter people with an excess of those 'Type-8' challenges: people who turn like a weathercock with the wind, people who listen but let nothing of themselves be seen, grey mice, twisters and wimps. In general he will be irritated by them. They form his Type 8 allergies.

Your pitfall was an indication of your positive quality. You can also arrive at your good qualities via the challenge and via the allergy in the core quadrant. The challenge for somebody with Type 2 could be, for instance, to assert his own needs in a direct manner. This points to the already-present quality of being able to look after others well. Type 4 could have as his challenge doing ordinary things with care. This says something about the quality of being special, of investing in things out of the ordinary. For Type 7 a challenge could be making choices and adopting relationships and/or responsibilities.

The quality is then the person's varied interests, and the capacity for being occupied with many things at the same time.

If we reason from his allergy then a Type 3, for example, could be irritated by people who talk a lot and do little, by lack of commitment to results, by flabby processing procedures. This provides information about the quality of Type 3's orientation towards results. A Type 5 can be upset by people who talk through their hats, who express unbridled emotions. This says something about Type 5's analytical capabilities and his capacity for remaining calm in crisis situations.

Imagination and evaluation

Once the strong qualities have been brought into the picture, then the next question is how they can be put to use more effectively. One possibility is to consider every morning how you are going to utilise your own strong qualities in the programme for the day, and to evaluate every evening to what measure that has succeeded. That demands only a few minutes per day.

Even more effective is to visualise how one can put one's strong qualities to good use. In other words, you imagine how something will proceed if you use your strong points completely. 'If you can dream it you can do it', as Walt Disney once said. This visualisation can be done in different ways: making a representation in thought, in drawing, in writing. One can even think of accompanying music.

Another effective method is utilising the strong qualities only in limited doses, as is suggested by the model of Ofman. Someone who exaggerates a quality makes it a negative trait.

Broadening the behaviour repertoire

Gareth Morgan quotes Abraham Maslow as saying 'If you only have a hammer every problem tends to become a nail.'[3] Someone's personal qualities influence what he perceives. But the situation in question may demand a different approach, for which that person does not have the natural talents. Thus stimulating others is one of the qualities of Type 2. There are, however circumstances in which it is of greater importance to analyse the situation well. A Type 5 is good at analysing a situation and choosing an adequate approach. When there is no crisis, he will want to analyse further. That might be at the expense of speed in acting which could also be important, for instance in order to seize a chance that comes along only once.

Taking speedy advantage of developments is precisely the strength of Type 8 – reacting quickly and carrying something out promptly and purposefully. Sometimes, however, a situation actually asks for caution and careful processing.

In order to be effective in every situation, people must avail themselves of a behaviour repertoire more extensive than that of their own types only (see 'Charismatic leadership').

Charismatic leadership

Ray goes to a coach because he wants to learn to be more charismatic and inspiring in his performance. He is director of an expansion-orientated subsidiary of a large company. His boss in the concern has told him that he is not charismatic enough and does not inspire his staff sufficiently. Actually Ray did not aim at having a directorship: it just happened that way. He finds the content of the work interesting, but he regards dealing with all those people as a burden.

Earlier he always said 'I don't have time', but now he has become a director, his staff apparently have a problem with this. They accuse him of not being interested in them. He wants to do something about that, without going over his own limits. He wants to learn how to keep people out of his office without them feeling rejected.

The coach does a typing interview with Ray. They come to the conclusion that he has Type 5. The coach now discusses with him the fact that he will always be a director in his own style. He will probably never be a great swayer of public opinion but he can learn to inspire people in his own way.

The coach plays roles with Ray, who practises how to empathise with the feelings of others and to react to them effectively. Thus, for instance, Ray has the feeling that one of his female employees, probably a Type 2, continually wants to take up his time. The coach practises with him a way of satisfying her without this costing him too much energy or too much time. In doing this they also examine in depth the question of what that employee actually wants from Ray.

Another employee seems untrustworthy: he says 'yes' to everything and then does nothing. The coach and Ray discuss what motives this worker could have for this. Thereafter they practise together the talk Ray is going to have with him about the reasons for his behaviour, and how the two of them could get along together more constructively.

This phase of role-playing occupies a number of sessions. As a result Ray obtains more feeling for the emotions of others and how he can deal with them without going over his own boundaries.

Different learning goals with the same type

It is important to realise that people of the same type can have different objectives in learning at first-order level.

For a Type 8 the goal could be, for instance, to allow others more space. Type 8's development aim, however, could also be to come to a more nuanced way of forming judgements, or to accept his own physical limits and work a little less hard, or to make a better distinction between objective truth and self-interest, or negotiation skills, or ... Type 1's learning objective could be to accept as a fact that mistakes are made and not to get upset about them. It could also be not to drive himself to unattainable heights, or to take enough time to enjoy himself, or to make himself open to other opinions, or to learn to make compromises, or … People with the same type therefore can have different accents in their learning objectives when they want to broaden their behaviour repertoire.

In principle everyone can acquire the skills of all the other types. From Type 1 it can be learned how one can strive for perfection, from Type 2 how people can be stimulated in their development, from Type 3 how one can present oneself better, from Type 4 what authenticity is in relationships, and so forth. These skills create alternatives for someone's automatic reactions. Someone who commands these skills can increase his effectiveness. Learning skills implies a certain amount of self-reflection and in this respect is a preview to second-order learning.

'Unlearning'

Sometimes someone wants to cure himself of his less desirable type behaviour. Unlearning is more difficult than learning. After all, the behaviour concerned has a function: it serves the basic motivation, is part of the survival strategy and forms with it a counterbalance to the basic fear. A person does not let go of that protective function so easily. At the level of first-order learning, it is worthwhile investing in 'unlearning' it only if something else comes in its place that fulfils the function concerned as well or better (see 'Discussion technique').

Discussion technique

Sandra tends to discuss things endlessly with people. It doesn't matter if they are clients, her boss or her colleagues. Her chief has said already a number of times that her telephone calls must be shorter and more businesslike. Because of the long discussions she makes far fewer calls than her colleagues and so brings in fewer new clients. She says she will try, but it doesn't work. Sandra gets a coach.

From the typing interview it transpires that Sandra has Type 9. The long discussions serve the basic motivation of wanting to establish harmony. Sandra cannot easily accept ending contact with her discussion partner while they are in disagreement and she tries to talk to the other person for just as long as it takes for him to agree with her. The coach discusses with her what other ways she could arrive at harmony. Is a compromise with which both parties can live acceptable enough? Is every subject worth the trouble of such a discussion, or should she keep her powder dry for more important matters? Could she achieve the same in less time but with a better discussion technique (Sandra is very indirect in her efforts to influence people)? She goes to a training course in negotiation technique.

In this example the coach respects Sandra's efforts to reach harmony. He takes this as the point of departure in changing her behaviour. At the level of first-order learning that is a good strategy. The basic pattern of the type is not yet open to discussion: it is regarded as an accepted fact. Changing behaviour then has more chance of success if linked to the type pattern.

Relationship between behaviour change and attitude

If someone changes his behaviour, that can influence his attitude. If he changes his attitude, that has consequences for his behaviour. Psychological research indicates that people who can be persuaded to change their behaviour also often change their convictions. This happens via the mechanism of *cognitive dissonance reduction*. That is to say, people try to stop conflict between what they do and what they think. For instance, if someone still drives at 180km per hour after all the publicity about speed restrictions, he can maintain to himself that this is not more dangerous than 120km per hour. No, driving slowly – that's what's *really* dangerous on the motorway! People who smoke believe deep in their hearts that only other people get lung cancer ('my grandfather smoked throughout his life and lived to 95'), or that the connection has not been proved. Fishermen think that fish do not feel pain; meat-eaters do not connect their pork chops with factory farming, and certainly do not regard themselves as people who mistreat animals; environmental polluters think the greenhouse effect will not turn out that bad after all.

If one succeeds in getting people to a point where they change their behaviour, then their views change with it. If people in their organisation are forced by a regulation to be more conscious of the environment in their dealings, then it will turn out, over the course of time, that they also begin to find environmental awareness more important. People who once could not be prised out of their cars but are now subsidised only for public transport by their employers are able, after a while, to be able to express some enthusiasm for this way of travelling: 'I couldn't miss my hour of reading'; 'I can wake up gradually'; 'I wouldn't like to be stuck again in the traffic jam every morning.'

Thus one can also acquire second-order learning via training in skills and behaviour change, or at least up to a point. Once someone with Type 8 has learned how to provide space for other people, then after a while he may also start to believe that other people ought to have space. Once someone with Type 1 has seen for himself that a combination of different views can also lead to good results, then he can distance himself from his trusty old dogma that there is always only one view that can be right.

Behaviour training and the centres

For first-order learning, several different training methods linked to the centres are in current use. A few examples:

- *Behaviour training.* Here one practices different behaviour in short, simple, successive, achievable steps. In this way one can see while working what is effective and what not, and one can try out alternatives. This suits orientation towards action, the belly centre.
- *Cognitive restructuring.* By changing one's own thinking and insight, one changes one's behaviour. Someone then develops a new conviction or thinks of a new approach which he puts into practice thereafter. This suits the head centre.
- *Becoming conscious of feelings* and working on this. This suits the heart centre.

In my experience it is not the case that head types benefit more from an intellectual approach, heart types from an emotional approach and belly types from an active one. It is true that a trainer with a corresponding approach can use attuning, and thus can often build up a working relationship quickly with the person involved. The approach the client likes best, however, need not be the most effective by any means. A head type can feel wonderfully at ease with an intellectual approach, while it would be more effective to keep him busy with his emotions. A belly type can find action great fun and may also demand it, while he could spend his energy more effectively on his cognitive capabilities. If you enjoy yourself thoroughly in training you should ask yourself if you are really learning something, or if you are actually busy confirming your normal pattern. On the other hand, I would be the last to assert that only suffering can lead to learning. However it is true that the desire to learn often arises only if people are confronted with problems which they cannot solve from within their type patterns.

See also 'Working with the centres', further on in this chapter.

General development interventions of the second order: clarifying the underlying thought pattern, reframing

In this section the following general development actions are discussed:

- self-observation
- opening typical basic assumptions to discussion
- interrupting type automatism
- working on type fixations
- de-identification with the type
- working with the three centres.

Self-observation

Regard the type as a horse you want to ride. As a rider, the more you know about your horse, the better you will be able to ride it (see 'Career orientation').

Career orientation

Charlotte comes to a career consultant. She has a high-level function with a bank and is regarded by her superiors as exceptionally talented. She herself finds her work dull and colourless – too much routine – and her colleagues (if that were possible) duller still. This is a work environment that does not make her heart beat faster. Her present employer, however, offers all sorts of practical advantages. She can work part-time, which suits her well with three small children. The salary too is very attractive, and there is nothing wrong with that considering she and her husband have just bought a very special house with a big mortgage. This means she can also benefit a lot from the outstanding mortgage facilities the bank offers its employees. She has looked round herself a little for other jobs but has not succeeded in finding out precisely what she wants.

From the typing interview she stands out as a Type 4 in the bloom of her type. Type 4 has difficulty with the ordinary, always looks for the unobtainable, and thinks more of 'there' and 'then' than of the 'here and now'. Charlotte gets self-observation homework to see what role the Type 4 pattern plays in her work and private life. The consultant discusses with her what this pattern means in her search for the ideal job. The next homework is external orientation to give the search for another function more realistic content. What are all the sorts of jobs that would be possible for her, not just in theory but also in reality? An impressive list results, varying from a lectureship at the university (her former professor is very willing to help her and is willing and able to create a job) to a partnership in a communications consultancy (the director/owner is a former fellow student with whom she still has contact). Now that all these jobs are really within reach, Charlotte begins to see the disadvantages (also part of the Type 4 pattern).The consultant discusses this pattern with her as well. It becomes clear that there are advantages and disadvantages in every job. Now her present director begins to pull on her: he certainly doesn't want to lose her. Finally Charlotte chooses another function at the bank: in the Marketing and Communications Department.

Gurdjieff spoke of the type as the 'robot person'. A robot has mechanisms and is programmed for automatic reactions. At the level of second-order learning you watch out for the automatic patterns, your emotions, the situations in which these emotions are aroused, and also how you act thereafter. You learn to know thoroughly the general pattern, the robot character, of your type. You investigate how this type pattern works for you personally. You become increasingly aware that, if someone pushes button X with you, you react automatically in manner Y. You also begin to regard these automatic reactions more and more as something that belongs to you and tend less to feel badly treated by the 'big bad outside world'.

You also become aware of the personal filling-in of your type. Thus one
Type 1 thinks very quickly that he is not treated correctly or is even
exploited; the next Type 1 reacts violently to injustice at work; and the third
Type 1 is troubled most of all by a chaotic and unpredictable environment
where the rules are constantly changing so that he can never do well.

Subjects for self-observation – all described in Chapters 7–9 – are the
qualities, pitfalls and remaining characteristics of one's own type and the
basic patterns that form their foundation.

People begin, for instance, to think in ever-more nuanced terms about
their qualities. It becomes clear to someone where he automatically directs
his attention. One is confronted more and more with one's own basic motivation. Because of these observations holes gradually form in the ideal self-
image – it becomes ever clearer that this self-image does not correspond with
reality. People become ever more aware of the 'spectacles' through which
they look at reality and with which they interpret it. It also becomes clear to
people under which circumstances they always run to their defence mechanism. They discover when they apply their survival strategy, and begin to
realise the extent to which it actually prevents them from achieving what
they want. The (faulty) reasoning that lies behind it also comes into the
picture.

It appears that self-observation is not a process in itself that really makes
one happier. And this is true. It is a step in a process – but one does eventually become happier as an outcome of that process. Self-observation is a
requirement for creating more distinction between horse and rider, between
one's type and one's real self. Only those who draw that distinction can
create personal mastery. If a horseman cannot ride his horse it will certainly
not make him happy, and it is not effective either. Thus, indeed, self-observation can be painful. But not being the master of one's self can be a lot more
painful still.

Looking back daily

One self-observation exercise is to look back every evening at the day gone
by, and in so doing recall not only the events but also the thoughts and
emotions experienced in them. Thus one not only looks back at what has
happened during the day but also investigates one's inner reactions to those
events. Someone who does this exercise evaluates what has satisfied him and
what aspects he finds capable of improvement.

Thus someone can think, for instance:

> That person did not treat me well, so I was justified in defending myself.
> I am content with that. But, at the same time, I felt a desire for revenge
> and went further than was necessary. I'm not content with that. What's
> more, perhaps the person actually had a good reason for the way he
> behaved.

Someone else can think, when he looks back on the day:

> I had to hang on the line for 40 minutes before I could speak to some-
> one in the emergency service. That makes me very angry; as a client I did
> not feel myself taken seriously. I am satisfied that I remained friendly
> towards the telephone operator. She can't help it if her organisation
> functions so badly. But I shouldn't have taken it so personally. They
> certainly don't do it to irritate me on purpose.

Self-observation is a continuous process in daily work and life. However, we
do not always pay conscious attention to it – we are too busy with other
things that demand our concentration. It helps to have fixed moments for
self-reflection.

Discussion partner

This exercise is with a permanent discussion partner daily, weekly or
monthly to talk about what is going on in both the people concerned.
Naturally that partner must be someone you trust. Here things that are less
pleasant also come to the fore: things that tarnish the ideal self-image or
which one is to some extent ashamed to bring up. If these things are explicitly named, they lose their power over the person who speaks of them.
Through this the freedom is created to act differently in daily life. For
instance, someone who wants to take revenge, and says this, thereby recognises that need. Through this arises the freedom to choose whether to
pursue this urge or not.

Diary

A diary can fulfil the function of a discussion partner. As long as you do not
envisage future publication, you can really write down everything. Even
then, it is not always easy to entrust the deepest motives to paper.

Opening typical basic assumptions to discussion

One can raise an assumption for discussion only if one realises there is any
question of an assumption in play in the first place. Frequently, however,
people are not conscious of this.

Becoming aware of typical assumptions

You can become aware of your typical assumptions by asking yourself what
kind of things arouse particular emotions in you. What irritates you? What
disturbs you? What makes you angry or indignant? What is the best way to
infuriate you? When are you driven crazy? And so forth.

For example, if someone always gets very angry if he has to wait, his implicit assumption is apparently that he must always be helped immediately. Formulating this in absolute terms ('I apparently expect that I will be helped immediately') is enough to raise the question: 'Is that actually realistic?' If someone is extremely irritated by every spelling error in a report, his assumption seems to be that not even one single spelling error may ever appear in a report. In the Netherlands there is an annual National Dictation Contest, and its results indicate that this last assumption is unattainable. One winner, acknowledged as the best speller in the country in that year, still made five mistakes. If someone becomes impatient and angry when a colleague, because of personal problems, does not finish a contribution to a project group, then his implicit view is apparently that employees ought not to have personal problems.

Behind one assumption can lie another assumption. Thus, for instance, the assumption 'I must always be helped immediately' can arise from convictions like 'If I am not helped immediately then I am not being taken seriously', 'Others are always going first', 'Nobody will look after me if I don't look after myself', and so forth. Under these deeper convictions yet more assumptions can lie. If we go on long enough with asking which assumption lies at the root of another assumption – for instance by continually asking such questions as 'why is that a problem?' – we finally arrive at our type's basic assumption.

It is possible, however, to reason from the other side, from the basic assumption of the type towards the practice. Someone who knows what type he has, and has therefore gathered insight into his basic assumptions, can start watching out in daily practice for the moments when a certain basic assumption comes into play, and may consider if the basic assumption concerned is justified in that specific situation or not.

Once we know our basic assumptions then we can open these for discussion.

Checking assumptions

If a person with Type 6 checks his assumption about the untrustworthiness and hidden agendas of the powerful, it can turn out that it is sometimes true and sometimes not. He can check his assumption, for instance, by questioning the powerful people involved or by comparing his own conception with those of colleagues.

The basic assumption of Type 9 is that only by complying with others' wishes will he be accepted by others – or at least this is what Type 9 supposes that other people expect. He can check this assumption by *not* conforming for once and seeing what happens. To his surprise, some people may actually find his standpoint interesting. He can also observe what happens when others do not conform, and establish that his assumption does not actually apply to everyone: many people actually attract others because they adopt a standpoint.

The basic assumption of Type 3 is 'I am accepted and loved only if I produce good results.' He can check this assumption by doing nothing for once, and experiencing the fact that he is not immediately driven from house and hearth. Stronger still, it is actually appreciated that he is available at home.

Absolute formulation of assumptions

By formulating an assumption absolutely it takes on a colouring of absurdity. Thus someone with Type 3 could formulate the view that it is wholly unthinkable that he could ever – even for one minute – be accepted as a person if he had done nothing to earn this acceptance. Someone with Type 6 could say that absolutely no one, speaking on any subject whatsoever, can be trusted even for the briefest moment.

Such absolute statements put things in perspective. The person who does this then invites a discussion with himself: when precisely does that sharply formulated assumption apply (if ever), and when not? Through that inner discussion the sharp edges of the position concerned will be rounded off in many cases. The next time that someone feels the urge to blow his top because his expectations are unfulfilled once again, he thinks back on this discussion he has had with himself (or perhaps with someone else).

Nuanced formulation of an assumption

After the last exercise the basic assumption can be formulated in nuanced terms. Type 3, for instance, could now say that in certain circumstances he is only valued for his work. The facilitator will now question him further on what those circumstances are. In his team? No, not there: they like him there. At home? No, not there either; they actually want him to relax a little more sometimes. Finally there remain the situations with a new client who has not yet got to know him as a person, and the Board of Directors who do not know him at all. The basic assumption, in any event at cognitive level, no longer has any general validity. One can proceed with the following development action.

Interrupting type automatism

A consultant is asked by a department to facilitate a number of team sessions. Some members are fed up with their chief Ben; others want to give him another chance. Everyone is agreed, however, that progress, speed of decision-making and innovative ability all leave a good deal to be desired. The responsibility for this is laid completely with boss Ben. The members complain of too much or too little freedom; they find that their tasks are unclear and they are dissatisfied about the projects to which they are assigned.

Ben has difficulties with some members who keep breathing down his neck. After all, he works as hard he can, doesn't he? He is in harness at the office from early in the morning until late in the evening, and then often still sits down behind his computer at home, to the displeasure of his family – 'Mom, who is that gentleman that cuts the meat on Sundays?' What more do they want?

The consultant has typing interviews with everyone. The chief turns out to have Type 9. He has difficulty making decisions and postpones things regularly until they are clearer. The team members who are most dissatisfied are Types 8, 3 and 7 – all rather action-orientated types. The other members, with Types 9, 5 and 6, complain much less but stay in the background in the verbal warfare of the team meetings.

In the first team session everyone talks about his own type and the consequences this has for communication. The communication pattern becomes clear. It also becomes clearer for everyone what drives the others have.

Thereafter the team members mutually exchange views on what each requires individually from the others, and they discuss how they can deal more effectively with each other, given each person's specific type. Finally a number of agreements are reached about a better way of communicating. The team also forms a few sub-groups of people with certain qualities to take on given tasks suited to these qualities. Thus a 'progress' sub-group is created with the Type 3 member as leader. Up to this point work is based on the principle that everyone simply has the type patterns that he has.

Subsequently the consultant raises for discussion the principle that people do not always have to carry through their automatisms but can also interrupt them. Now the team discusses what signals each can recognise for himself if he switches to his automatic type robot and how his colleagues can help with this recognition. At the same time there is discussion as to how everyone can interrupt his type automatism and what he needs from his colleagues for this. (Don't think now that every team session with the enneagram is a heavy meeting. People often laugh a lot and all sorts of creative methods can be used.)

Interrupting automatic reactions, which the consultant speaks of with the team, is in essence holding back the type energy. If, for instance, someone with Type 3 notices that his colleague looks like being better at his work than he is himself, then his automatic reaction is something like: 'Oh, oh, that's bad news! They'll value my colleague more than me. My status is in danger of slipping. I feel I'm bursting with energy. I must do something!' That 'do something' can consist of this person trying to present himself more favourably. In this, it would not be bad to exaggerate certain details a little and leave less favourable aspects out. Perhaps he points out that his colleague actually owes the good performances to him. Or perhaps he informs his superiors in advance of the results of a project which they actually do together. And so on.

This person with Type 3, however, can also decide to do none of this and to interrupt his automatic reaction. In that case he examines his own feeling under the magnifying glass: 'How serious is it really if my colleague is better than I am? Can I survive that? Or can I try to be just as good instead of using up my energy in presenting myself more favourably? If I become as good as my colleague I create added value; if I present myself better I don't do that.'

The first step particularly, accepting that one is not the best, is not easily taken by Type 3. The type remains spluttering for a while ('Do something!'). The type, after all, does not give up so easily. Furthermore, someone with Type 3 will feel uneasy in that situation: the type energy, after all, prefers to be converted into action. The tension level is increased.

The following exercises serve to interrupt type automatisms:

Contrary action

This exercise consists of consciously doing the opposite of one's pattern and observing what happens within oneself. The Jesuits called this *agere contra* (literally 'to act against'). Somebody with Type 5, in that case, tries to open himself up instead of withdrawing; someone with Type 4 tries to enjoy what there is here and now; and somebody with Type 7 faces up to painful situations instead of getting rid of them as quickly as possible. And so on. This exercise is also used to loosen up the type fixations.

Turning round the focus of attention

A way to interrupt the type automatism is to shift the focus of attention. If someone with Type 4, for instance, notices that his attention is directed towards the best that is not available and the worst that is, he can consciously direct attention to the best that is available. He can also focus it on what others need at the moment instead of what he himself requires. If someone with Type 3 notices that his attention goes to the impression he makes on others, then he can direct it to what he finds important for himself. Or he can focus it on intrinsic perfection, irrespective of the evaluation of others.

By consciously shifting the focus of attention we interrupt the type automatism.

Affirmations

The automatic type reactions are interrupted by expressing an *affirmation*. An affirmation is a positive statement which has to be expressed with complete conviction and which must conflict with one's own automatism. Examples of affirmations are:

- *Type 1:* 'I am perfect as I am'
- *Type 2:* 'I am complete in myself'
- *Type 3:* 'I am worthwhile as a person'
- *Type 4:* 'I am satisfied with what is now available'
- *Type 5:* 'There is always enough for me'
- *Type 6:* 'I trust myself, the world and the future'
- *Type 7:* 'Both the sunny and shadowy sides of life provide fulfilment for me'
- *Type 8:* 'I am sensitive and vulnerable'
- *Type 9:* 'I am of value'

These examples of affirmations are meant only as a source of inspiration. It is very important to choose an affirmation that applies to you personally. This cannot always be picked from a general list. Professionals who work with others will sometimes have to search for a while and try out alternatives before they find the affirmation that works best for a specific individual.

There are a number of rules for working with affirmations:[4]

- Formulate an affirmation in the present tense, as if this were already reality.
- Affirm only what you want, not what you don't want: the subconscious does not know the word 'not' and reacts to the content. Had Moses known this he might have formulated the Ten Commandments differently. Most of them are formulated as 'Thou shalt not …' And what do most people do? Exactly. Therefore, formulate positively. Not 'I am not dependent on other people', but 'I am independent.'
- Keep the formulation short and forceful, without conditions and 'buts'. The longer the story, the more it loses its emotional effect. Compare 'I am vulnerable' (ouch!) with 'In certain situations I have no trouble in appearing vulnerable, but that does not mean that people can pull my leg.'
- Choose affirmations which apply to you personally and which you can cope with at that moment.

If you cannot believe in a given affirmation, or have too great a resistance to it, look then for one that goes a step less far. If 'I am perfect as I am' is a bridge too far, choose then, for example, 'I am good enough.' It is important that you can believe sincerely in the affirmation you choose.

One can work with affirmations in different ways. One is the 'punishment lines method'. Write down the affirmation concerned ten or twenty times every day. Another possibility is to speak the affirmation out loud. Look at yourself steadily in the mirror in the morning and pronounce it a number of times to your reflection. Yet another possibility is to practise with someone else. Or one can make a song with the affirmation and sing that throughout the day. Whatever method one chooses it is important to carry out the affirmation with conviction and belief.

Mental picture of alternatives

When you catch your type automatism setting in and interrupt this, you can then imagine how you could do something otherwise. One way of doing this is to form a mental picture in which the alternative method is put into practice on a future occasion. Such mental pictures help people to build up a repertoire of other behaviour and have it ready at the moment it is needed.

Top sports people are trained like this. They imagine they are jumping higher, running faster or skiing quicker.[5] The mental preparation forms the basis for the new behaviour. It is a well-known phenomenon that, when a sportsman breaks a record, others improve on the old record not long afterwards. This has to do with the belief that it is possible.

Working on the type fixations

A fixation is an idea which involves emotions. This idea has rooted itself in someone's system. For example:

- 'I am not the kind of person people love'
- 'I can survive only by being powerful and strong'
- 'No one can be trusted'.

In order to free oneself from a fixation it is necessary to come in contact again with the feelings that originally led to it. Countless methods that are used in psychotherapy and counselling fall outside the framework of this book, but include talking about the original feelings, entering a dialogue about them, acting them out, calling them again to mind, working on the muscular tension connected with them (memories are stored not only in the brain but also in the muscles: after several years of intuitive training I had lost so much muscular tension that I needed a bigger shoe size and was 3 cm taller), and so forth. In most cases guidance is needed here, because the type level continually resists strenuously against this freeing action.

What does not work is pretending the fixation does not exist. Advice such as 'Pay no attention to it', 'Just leave it behind you', or 'Set your sights on higher things' works only for people who have already resolved a lot of fixations, or were born almost enlightened.

In the first place it is important not to deny the fixation but to examine it and discover all its aspects – both positive and negative. Once a person has really 'taken possession' of his type, then he can go to work thereafter, whatever the method may be.

Disidentification with the type

Self-observation, opening one's suppositions to discussion, interrupting one's automatic pattern and freeing oneself from the type fixation are all forms of 'disidentification'. Disidentification means that someone no longer regards his type as his 'total person' but knows how to draw a distinction between that type and his own self. The type is no longer the complete identity: someone is no longer his type, but has a type. Here a few specific disidentification methods are discussed.

Exaggerating the pattern

A way of disidentifying is to exaggerate the type pattern, and to experience what then happens within.

A conflict-evading Type 9 by way of exercising now actually avoids every form of confrontation, difference of opinion or discussion. A Type 3 does everything imaginable to put himself in the picture, like someone in the background of an outside TV broadcast who tries constantly to get his head into the camera shot. A Type 7 interprets everything, but then *really* everything, as cheerful, optimistic. And so forth.

It is extremely difficult, if not impossible, to keep this exercise up for long. Very soon the feeling arises that this cannot really be the meaning of life. Through this someone gets his own pattern into perspective, thus disidentifying with it.

Consciously opposing the command or interdict of one's type

One method of disidentification is to grant oneself permission to oppose a type command or type prohibition. Thus a Type 1 could say to himself: 'You can relax and enjoy yourself, even if everything is perhaps not finished. They love you as well if you make mistakes. You have wishes, needs, feelings and moods, and those are welcome in the world.'[6]

Rational Emotive Training: the ABC method

Another method that can be applied for disidentification is Rational Emotive Training (RET), developed originally by the American Ellis and worked out in the Netherlands by R.F.W. Diekstra.[7] Ellis found out that he himself could determine how he felt as a result of an event by thinking differently. If he tried to date a girl he was rejected regularly. Instead of thinking as a result 'D'you see? I'm really unattractive after all', he thought: 'Another step nearer my goal of asking out a really nice girl!' and that made him feel a bit better.

The RET method, also called the ABC method, works as follows:

■   A is the actual event. This is the external stimulus which calls up the standard type reaction.
■   B is what one thinks as a result of the event (this is the standard type reaction).

- C is the feeling which is called up by that thought (this is also a standard type reaction). What someone thinks and feels as a result of actual events is, after all, determined partly by the way he perceives the world, thus through his own type.

Example of ABC analysis

A   Event: the boss raises an eyebrow while he reads the piece by the employee and does not look at him.

B   Various types will think differently about A. For instance:
   - Someone with Type 2 could think: 'I have the feeling he does not think the piece is good and that he rejects me – even though I have done my very best for him!'
   - Someone with Type 6 could think: 'I have the feeling he thinks the piece is not up his political street. Could he have changed course behind my back? I already thought he was not to be trusted.'
   - Someone with Type 7 could think: 'I have the feeling he is pleasantly surprised by my interesting line of thought. That will be a nice discussion.'

C   The various thoughts under B will call up different feelings. For example:
   - The person with Type 2, reacting to the thought of being rejected, could have the feeling: 'I feel angry. He could at least show a little more appreciation now I have made so much effort for him.'
   - The person with Type 6, as a reaction to the thought of the chief having changed course behind his back, could have the feeling: 'I am indignant.'
   - The person with Type 7, reacting to the thought that the chief is pleasantly surprised, could have the feeling: 'I'm happy and look forward to the interesting discussion we're going to have.'

The following steps are now:

- D: Putting B up for rational discussion.
- E: Choosing how one feels.

Once more we consider how the different types in our example could do this.

Example of DE analysis

D   Putting B up for rational discussion.
   - Someone with Type 2 could think 'He can actually raise his eyebrow for all sorts of reasons. Perhaps he has an itch or a nervous twitch or

his attention is distracted for a moment and he is thinking of a very
different situation: for instance that his son doesn't want to do his
homework. If he is reading my piece attentively, he can't look at me
at the same time.'

- Someone with Type 6 could think 'Is my boss normally in the habit of
not keeping me informed if he changes direction? How often has that
actually happened?'
- Someone with Type 7 could think 'What indication is there that he
finds my train of thought interesting?'

E   Choosing how one feels.
As long as someone has no clear indication of the reasons why the boss
raises his eyebrow, he can have a neutral feeling about it. And even if he
does have a hypothesis he can choose how he feels. For example:

- The person with Type 2 in this example: 'Imagine the chief actually
does think my piece isn't good; then we can also have a discussion on
how I can improve it, without me feeling rejected as a person. That
could be interesting.'
- The person with Type 6 in this example: 'Imagine he has really
changed course; then this is a good opportunity for him to inform me
about it without me having to feel indignant. I'm looking forward to
the discussion.'
- The person with Type 7 in this example: 'Imagine he finds my line of
thought interesting; then I can also remain interested in the criticism
he might have. I feel worried.'

Occupying a position other than the type fixation[8]

Here you imagine you are sitting in a theatre. Being acted on the stage is a
piece in which you yourself have the leading role. It concerns a scene from
the past which has troubled you, or a situation you must tackle shortly and
which you are not looking forward to. What is the title of the play?

The piece begins. The first performance is of the situation which has
occurred, or as you expect it will probably occur. From your position in the
theatre you see yourself on the stage. In this scene you perhaps see how you
act out your automatic type pattern.

Then a second performance follows. The subject is the same situation, but
now you imagine that you possess infinite wisdom on the stage. How does
the scene progress now? What is the title now?

The third performance: now you imagine the infinite wisdom also lies
with the other person or persons in the situation concerned. Enact the scene
again. What happens differently now? What title does the piece have now?

In this exercise you fix your attention in different positions: the position
of actor on the stage and that of spectator of the play in which you yourself

have the leading role. In the latter position you distance yourself from your type position. The position of spectator is the position of the real self, the inner guide.

A variant of this is to think of what advice you would give another in your position. This is something at which people are often very good (the best coaches are on the sidelines ...). We know perfectly well what effective behaviour is; the trouble is in applying it to one's own situation. Regularly I say to myself if something does not go according to plan: 'What is it I always say to students on my courses if they bring up this sort of situation?'

Imagining oneself in the type fixation and in the disidentification with the type

Another way of taking a position other than the type fixation is the following:[9] First you think of a situation in which you let yourself be carried along by your type fixation. Identify yourself completely with the situation. What did you feel? What was your body language; the position of head, hands, and so forth. What does the world look like, seen from this position? What do you normally say? What does your voice sound like? Are there special memories connected with this position? Certain smells or tastes?

Now walk round and try to exaggerate this position. What happens to your feelings, body language, tension or relaxation, way of looking, and so forth?

Write down what has struck you most so far.

Now think of what the opposite is of your enneagram fixation. When are you most yourself, the least compulsive, the most in contact with your real self? Can you remember instances of this? Identify yourself completely with this situation. What do you feel now? What is your body language, the position of the head, hands, and so forth? How does the world look, seen from this position? What do you now say? What does your voice sound like? Are there certain smells or tastes connected with this position?

Now walk round and try to express this position. What happens to your feelings, body language, tension and relaxation, way of looking, and so forth? Exaggerate this as much as possible.

Write down what strikes you most in this position.

Autogenic training

Autogenic training in connection with the enneagram means that you train yourself in convictions such as: 'I have a type, I am not my type', 'I have emotions, I am not my emotions', 'I have thought patterns, I am not my thought patterns.' You do this training by repeating these sentences in relaxed circumstances like a kind of mantra.

A second step is to fill in the concepts concerned concretely during the exercise. In that case think specifically about your own type pattern and say to yourself: 'I have this type, I am not this type.'[10]

What if I did not have these qualities?[11]

Write the qualities that suit your type on separate pieces of paper. Then lay these sheets in order – that to which you are least attached on top, that which is most characteristic of you at the bottom.

Thereafter, one by one, you imagine *not* having each quality. Who would you then be? You begin with the topmost paper and work through them all in succession until you have had the last one as well.

If you have Type 1, for example, and your topmost paper says 'diligence', then you imagine you are no longer diligent. 'If I weren't diligent, who would I be then?' Your second sheet says perhaps 'ethical'. You imagine you are no longer ethical. Who would you be then? When you have had been through all the papers an idea remains about who you would be without your type.

The soul is pure[12]

One of my favourite exercises is making a distinction between type patterns and the soul that is pure. This proceeds as follows:

You imagine yourself with all your good characteristics. Then you say to yourself: 'My soul is pure.'

Thereafter you imagine yourself with all your less good characteristics – the things you are a little ashamed of and which you try to hide. These are characteristics you know some people in your surroundings have trouble with, your less charming tendencies, your type automatism. Once more you say to yourself: 'My soul is pure.' In this way you again draw a distinction between your type pattern and your real self.

You can also use this exercise to disidentify yourself from your sometimes negative automatic reactions to the behaviour of people with whom you work.

Imagine first that you meet someone with whom you have a good relationship. You find the type patterns of that person pleasant, and you say in thought to the person concerned: 'Your soul is pure.'

Thereafter you conjure up someone with whom you have a neutral relationship. His type patterns give you no trouble, and also no pleasure. Again you say to yourself: 'Your soul is pure.'

Then you imagine someone with whom you have a decidedly bad relationship. The type patterns of that person press on all your 'type buttons'. You really have trouble with him. Even so you say to yourself about that person as well: 'Your soul is pure.' In this way you make a distinction between that person and his type pattern. That makes it easier if needs be to disapprove of his conduct without rejecting him as a person. And that puts one's own reaction in perspective. My experience is that this exercise is of great help in gaining space in which to solve mutual problems, instead of becoming stuck in a 'I'm good – you're bad' dynamic.

Working with the three centres

As we have remarked earlier, three development paths are described in many traditions. These are coupled to the centres. The paths are:

- *The path of the mind*, mental training. This is the path of the head centre.
- *The path of the heart*, devotion. This is the path of the heart centre.
- *The path of control of the body*, action, daily practice. This is the path of the belly centre.

We now describe for each centre a number of exercises which one can do to activate the separate centres and let them function better. These exercises involve more than one level of learning. For this reason I have placed this section between the sections about second-order and third-order learning. First, examples are discussed of exercises whereby each of the three centres can be trained. Afterwards some remarks follow about the use of these exercises in relation to the enneagram.

Exercises for the belly centre

Someone who is well grounded or earthed will not easily lose his balance. This applies both literally and metaphorically. In Japanese martial arts like aikido one must concentrate the attention in the *hara* (the Japanese word for 'belly centre'). Someone who has his attention there literally cannot be overthrown. An aikido teacher once told me that his little children could not be lifted if they concentrated their attention in the hara. Metaphorically someone who lets himself be carried along by negative fantasies and interpretations (head) is much easier to unbalance than someone who concentrates wholly on objective reality and what he wishes from within himself (belly).

Grounding

The trainer does role-playing with manager Derek. Derek's aim in learning is to gain the co-operation of staff for his objectives. In the role play it transpires that Derek does not check his assumptions of what goes on in a worker's mind. Because of those assumptions he begins to feel uncertain. For this reason his proposals are not brought over properly. He presents them hesitantly, and leaves out half of what he had meant to say if his discussion partner interrupts him. The trainer now does a number of grounding exercises with him. Playing the next role proceeds much better. Derek is clear about what he wants, and the employee also takes this seriously.

An exercise for grounding is thus situating the attention in the belly centre. Further, one can think of bodily movement such as stamping the feet, jogging, African dancing, or working in the garden with hands and feet in the earth.

One can also ground oneself with the help of visualisation (in this case the head centre is brought in to let the belly centre function better). You can imagine, for instance, that roots grow from your feet into the ground, or that you are connected by a cord to the centre of the earth. One of the exercises the trainer did with Derek, for instance, was to ask him to concentrate himself wholly on the idea that roots grew from his feet into the ground and to begin the discussion anew with that idea in his head. That indeed made a difference: Derek came across much more confidently. Obviously all these exercises work only if one takes them seriously.

Everything that promotes vitality has a positive influence on the functioning of the belly centre.[13] A healthy lifestyle includes sufficient sleep, healthy and digestible food, not smoking, moderation with alcohol, drinking sufficient water, sufficient bodily movement, good social contacts, a positive attitude to life (every type can make himself familiar with these).

Oscar Ichazo, mentioned in Chapter 4, developed special movement exercises, which he called 'psychocallisthenics'. These were aimed at awakening vital energy in organs, glands and tissues. Stress-reducing body exercises, such as relaxation exercises, hatha yoga and some forms of meditation, make a contribution to vitality as well.

One can also situate the attention in the belly centre by means of some breathing exercises. Belly-breathing meditation is sometimes associated with the head centre because the attention comes from the head, but this exercise can be associated equally well with the belly centre because the attention goes to the belly. (This example illustrates, by the way, that many exercises are related to more than one centre.) In belly-breathing meditation you breathe only by expanding and contracting the abdominal wall. In doing this concentrate completely on this abdominal movement, and count your breaths. As soon as a thought arises or your attention strays you begin to count again. It is a great art to reach 10.

With T'ai Chi, for instance, a series of exercises based on Chinese martial arts which is aimed at letting the life energy (chi) circulate freely, or with meridian massage (meridians, used in acupuncture among other things, are paths in the body through which vital energy passes), you can bring the energy flow in the body into equilibrium. The basis of this philosophy is that an imbalance between yin and yang leads to diminished vitality and illness. It is not nonsense: the energy flow in the meridians can be measured with the help of modern technical aids.[14]

Exercises for the head centre

With exercises for activating the head centre one can start by thinking of visualisation exercises, like the theatre exercise described earlier in this chapter. What are involved specifically are mental visualisations. Visualisations with materials – for example paintings, drawings, modelling – call upon more centres.

Another category of exercise is thought exercise, such as raising assumptions for discussion or training in truly logical thinking.

A further group is that of intuitive training. This is discussed in this chapter under third-order learning. Such training can involve the head centre particularly, or be based on all centres.

A fourth category is that of attention exercises. The attention, for instance, can be placed in the centre of the surrounding space, on the farthest wall, or at reading distance; in one's own person, listening to another from one's own person, or identified with the other.[15]

Other examples of attention exercises are the so-called 'Gurdjieff movements'. Gurdjieff claimed to have learned of these in his secret monastic society. They are movement exercises to music whereby arms, legs and head are moved independently of one another. This demands the utmost concentration. Every distracting thought or emotion is punished.

In Zen monasteries monks work with problematic assignments which cannot be solved logically, the so-called *koan*. The best known example of a koan is 'What is the sound of one hand clapping?'[16] An apprentice monk can spend years on one koan.

Exercises for the heart centre

The heart centre has to do with altruistic love, called *agape* by the ancient Greeks (and thus not the physical sort, *eros*, which belongs to the belly centre).

By thinking and talking positively about oneself and others, one can have a positive influence on the functioning of the heart centre. Exercises in sympathising with the feelings of others, instead of shutting oneself off from them or passing personal judgement on them, are also exercises that 'open' the heart centre.

One can reduce tension in the heart area with physical exercises. For instance, lean backwards with arms raised and spread above the head. A good back support is necessary here.

There is a relationship between psychic and physical functioning. By relaxing physically one also relaxes psychologically – and vice versa. One cannot relax the body completely, for example, and then remain angry. Thus we know the phenomenon of psychosomatic illness – somatic anomalies which are caused by a psychic condition. The stomach ulcer is a well-known example. This usually has a psychic cause: matters lie heavily on the stomach; one cannot 'digest' certain situations.

Certain forms of singing (for instance, those encountered in devotional practices) have a positive influence in the same way on the functioning of the heart centre.

One of the heart centre's functions is to distinguish between emotions which connect someone with himself (his true self) and others, and emotions whereby he injures himself and possibly others. For example, someone who does not forgive another and continues to nurse resentment 'hardens his heart'.[17] In this manner he also stands in his own way. Every hardening is a fixation, and as Elliot Ginsburg once said: 'The hardened heart must be broken before we can grow.'[18] One can prevent that painful process by really forgiving the other from within. Needless to say, that will not always be simple; sometimes one will have to work hard at it. Techniques one can use in this are, for example:

- Visualising a talk with the person concerned.
- Writing a letter. This does not have to be sent (often it is better not!). Sometimes you may work for weeks on a letter which is never sent but is a means for developing your inner process.
- The exercise 'The soul is pure' which was described earlier in this chapter.

However difficult it can be to forgive another, it is sometimes even more difficult to forgive oneself. With methods like psychodrama, bio-energetica and bio-release, and through breathing exercises, old emotions can be loosened so that one can let them go.[19]

Perhaps one of the best methods is to 'slow down'. This means working less hard and for fewer hours and to relax regularly – *really* relax. An international manager with severe burn-out complained that he had always relaxed enough: so how could this now happen to him? On further questioning it turned out that he sometimes drove from the aeroplane to the hockey pitch. There he did his very best to win. After this 'relaxation' he went to work again immediately, sometimes even going back directly to the airport. And in the aircraft you sit quietly with your documents, don't you? The tempo of the heart is slower than that of the head, and someone who is too busy with his head cannot hear the voice of his heart.

Which exercises for which enneagram types?

In my experience it is not true that head types always benefit most from a head approach, or heart types from an emotional one, and so forth. What is often the case, however, is that such an attuned approach holds the attention longer. If there is theoretical talk of greater than normal length, someone with Type 5 can enjoy it while someone with Type 8 begins to wriggle on his chair and says: 'When are we going to exercise again? Let's go and do something!' But it could be that Type 5 would profit most from the practical exercises, while Type 8 would progress more with a new way of thinking. It is comfortable for course participants to train in their own old patterns, but it is not always most effective (depending on the aims of learning). In this a facilitator is faced with a dilemma. He makes himself more popular by attuning to existing patterns – and in the first instance he must do this in order to win trust. But thereafter he will have to direct himself towards the other centres also.

In addition culture has something to say too. In present-day organisations the heart centre has become a somewhat neglected child while the head centre has acquired a very heavy accent, at least in the way people talk about it. I once called this the 'myth' of the rational organisation. Everyone knows perfectly well that decision-making in organisations is often not at all rational, and in many cases that is just as well. When all is said and done no rational certainty about the future can be obtained, and a good corporate planner needs his intuition badly – all the more reason to work on the optimal functioning of all three centres.

General development interventions of the third order: transformation learning, transcendence of the type fixation

In this section the following general development interventions are dealt with:

- contact with the real self
- training the moral will
- developing intuition
- solving type fixations
- growing to the higher aspects of the type.

It will be clear that these development actions are linked with the higher levels which we discussed in Chapter 11, *Anatomy of consciousness*.

Coming into contact with the real self

According to Zimmer and Jung, someone comes automatically to his real self if he 'peels off the skin of the personality'.[20] Second-order learning should therefore lead in itself to the real self. In fact, the real self can be regarded as the turning-point between second-order and third-order learning. However, there are also exercises one can do specially in order to come in contact with the real self.

Inner dialogue

As we saw in Chapter 11 we have different voices within ourselves.[21] One voice wants this, the other voice wants that. This is illustrated by the following inner dialogue of a Type 1:

Voice A: I must do as well as possible in this project. I have a clear idea of what I want to attain. I'll go for it.

Voice B: The last time I felt that two people became overstressed, and I nearly did too. That is morally irresponsible.

Voice C: I feel like doing nothing for a week for a change: visiting museums, sleeping late, going out, getting into nature.

Voice A: It makes me completely stressed. This way the project will come to nothing!

Voice B: But the last time when I walked around chasing people up I didn't reach my goals either, and a lot of people had trouble with it.

Voice A: Yes, that went very wrong; it has to be better this time.

Voice C: If I plan it more broadly I can go on a spree this week-end.

Thus various voices are present within an individual. There remains, however, an identity that 'conducts' these voices, as it were. This decides which voice has the say, and to what extent. It draws conclusions from the dialogue that goes on. The conductor is the real self.

If you want to carry on an inner dialogue you can write down the utterances of the various voices on paper. You can also arrange as many chairs as there are voices and physically sit in the various positions. If you have done this your conductor can say: 'Alright, I've heard everyone. What conclusion does it bring me to?'

Listen to yourself

Another way of coming in contact with the real self is 'to listen to yourself'. The real self has another quality of feeling than the unreal self. Peace rules the real self and a feeling of quietly knowing, while the unreal self has a quality of obligation, of restless energy, of fanaticism, sometimes of uncertainty, of fear. If you have the idea that something must be done, or that you have to undertake a certain action, you can then investigate by yourself what feeling is connected with that thought: the peaceful feeling of knowing, or the restless, wound-up feeling. In this you can work with visualisations. You then imagine that your idea has been realised, as concretely as possible, and with all the consequences attendant on it. Thereafter you pose to yourself the question of whether what you want to attain is real. This is a technique that is also used in 'visioning'.

Training the moral will

Transcendence of the type level is not a question of pressing the right button one day and from then on perceiving things exclusively from the higher perspective. What is concerned here is a choice that people have to make anew every day, and with which they often have to struggle.

An aspect of transcending the type is training the moral will. It can be trained by allowing the moral aspect to be a continuous part of one's decision-making – not just in major decisions, but every day and every hour. One keeps asking questions like the following:

- 'My type wants this, but is it also ethically sound?'
- 'What consequences do I bring about if I do that this way?
- 'Is this going to contribute to forgiveness, or actually to hardening of attitudes?'
- 'Is this justice or revenge?'
- 'Am I doing this with the right motivation?'

Every tendency is examined under the microscope, from 'I don't feel like this' to 'Yippee! That's what I'll do!' That aspect of constantly acting consciously leads fairly often to people doubting this exercise. I often hear people say: 'Can't I ever again do something naturally impulsive then?' A justifiable question! Go ahead and be impulsive, but realise which level this wish comes from.

A philosophy of life or religion, of whatever sort, can be an important support in training the moral will. Someone who takes his religion or philosophy of life seriously can no longer let himself be led exclusively by the type level. This is daily life as exercise. In everything one does one considers if one's action is in fact ethically responsible, what one is putting into the world with this, what chain of consequences is linked to it, and whether an activity is actually something on which one should expend one's energy.

The subject is alive in 'management land'. Some years ago management consultancy KPMG brought the game *Cards on the table, Ethics and Business* on to the market; I have also heard of Corporate Integrity departments. The proverbial capitalist businessman who earlier wanted to maximise the profit of his company at all costs no longer exists – at least not beyond criminal circles.

Developing intuition

In developing intuition we can use the five Rs as a guideline:[22]

- Relaxing
- Recalling
- Receiving or Remaining open
- Relying
- (Re)acting accordingly.

Relaxing

Relaxation is the generally favourable condition for intuition. True, people sometimes do actually receive inspiration under stress, but more frequently it happens if someone is relaxed. Vaags investigated where managers get their ideas.[23] Often this was not behind their desks but in bed, while shaving or showering, while driving, and so forth: at times, therefore, when they were not concentrating hard on work or were busy thinking. Relaxing can happen physically (with relaxation exercises, yoga, and suchlike) and mentally (for instance with meditation or imagination exercises under guidance).

Recalling

One often receives intuitive inspiration spontaneously. But one can also 'recall' or 'evoke' intuition with the help of *intuitive exercises*. With the help of these exercises information – information which you were not aware you had – is made available to you.

Intuitive exercises can be divided into three groups: making the the left side of the brain less active, using the right side of the brain more, and making use of the principle of synchronicity.

- *Deactivating the left side of the brain.* The left side of the brain becomes less active when one carries out routine tasks. In doing this one hardly has to think about something, or not at all. Examples are walking, cycling, driving, washing the dishes, ironing, showering, and so forth. Einstein said himself that he got his best ideas while shaving. Relaxation exercises can also make the left side of the brain less active, as can various forms of meditation.
- *Activating the right side of the brain.* The right side of the brain can be activated by calling on one's own imaginative powers, for instance in the form of visualisation or by painting. With intuitive painting or writing, one creates something one has not thought of beforehand. One lets it come into being, as it were. The painting or writing hand is the medium of a higher level of consciousness. Later someone can be surprised at what he has painted or written. Subsequently the concern is to understand the message in the painting or writing. A discussion partner can be helpful in this.

  Another possibility is to work with dreams.[24] Not all dreams have anything important to say. Many represent digestion of what has happened that day or in the same period. Sometimes, however, a dream does contain a reasonably important message (not all dreams are delusion). An indication of this is, for instance, a recurring theme in dreams.
- *Synchronicity.* Synchronicity is the meaningful coincidence of events in time, without there being any question of a causal connection. A famous example was recorded by the psychologist Jung. One of his clients had dreamt of a golden beetle. While she related this, she heard a tick and saw a gold-coloured beetle on the outside of the window. This became a turning-point in the therapy. We see here two instances of synchronicity: the

beetle of which the client dreamed had ticked on the window, while in ancient Egypt the beautiful dung-beetle was the symbol of transformation, a process that could now proceed within the client.

When I was writing my first book, someone mentioned to me one morning the name of someone who might possibly be interested in publishing it. I had never heard before of the person concerned, but the same evening I met her 'by accident' in totally different circumstances. She did indeed publish the book.[25]

By being attentive to what happens to you, to those you meet or come across, and by finding the meaning in these events, you exercise your intuition. Those who dismiss synchronicity as 'pure accident' ('Oh, that way you can look for something behind everything') deny themselves intuitive information from which they might draw advantage.

Receiving or Remaining open

Receiving or remaining open means that you take your intuition seriously.

Perhaps you know the story of the great flood. A boy rings the doorbell of a man to warn him that the water is rising fast and that he must leave. But the man in the house says 'I don't have to leave. God will save me.' The water has risen to the first floor when a boat comes along. The people in the boat shout 'Quick, jump in!' But the man in the house says 'I don't have to leave. God will save me.' When the water has risen to the second floor a raft comes along. The people on the raft shout 'Quick, jump on, the water's still rising!' but the man in the house says 'I don't have to leave. God will save me.' When the water has risen to the crest of the roof a helicopter flies over. The people in the helicopter shout 'Quick, grab the rope ladder!' but the man, who is now sitting on the ridge of the roof, calls 'I don't need to leave. God will save me.' And then he drowns. He is furious when he reaches the gate of heaven. 'How can that be?' he asks St Peter. 'I've always trusted in God and still I've drowned!' 'Well', says St Peter, 'we don't understand it either. We sent a boy, a boat, a raft, a helicopter ...'

In other words, one has to remain open to the information that one receives. Do not push aside rising sensations, feelings, thoughts or moments of inspiration, but take them seriously and investigate their meaning. An important part of intuitive training consists of taking seriously what goes on inside yourself.

Relying and Reacting in harmony

If you then do what your intuition inspires in you, you develop naturally trust in your intuition's reliability. You learn in practice to distinguish something that is true intuition from something that is merely an idea, perhaps inspired by your type fixation, by greed, by fear, and so on. I was once asked to speak at a congress on a subject with which I had done little work for some years. My first thought was 'Am I still good enough at that?' I asked for time to think it over. The same week I participated in a congress on a related subject. Listening to one of the speakers I suddenly knew clearly what I had to say at the congress to which I had been invited. The first thought was not intuition, the second was.

If you keep a record of your inspirational ideas and their results when you put them into practice, that can help you to make a clearer distinction between true intuition and other thoughts.

Growing to the higher virtues and ideas of the type

Exercises are also possible at the level of the higher virtues and ideas.

Imagining

You can imagine how your life and work would change in real terms if you realised the higher virtues and ideas of your type. You live this situation completely.

- Someone with Type 1 imagines, for instance, how it would be if he accepted that it is at this moment as good as it can be at this moment.
- Someone with Type 2 can imagine the situation in which his feeling of personal value is not dependent on others, and in which the things he needs come to him without him having to manipulate people.
- Someone with Type 3 can feel what it is like if he is accepted as the person he is, without him having to do anything further about it.
- Someone with Type 4 can imagine that his life in the here and now is fulfilling and fulfilled.
- Someone with Type 5 can imagine that he always has enough energy available and that he always has the right knowledge available on time.
- Someone with Type 6 can imagine trusting in himself, in others, in the world and in the universe.
- Someone with Type 7 can visualise that he accepts painful and pleasurable matters in equal measure as part of life and works adequately with them in the here and now.
- Someone with Type 8 can see before him how he no longer has to exercise control and can open himself to the real truth.
- Someone with Type 9 can imagine being worthwhile in actual fact and choosing what is essential for him personally.

Most people will not change definitively right away when they first experience this higher level. They simply turn back to the old daily reality, with their type fixations. Further still, only striving for the higher level without working on the type fixation can strengthen the lower level. One wants to, but it doesn't work. The 'old person' is persistent.

One can only put a radical change into effect by confronting directly what one would really rather avoid, and to develop the ego (the level of type fixation) to such a degree that one is in a position to let it go, according to Condon.[26] In addition one can do the exercises concerned with the level of higher virtues and ideas.

Meditation on the higher virtues and ideas

Another exercise for developing consciousness of the higher virtues and ideas is to meditate on these higher qualities. This exercise is like the previous one, but is nonetheless a little different. After you have relaxed using your own preferred techniques and brought yourself into a meditative frame of mind, you concentrate on one of the qualities.

Imagine you are completely filled with this quality and that this is also all around you. You become this quality. Note mentally what you experience.

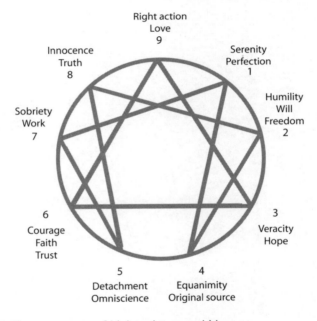

Figure 17.2 The enneagram of higher virtues and ideas

In this chapter general interventions were discussed at three levels of learning. These are interventions which are good for everyone, irrespective of type. In the next chapter we go into type-specific interventions, and also at three learning levels.

CHAPTER 18

Type-Specific Development Interventions

The type-specific interventions form the subject of this chapter. Once more we are concerned here with the notorious 'average type', that unavoidable stereotype. Different people may well find themselves individually in another stage of development. That is why every individual may need different interventions in order to be able to develop further. Someone who is just beginning to develop in his type often needs a lot of unconditional acceptance, while an advanced type can well use some confrontation.

Sometimes one ought not to use the interventions that suit someone's own type, but those that belong to his stress or relaxation point. Thus a Type 9 who goes under stress to 6 can then benefit from an analysis of calamities, a Type 6 type-specific intervention. Sometimes one can use an intervention that suits one of someone's wing types.

In type-specific interventions distinction can also be drawn among the three levels of learning which are described in Chapter 16:

- *First-order learning*: changing behaviour and broadening the behaviour repertoire
- *Second-order learning*: making the underlying patterns clear, reframing
- *Third order learning*: transformation learning, transcending the type fixation.

In fact, the type-specific development interventions in this chapter are less concerned with interventions than with themes. One can use various methods for working on those themes. For instance, learning to stand up for one's own needs is a Type 1 theme. He can learn this in various ways: by exercising in role-playing, by writing down what he actually wants, by using his anger as a signal that he really wants something else, by learning to box, and so on. In this chapter we deal with the themes, not the learning methods.

No sharp dividing-line can be drawn between the levels, and placing any theme at one level of learning is consequently debatable. Sometimes this depends on the manner of execution. Thus the theme 'learning to receive' for someone with Type 2 can be a form of first-order learning. Someone with Type 2 learns to pay attention to a compliment instead of saying immediately 'It really doesn't mean anything, you know', or 'You did it very well too – how are you, by the way?' If someone offers him help, Type 2 learns to make use of it.

For Type 2 learning to receive can also be a form of second-order learning. Then someone with Type 2 opens to discussion his natural urge to give. And learning to receive can also be a form of third-order learning: then the person with Type 2 in this example leaves the Type 2 fixation behind him.

As a result, the division into learning of the first, second and third orders in the summary below is rather fuzzy. Nonetheless I think it is worthwhile attempting the distinction. It is then clearer what one is occupied with, why certain things (still) do not work and what still remains too far advanced, and what could be a suitable intervention level for a certain aim by a certain person with a certain degree of development.

I provide now a summary of themes for the various types which can make a contribution to their development. Once again, perhaps to excess: not every theme will be relevant for every representative of a certain type. Thus this summary is intended to be more of a check list. In using it each person can find out which themes are relevant for himself or for his clients. In this the individual person must always remain in the forefront.

Now follow the various themes, arranged according to type, and within that by level of learning. At the end of the summary I shall discuss briefly working with the themes in practice.

Type 1

First-order learning

- Practising with the '80/20' rule (80 per cent is good enough – 80 per cent of the result costs 20 per cent of the effort; the remaining 20 per cent of the result costs 80 per cent of the effort).
- Thinking of alternatives, instead of in terms of 'one best way'.
- Promoting pleasure and relaxation as a duty.
- Learning from mistakes.
- Reacting to what others need, not to what is correct.
- Paying attention to what goes well; not offering only negative criticism.
- Standing up for one's own wishes.

- Showing understanding for different ways of thinking, seeing and acting.
- Expressing emotions, including anger.

Second-order learning

- Recognising anger, holding back and resentment as signals that one's own wishes are not being fulfilled.
- Recognising transferred aggression. Is event X of the present moment the true cause of anger, or have you perhaps held back earlier with event Y; and is event X more a pretext for expressing, after all, the anger bottled up about event Y?
- Finding out what one's own wishes are.
- Perceiving one's own critical attitude.
- Opening to discussion one's own norms and rules.

Third-order learning

- Accepting that things are good today as they are today: that in this way there is already perfection.
- Accepting that there are many ways to perfection.

Type 2

First-order learning

- Expressing one's own wishes clearly and standing up for them; directness.
- Staying out of the way if another receives attention.
- Taking time for oneself, being alone, and undertaking things that are independent of other people, that are of value to and meaningful only for one's self.
- Not regarding criticism as personal (professional criticism is not personal rejection) but reacting to it objectively.
- Working for the content, and not just for a person.
- Recognising when you are really needed and when not.
- Asking for help and accepting it.
- Discussing the feeling of being rejected, instead of trying to secure attention by manipulation or wanting to take revenge.

Second-order learning

- Recognising the wish to please and the tendency to adapt one's self-presentation.

- Recognising that real love and acceptance are independent of presentation.
- Distinguishing between real emotions and emotional display.
- Recognising anger and hysteria as signals of one's own needs.
- Noticing when you value (or do not value) your own talents.
- Accepting that you cannot be everyone's best friend.
- Recognising and accepting one's own needs.
- Learning to receive.
- Realising that lack of attention from others does not have to be rejection; they are simply busy with something else.

Third-order learning

- Experiencing personal will and personal freedom.
- Trusting that one's own needs will and can be fulfilled without needing to manipulate other people.
- Actual altruism.

Type 3

First-order learning

- Slowing down; creating moments or periods without a task, so that there can be attention to one's own feelings (and not making a task of this as well).
- Tackling and solving problems instead of re-framing them or escaping from them.
- Taking account of feelings, interests and wishes of others.
- Respecting the territory of others.

Second-order learning

- Using obstructions as a signal to mark time and reconsider instead of pushing on or beginning another project.
- Perceiving body signals for recognising feelings and fatigue.
- Observing when feelings are postponed.
- Perceiving when feelings become a task.
- Noticing when success fantasies replace real capabilities and performances.
- Noticing fear of failure if there is less work.
- Noticing when personal value is derived from performances and image.
- Noticing when one adapts one's own presentation and why.
- Noticing when one is not truly sincere.
- Recognising one's own weaknesses and faults.
- Observing one's own uncertainty.

Third-order learning

- Being good enough as oneself and being honest about this to oneself and to others.
- Experiencing real feelings.
- Trusting easily that the universe will supply what one needs, without one having to set this in motion oneself.

Type 4

First-order learning

- Being in the here and now, directing attention to what is positive now.
- Directing the attention to future consequences when Type 4 lets himself be led along by his feeling.
- Keeping drama within limits.
- Creating supporting points and structures.
- Ceasing to sabotage oneself.
- Bringing attention to others and to oneself into better balance.
- Physical activity as a means of grounding.

Second-order learning

- Appreciating the ordinary.
- Recognising that wanting to be special is a strategy to avoid being let down.
- Realising that being let down is something from the past and need not happen in the present.
- Seeing through the pattern of attraction and rejection.
- Recognising the power of attraction of sorrow and suffering, and seeing sorrow as a reality that can be relinquished after mourning.
- Realising that sarcasm and anger are ways of laying the blame on others for one's own inabilities.

Third-order learning

- Appreciating one's personal qualities such as idealism, empathy and the capacity for dealing with the diffculties of others
- Fulfilment in the here and now
- Feeling of oneness and contact with the universe.

Type 5

First-order learning

- Protecting one's space without isolating oneself.
- Dealing effectively with 'intrusive' people and with people's feelings.
- Attention to feelings; coming in contact with them, for instance through body work.
- Physical activity for grounding.
- Talking about feelings and anxieties.
- Revealing who one is and what one does, opening oneself up.
- Organising group meetings alongside bilateral contacts.
- 'Here and now' behaviour.
- Not intellectualising.

Second-order learning

- Noticing how one keeps knowledge, time, energy, thoughts, space and feelings for oneself, and what role compartmentalising work and life plays in this.
- Perceiving how one exercises control by setting up rules about what one gives, and to whom and when.
- Noticing that by withdrawing oneself, one yields to another the role of initiator and invites his invasion.
- Relinquishing control of time, energy, and so on.
- Noticing, and living with, the feelings and thought processes of others and dealing effectively with them.
- Noticing the difference between thinking and experiencing.
- Experiencing the difference between one's own feelings when someone is and someone is not present.
- Perceiving whether feelings are always painful; noticing pleasant feelings as well.

Third-order learning

- Trusting that there is always enough life energy.
- Trusting that the right knowledge is present at the right moment.
- Have close relationships with others without this costing energy.

Type 6

First-order learning

- Checking fantasies of calamity against reality.

- Thinking up ridiculously, exaggeratedly bad scenarios, so that one can see worst-case scenarios in perspective.
- Thinking up positive scenarios.
- Organising support.
- Undertaking physical activities and other action for emptying the head of energy.
- Acting as if there were a state of trust.
- Making choices and carrying them out in spite of doubt.
- Taking risks.
- Inventing possible alternative meanings in cases of mistrust.
- Looking for points of agreement when doubting authorities.
- Establishing one's own authority instead of making oneself dependent.
- Perceiving one's own successes and good performances and celebrating them.

Second-order learning

- Recognising fear signals and 'worst-case' thinking.
- Recognising when these ideas are real and when they arise only from one's imagination.
- Recognising the tendency to fight or to fly.
- Making a distinction between intuition and projection, realising that projections do not always correspond with objective reality.
- Investigating the function of projection.
- Noticing the tendency to experience success as greater vulnerability.
- Appreciating one's own strength and qualities.
- Contraphobic: asking oneself why one takes action.

Third-order learning

- Being courageous.
- Believing and trusting in oneself, in others, in the world and in the universe.
- Experiencing the feeling of being supported and carried by the universe.

Type 7

First-order learning

- Taking time to experience problems and painful matters.
- Looking at the positive and negative sides of a situation.
- Dealing with criticism and conflicts.
- Making choices, not taking on too much, doing one thing at a time.
- Taking responsibility.

- Organising matters well to ensure there is no gap when interest wanes.
- Doing less interesting jobs if necessary.

Second-order learning

- Perceiving mental evasion strategies.
- Recognising positive re-labelling, examining the facts.
- Investigating, when the attention goes to something attractive, whether this is a flight from something unpleasant.
- Seeing anger as a signal that something is being avoided.
- Registering the feeling of being trapped if there are limitations.
- Recognising one's own subtle feeling of superiority.
- Distinguishing ideas from reality.
- Evaluating the need for stimulation and options.

Third-order learning

- Making choices and carrying them out in the here and now; entering into genuine commitments
- Accepting the whole of life – both the sunny and the shadowy sides.

Type 8

First-order learning

- Listening to others, empathising with the standpoint and the feelings of the other, giving others space.
- Applying strategy and tactics; negotiating, particularly in conflicts.
- Signalling and posing questions instead of imposing one's own opinion and being confrontational.
- Moderating impact.
- Looking for points of agreement in differing standpoints, looking for compromises and win/win possibilities.
- Restraining impetuosity, considering the consequences before acting.
- Striving for effect in the long term instead of wanting to obtain results immediately.
- Postponing incentives and rewards.

Second-order learning

- Recognising one's role in negative situations.
- Examining vulnerability and weakness, feeling fear.
- Experiencing weaker feelings as an indication of progress.
- Realising one's influence on others and asking others about this.

- Realising that a compromise is not the same as capitulation.
- Noticing when one polarises and escalates conflict situations.
- Investigating why one breaks rules.
- Realising the function of extravagant behaviour and confrontation; real feelings can lie at the root here.
- Recognising when one's own boundaries or those of others are not being respected, and why not.
- Noticing why one stands up for the weak.
- Finding the positive in moderation.

Third-order learning

- Letting things come to one with the open-mindedness of a child without having to control them
- Seeing the truth that transcends the individual.

Type 9

First-order learning

- Learning to express anger and intuitive feelings.
- Asking oneself what one wants.
- Finding out what one does want by eliminating what one does not want.
- Practising taking up a standpoint, confronting, expressing oneself clearly.
- Constantly re-evaluating one's priorities.
- Saying no to new obligations when one has too much on one's plate already.
- Dealing positively with change.
- Being less evasive, tackling more conflicts and resolving them constructively.
- Choosing a focus, making plans with time schedules and deadlines, and aids for keeping oneself to them.
- Learning assertive leadership skills.

Second-order learning

- Noticing when one's attention is focused upon the expectations of others.
- Noticing when consideration of a subject from all sides slows things down.
- Recognising passive aggression, obstinacy and resistance and realising the underlying wish; investigating what other strategy could possibly realise that goal.

- Recognising which feelings are being repressed and what is being avoided by doing unimportant things.
- Accepting change as an unavoidable part of life.
- Recognising when one lays the blame on others if something goes wrong, instead of taking the responsibility for it oneself.
- Recognising how one determines whether or not one is in agreement with others.
- Not belittling oneself; finding one's own wishes important.
- Accepting that criticism does not have to be negative.

Third-order learning

- Love of oneself and self-esteem, and genuine love for others.
- Giving priority to one's own personal path of development and taking action on it.

Working in practice with type-specific themes

With all these themes, the right dose is always of first importance. Thus Type 1, from his type, is too perfectionist. His development goal, however, is not to abandon every form of perfectionism: he can continue to strive for ideals. In the same way Type 1, Type 2 and Type 9 want to become more conscious of their own needs. This is not to say, however, that they must strive for unlimited egoism. The concern is more to search for a better balance between their own needs and those of others. Type 4 and Type 7 develop themselves by coming more 'into the present'. No one, however, can live exclusively in the present. Without any form of future perspective, someone does not know if he is going upstairs or downstairs, or what the reason was for writing a note. Nor can people live without consciousness of the past – it is still handy to know what the client had asked for. In this example, we are concerned with establishing the correct dosage of 'living in the present'. It is the same with all themes. It is not about throwing one's own strong points overboard or turning round 180 degrees. The aim is to reach a better balance.

In Conclusion

....

If you want to study the enneagram in greater depth for your personal development, or if you wish, as a professional, to attain further proficiency in the field of the enneagram, there are the following possibilities.

- *Advanced reading.* In the Appendix you will find a list of books, together with indications of the authors' enneagram types. As is noted in Chapter 1, what every author writes is also perceived through the 'spectacles' of his or her own type, and every author naturally also has aspects of the enneagram which are of special personal interest. It can therefore be useful to read books by different authors with different types alongside one another.
- *Self-development.* There are many exercises in this book which you can do independently.
- *Training or coaching.* You can undergo training in the field of the enneagram to deepen your knowledge of it. You can also take part in training in the field of the general interventions in order to develop further as a person (see Chapter 17), or you may let yourself be coached individually.
- *Intercollegiate consultation.* If you want to work as a professional with the enneagram you will need this. Continuous learning, an aspect of professionalism, can be acquired by supervision, intervision (mutual supervision), coaching, peer review and advanced training.

A journey round the world begins with the first step. Everyone is where he is and has his own individual path of development. What matters is finding your own way and your own next step.

I wish you a fascinating and instructive journey.

Hannah Nathans
Nathans Aviesbureau voor Organisatie en Opleiding BV
Fransen van de Puttelaan 34–36
3707 EH Zeist
t +31 30 693.19.14
f +31 30 692.11.62
e office@nathans.nl

APPENDIX

Authors on the Enneagram, by Type

Type 1

- Richard Rohr. For example, Richard Rohr and Andreas Ebert, *Discovering the Enneagram: An Ancient Tool for a New Spiritual Journey*. New York: Cross Road Publishing, 2002.

Type 2

- Renee Baron. For example, Renee Baron and Elizabeth Wagele, *The Enneagram Made Easy: Discover the 9 Types of People*. San Francisco: HarperSanFrancisco, 1994.

Type 3

- Kathleen Hurley. For example, Kathleen V. Hurley and Theodore E. Donson, *What's My Type?* San Francisco: HarperSanFrancisco, 1992.
- Janet Levine, *The Enneagram Intelligences*. Westport, Conn/London: Bergin & Garvey, 1999.
- Howard A. Addison, *The Enneagram and Kabbalah: Reading Your Soul*. Woodstock, Vermont: Jewish Lights Publishing, 1998.
- Oscar David, *The Enneagram for Managers: Nine Different Perspectives on Managing People*. Lincoln: iUniverse.com, 1999.

Type 4

- Theodore E. Donson. For example, Kathleen V. Hurley and Theodore E. Donson, *What's My Type?* San Francisco: HarperSanFrancisco, 1992.
- Russ Hudson. For example, Don Richard Riso and Russ Hudson, *The Wisdom of the Enneagram: The Complete Guide to Psychological*

and Spiritual Growth for the Nine Personality Types. New York: Bantam Books, 1999.

Type 5

- Don R. Riso. For example, Don Richard Riso and Russ Hudson, *The Wisdom of the Enneagram: The Complete Guide to Psychological and Spiritual Growth for the Nine Personality Types*. New York: Bantam Books, 1999.
- Claudio Naranjo, *Character and Neurosis: An Integrative View*. Nevada City: Gateways/IDHHB Inc. Publishers, 1994.
- A.H. Almaas, *Facets of Unity: The Enneagram of Holy Ideas*. Berkeley, Calif.: Diamond Books, 1999.
- Elisabeth Wagele. For example, Renee Baron and Elizabeth Wagele, *The Enneagram Made Easy: Discover the 9 Types of People*. San Francisco: HarperSanFrancisco, 1994.

Type 6

- Helen Palmer. For example, Helen Palmer, *The Enneagram: Understanding Yourself and the Others in Your Life*. San Francisco: HarperSanFrancisco, 1991; *The Enneagram in Love and Work: Understanding Your Intimate and Business Relationships*. San Francisco: HarperSanFrancisco, 1996.
- David Daniels, in David Daniels and Virginia Price, *Stanford Enneagram Discovery, Inventory and Guide* (SEDIG). Redwood City, Calif: Mind Garden, 1997.

Type 7

- Michael Goldberg, *The 9 Ways Of Working*. New York: Marlowe & Co., 1996, 1999.

Type 8

- Karen Webb, *Principles of the Enneagram*. New York: HarperCollins, 1996.

Type 9

- Hannah Nathans, *The Enneagram At Work: Towards Personal Mastery and Social Intelligence*. Schiedam, the Netherlands: Scriptum, 2000 (in Dutch), 2003 (in English).

NOTES

Preface

1. Ecclesiastes 1:10.
2. Hannah Nathans, *Adviseren als tweede beroep: resultaat bereiken als adviseur*. Deventer, the Netherlands: Kluwer Bedrijfsinformatie, 1995 (2nd edition).
3. Mystic and ethicist writing in Hebrew (Padua 1707–Akko, Palestine 1746).
4. 'If I have seen further it is by standing on the shoulders of giants': Newton in a letter to his countryman and fellow physicist Robert Hooke, 5 February 1675.

Introduction

1. The 'narrative tradition' is a method of working whereby people give information about their own type. See Chapter 13 about panel interviews.
2. *Enneagram Monthly*, editors and publishers Andrea Isaacs and Jack Labanauskas, New York.
3. Interview series *Van de schoonheid en de troost*, VPRO, 2000.
4. John Naisbitt, *Megatrends – Ten New Directions Transforming Our Lives*. New York: Warner Books, 1982.
5. Harry Starren and Twan van de Kerkhof, *De 21 geboden van modern leiderschap*. Hilversum, the Netherlands: Teleac/NOT, 1999.
6. Peter M. Senge, *The Fifth Discipline: The Art & Practice of The Learning Organization*. New York: Doubleday, 1990.
7. Mathieu Weggeman, *Kennismanagement: inrichting en besturing van kennisintensieve organisaties*. Schiedam, the Netherlands: Scriptum, 1997.
8. Jos Kessels, *Het Corporate Curriculum* (inaugural speech). Leiden, the Netherlands: Rijksuniversiteit Leiden, 1996.
9. David Daniels and The Enneagram Business Alliance. Papers *The 9 ways of effective leadership*. Workshop Nederlands Studie Centrum, 1999.
10. Vincent Nolan, *The Innovator's Handbook: The Skills of Innovative*

Management: Problem Solving, Communication, and Teamwork. London: Sphere Books Ltd, 1987.

11. For an excellent explanation see Ken Wilber, *The Marriage of Sense and Soul: Integrating Science and Religion.* New York: Broadway Books, 1999.

12. Leon Wieseltier, *Kaddisj.* New York: Knopf, 1998.

Chapter 1. The Enneagram

1. Names are derived from Kathleen V. Hurley and Theodore E. Donson, *What's My Type?* San Francisco: HarperSanFrancisco, 1992; J. Jorritsma and W.J. van de Wetering, *Ontdek je sterke kanten.* Blaricum, the Netherlands: Andromeda; Janet Levine, *Nine Styles of Teaching: How Educators Teach.* Companion Guidebook to Video, 1996; Janet Levine, *The Enneagram Intelligences.* Westport, Conn./London: Bergin & Garvey, 1999; E. McInnis, 'The Enneagram and Christianity', Part 1. *Enneagram Monthly*, November 1998; E. McInnis, 'The Enneagram and Christianity', Part 2. *Enneagram Monthly*, December 1998; Helen Palmer, *The Enneagram: Understanding Yourself and the Others in Your Life.* San Francisco: HarperSanFrancisco, 1991; Helen Palmer, *The Enneagram in Love and Work: Understanding Your Intimate and Business Relationships.* San Francisco: HarperSanFrancisco, 1996; Don Richard Riso and Russ Hudson, *The Wisdom of the Enneagram: The Complete Guide to Psychological and Spiritual Growth for the Nine Personality Types.* New York: Bantam Books, 1999; Klausbernd Vollmar, *Das Enneagramm. Praktische Lebensbewaltigung mit Gurdjieffs Typenlehre.* Munich: Goldmann, 1995; Willem Jan van de Wetering, *Het enneagram als weg naar verandering: persoonlijkheids typologie.* Blaricum, the Netherlands: Andromeda, 1999.

2. By *interventions*, we mean anything that a professional can do to make the change process more effective and efficient, and to support individuals with their development. Part IV of this book deals largely with interventions.

3. See, for example, Robert Hargrove, *Masterful Coaching: Extraordinary Results by Impacting People and the Way They Think and Work Together.* San Francisco: Pfeiffer & Co., 1995; Peter M. Senge, *The Fifth Discipline: The Art & Practice of The Learning Organization.* New York: Doubleday, 1992; David Daniels and The Enneagram Business Alliance, Papers *The 9 ways of effective leadership.* Workshop Nederlands Studie Centrum, 1999; M. Bast Monaghan, 'Transformational Change in Organisations'. *Enneagram Monthly*, April 1999.

4. Flauttt and J. Richards, 'Enneagram and MBTI: Their Relationship and Complementary Use'. Presentation at IEA (International Enneagram Association) conference, 1999.

5. Statistical significance means that the chance that a certain event (in this case the combination of a certain enneagram type with a certain MBTI type) is coincidental is less than a certain percentage (usually 5 per cent). Statistical significance only says something about large numbers, and does not say anything about the possibility of an individual event. A statistical significance of 5 per cent does not mean that everyone with a certain enneagram will have the corresponding MBTI type.

6. See, for example, Renee Baron and Elizabeth Wagele, *The Enneagram Made Easy: Discover the 9 Types of People*. San Francisco: Harper-SanFrancisco, 1994.

7. When large quantities of data are correlated with each other, time and again 5 per cent of the combinations will be statistically significant, although that does not mean this has any significance.

8. Even more so considering the quality of the relevant research. The way to discover the personality type (with a questionnaire; see Chapter 10 for the value of questionnaires) didn't carry off the palm.

9. Geert Hofstede, *Cultures and Organizations – Software of the Mind*. New York: McGraw-Hill, 1996 (revised edition).

10. Jürgen Gündel, *Das Enneagramm: Neun Typen der Persönlichkeit*. Munich: Wilhelm Heyne Verlag, 1997.

11. See, for example, D. Shank, 'The Diamond Approach to the Holy Ideas'. *Enneagram Monthly*, February 1998.

12. Tom Condon, 'Steps to Change, Excerpts from The Dynamic Enneagram'. *Enneagram Monthly*, July/August 1999.

13. Rolph Pagano, *Wie is hier de baas? Een boek over leiderschap, doelgerichtheid en communicatie*. Schiedam, the Netherlands: Scriptum, 1999.

14. Wilbert Friederiechs, 'Franciscus achterna'. *Koorddanser*, March 2000. St Francis of Assisi lived from 1181/2 until 1226.

15. David Daniels, 'Nature and Nurture: On Acquiring a Type'. *Enneagram Monthly*, March 2000.

16. *Winkler Prins Encyclopedie*, 6th edition, part 13, Amsterdam/Brussels, 1952.

17. Dirk van Delft, 'De wereld om Mekka'. *NRC Handelsblad*, Wetenschap en Onderwijsbijlage, 8 January 2000.

Chapter 2. The Enneagram in Organisations

1. Ruth Benedict, *Patterns of Culture*. Boston: Houghton Mifflin, 1989.

2. See Helen Palmer, *The Enneagram Advantage: Putting the 9 Personality Types to Work in the Office*. New York: Three Rivers Press, 1998.

3. *ibid.*

4. David Daniels and The Enneagram Business Alliance. Papers *The 9 ways of effective leadership*. Workshop Nederlands Studie Centrum, 1999.

Chapter 3. The Enneagram as a Process Description

1. J.G. Bennett, *Enneagram Studies*. York Beach, Maine: Samuel Weiser, 1983.
2. J.E. Piederiet, *Enneagram en outplacement*. Rotterdam: Van Ede & Partners, 2000.
3. See, for example, Sterling Doughty, 'The Enneagram of Cooking Perfect Rice – The White Cloud Way'. *Enneagram Monthly*, April 1999; or P.D. Ouspensky, *In Search of the Miraculous: Fragments of an Unknown Teaching*. San Diego, Calif.: Harcourt Brace, 1974.
4. P.D. Ouspensky, *The Fourth Way: An Arrangement by Subject of Verbatim Extracts from the Records of Ouspensky's Meetings in London and New York, 1921–46*. New York: Random House, 1971.
5. See, for example, S. de Vries, *Hindoeïsme voor beginners*. Amsterdam: Forum, 1996.
6. Z'ev ben Shimon Halevi, *Adam and the Kabbalistic Tree*. York Beach, Maine: Red Wheel/Samuel Weiser, 1990 (reprint edition); *281 Zen Koans With Answers*. York Beach, Maine: Samuel Weiser, 1990.
7. See, for example, *I Tjing, het boek der veranderingen*. Deventer, the Netherlands: Ankh-Hermes, 1953.
8. See, for example, Martin Palmer, *Yin and Yang: Understanding the Chinese Philosophy of Opposites and How to Apply It to Your Everyday Life*. London: Piatkus Books, 1998.
9. See, for example, Bernhard Delfgaauw, *Beknopte geschiedenis van de wijsbegeerte: van Thales tot Lyotard*. Baarn, the Netherlands: Wereldvenster, 1965.
10. E. McInnis, 'The Enneagram and Christianity', Part 1. *Enneagram Monthly*, November 1998.

Chapter 4. History of the Enneagram

1. Woody van Olffen and Arjen van Witteloostuijn, 'Marktgerichte universiteit levert niets op'. *NRC Handelsblad*, 5 July 1999.
2. J.G. Bennett, *Enneagram Studies*. York Beach, Maine: Samuel Weiser, 1983.
3. Prof. dr. F. M. Th. Böhl writes, among other things: 'In Genesis 11:28 the home town of Abraham is called "Ur of Chaldea", as this town was also in the region that from 1200 BC was considered part of Chaldea. For the era of the patriarchs this name is an anachronism.' Böhl, 1949, p. 696.
4. Fr. Michell Pacwa SJ, 'Tell Me Who I Am, O Enneagram'. *Christian Research Journal*, Fall 1991.
5. L. Nygaard, 'The Origin of the Enneagram'. *Enneagram Monthly*, March/April 1999.

6. *ibid.*
7. *Plato, schrijver, teksten gekozen en vertaald door Gerard Koolschijn* [Plato, writer, texts selected and translated by Gerard Koolschijn], Amsterdam: Bert Bakker, 1998.
8. Anselm Grün, *Der Himmel beginnt in Dir. Das Wissen der Wüstenväter für Heute.* Freiburg, Germany: Herder, 1999.
9. G.I. Gurdjieff, *Meetings With Remarkable Men.* New York: E.P. Dutton, 1991.
10. James Moore, 'Gurdjieff, The Man and the Literature'. *Gurdjieff International Review*, Internet 2000.
11. Gurdjieff, *op. cit.*
12. Among others Susan Zannos, *Human Types: Essence and the Enneagram.* York Beach, Maine: Samuel Weiser, 1997; Klausbernd Vollmar, *Das Enneagramm. Praktische Lebensbewaltigung mit Gurdjieffs Typenlehre.* Munich: Goldmann, 1995.
13. E. McInnis, 'The Enneagram and Christianity', Part 1. *Enneagram Monthly*, November 1998; E. McInnis, 'The Enneagram and Christianity', Part 2. *Enneagram Monthly*, December 1998.
14. See, for example, Laleh Bakhtiar,*Traditional Psychoethics and Personality Paradigm* (*God's Will Be Done*, Vol. I). Chicago: Kazi Publications, 1994; Laleh Bakhtiar, *Moral Healer's Handbook: The Psychology of Spiritual Chivalry* (*God's Will Be Done*, Vol. II). Chicago: Kazi Publications, 1994; Laleh Bakhtiar, *Moral Healing Through the Most Beautiful: The Practice of Spiritual Chivalry* (*God's Will Be Done*, Vol. III). Chicago: Kazi Publications, 1994.
15. Helen Palmer, *The Enneagram: Understanding Yourself and the Others in Your Life.* San Francisco: HarperSanFrancisco, 1991; Helen Palmer, *The Enneagram in Love and Work: Understanding Your Intimate and Business Relationships.* San Francisco: HarperSanFrancisco, 1996.
16. Oscar Ichazo. *Interviews With Oscar Ichazo.* New York: Arica Institute, 1982.
17. L. Nygaard, 'The Origin of the Enneagram'. *Enneagram Monthly*, March/April 1999.
18. *ibid.*
19. Alexander Roos, *Alchemie en mystiek.* Cologne: Taschen/Librero, 1997.
20. *ibid.*
21. Oscar Ichazo. *op. cit.*
22. See, for example, Claudio Naranjo, *Character and Neurosis: An Integrative View.* Nevada City: Gateways/IDHHB Inc. Publishers, 1994.
23. Helen Palmer, *The Enneagram: Understanding Yourself and the Others in Your Life.* San Francisco: HarperSanFrancisco, 1991; Helen Palmer, *The Enneagram in Love and Work: Understanding Your Intimate and Business Relationships.* San Francisco: HarperSanFrancisco, 1996.
24. See, for example, Don Richard Riso and Russ Hudson, *The Wisdom of*

the Enneagram: The Complete Guide to Psychological and Spiritual Growth for the Nine Personality Types. New York: Bantam Books, 1999.

25. See, for example, Kathleen V. Hurley and Theodore E. Donson, What's My Type? San Francisco: HarperSanFrancisco, 1992.

26. See, for example, Richard Rohr and Andreas Ebert, Das Enneagramm. Die 9 Gesichter der Seele. Munich: Claudius Verlag, 2002.

Chapter 5. The Centres

1. See, for example, P.D. Ouspensky, The Fourth Way: An Arrangement by Subject of Verbatim Extracts from the Records of Ouspensky's Meetings in London and New York, 1921–46. New York: Random House, 1971.

2. P.D. Ouspensky, The Psychology of Man's Possible Evolution. New York: Random House, 1973 (2nd edition).

3. Helen Palmer (ed.), Inner Knowing: Consciousness, Creativity, Insight, and Intuition (New Consciousness Reader). New York: Tarcher/ Putnam, 1999.

4. P.D. Ouspensky, The Fourth Way: An Arrangement by Subject of Verbatim Extracts from the Records of Ouspensky's Meetings in London and New York, 1921–46. New York: Random House, 1971.

5. Kathleen V. Hurley and Theodore E. Donson, What's My Type? San Francisco: HarperSanFrancisco, 1992.

6. Kathleen Hurley and Theodore Donson. 'The Enneagram: Key to Opening the Heart'. Enneagram Monthly, May 1998; Don Richard Riso and Russ Hudson, 'The Imbalances of the Centers'. Enneagram Monthly, November/December 1999 and January 2000.

7. Helen Palmer, The Enneagram: Understanding Yourself and the Others in Your Life. San Francisco: HarperSanFrancisco, 1991; Helen Palmer, The Enneagram in Love and Work: Understanding Your Intimate and Business Relationships. San Francisco: HarperSanFrancisco, 1996.

8. See, for example, C. Scott Littleton (ed.), Eastern Wisdom: An Illustrated Guide to the Religions and Philosophies of the East. New York: Henry Holt, 1999.

Chapter 6. The Type Descriptions

1. Psychologist René Diekstra once asked during a lecture which people might be considered crazy: coach potatoes watching news on television and seeing starved children, acts of war, corpses in a variety of conditions, torn-off limbs and awful train accidents; or people who are too neurotic to see such misery. Diekstra's conclusion was that what we consider 'normal' actually involves the exclusion of consciousness.

2. Tom Condon, 'In a Deep Trance'. *Enneagram Monthly*, June 1998.
3. See, for example, Piet Vroon, *De tranen van de krokodil: over de snelle evolutie van onze hersenen*. Baarn, the Netherlands: Ambo, 1989.
4. Peter M. Senge, *The Fifth Discipline: The Art & Practice of The Learning Organization*. New York: Doubleday, 1990.
5. M. Bast Monaghan, 'The Idealized Image and Stress'. *Enneagram Monthly*, July/August 1999.
6. P. O'Hanrahan, 'Working with the Instincts and Sub-types', Part 1. *Enneagram Monthly*, July/August 1998.
7. Katherine Chernick Fauvre, *Enneagram Instinctual Subtypes: The 3 Drives That Fuel The Passion Of Enneagram Type*. Enneagram Explorations, 1995, rev. 1997.
8. Based on P. O'Hanrahan, 'Working with the Instincts and Sub-types', Part 1. *Enneagram Monthly*, July/August 1998; Katherine Chernick Fauvre, *Enneagram Instinctual Subtypes: The 3 Drives That Fuel The Passion Of Enneagram Type*. Enneagram Explorations, 1995, rev. 1997.
9. Karen Webb, *Principles of the Enneagram*. New York: HarperCollins, 1996.
10. L. Nygaard, 'The Origin of the Enneagram'. *Enneagram Monthly*, March and April 1999.
11. See, for example, Claudio Naranjo, *Character and Neurosis: An Integrative View*. Nevada City: Gateways/IDHHB Inc. Publishers, 1994; Don Richard Riso, *Understanding the Enneagram: The Practical Guide to Personality Types*. Boston: Houghton Mifflin, 1990.
12. See, for example, David Daniels, 'The Core Dilemmas of the Nine Types: A Key to Effective Therapy'. *Enneagram TALK*, August 1998; D. Shank, 'The Diamond Approach to the Holy Ideas'. *Enneagram Monthly*, February 1998; A.H. Almaas, *Facets of Unity: The Enneagram of Holy Ideas*. Berkeley, Calif.: Diamond Books, 1999.
13. I. Briggs Myers and M.H. McCaulley, *A Guide to the Development and Use of the Myers Briggs Type Indicator*. Palo Alto, Calif.: Consulting Psychologists Press, 1985.
14. Michael J. Kirton (ed.), *Adaptors and Innovators: Styles of Creativity and Problem-Solving*. London: Routledge, 1989.
15. Michael J. Kirton and P.P. van der Molen. *Programma en handleiding voor de licentietraining*. Amsterdam: Chain, 1990.
16. If you want to cancel out this stereotyping by reading more books by different authors, the following are suitable: A.H. Almaas, *Facets of Unity: The Enneagram of Holy Ideas*. Berkeley, Calif.: Diamond Books, 1999; Katherine Chernick Fauvre, *Enneagram Instinctual Subtypes: The 3 Drives That Fuel The Passion Of Enneagram Type*. Enneagram Explorations, 1995, rev. 1997; Kathleen V. Hurley and Theodore E. Donson, *What's My Type?* San Francisco: HarperSanFrancisco, 1992; Janet Levine, *The Enneagram Intelligences*. Westport, Conn./London: Bergin & Garvey, 1999; Claudio Naranjo, *Character and Neurosis: An*

Integrative View. Nevada City: Gateways/IDHHB Inc. Publishers, 1994; P. O'Hanrahan, 'Working with the Instincts and Sub-types', Part 1. *Enneagram Monthly*, July/August, 1998; Helen Palmer, *The Enneagram: Understanding Yourself and the Others in Your Life*. San Francisco: HarperSanFrancisco, 1991; Helen Palmer, *The Enneagram in Love and Work: Understanding Your Intimate and Business Relationships*. San Francisco: HarperSanFrancisco, 1996; Helen Palmer, *The Enneagram Advantage: Putting the 9 Personality Types to Work*. New York: Three Rivers Press, 1998; Don Richard Riso, *Understanding the Enneagram: The Practical Guide to Personality Types*. Boston: Houghton Mifflin, 1990; Don Richard Riso and Russ Hudson, *The Wisdom of the Enneagram: The Complete Guide to Psychological and Spiritual Growth for the Nine Personality Types*. New York: Bantam Books, 1999; Richard Rohr and Andreas Ebert, *Das Enneagramm. Die 9 Gesichter der Seele*. Munich: Claudius Verlag, 2002; Karen Webb, *Principle of the enneagram*. New York: Harper Collins, 1996.

17. Benjamin Disraeli (1804–1881).
18. David Daniels and Virginia Price, *Stanford Enneagram Discovery, Inventory and Guide (SEDIG)*. Redwood City, Calif.: Mind Garden, 1997.

Chapter 7. The Heart Types

1. The description of the sub-types of the nine types is also based on Katherine Chernick Fauvre, *Enneagram Instinctual Subtypes: The 3 Drives That Fuel The Passion Of Enneagram Type*. Enneagram Explorations, 1995, rev. 1997; P. O'Hanrahan, 'Working With The Instincts and Sub-types', Part 1. *Enneagram Monthly*, July/August 1998; Helen Palmer, *The Enneagram: Understanding Yourself and the Others in Your Life*. San Francisco: HarperSanFrancisco, 1991; Helen Palmer, *The Enneagram in Love and Work: Understanding Your Intimate and Business Relationships*. San Francisco: HarperSanFrancisco, 1996.

Chapter 10. The Nature of Consciousness

1. Tom Condon, 'In a Deep Trance'. *Enneagram Monthly*, June 1998.
2. Stephen Wolinsky, with contributions by Margaret O. Ryan, *Trances People Live: Healing Approaches in Quantum Psychology*. Falls Village, Conn.: The Bramble Company, 1991.
3. Karlfried Graf von Dürckheim, *Meditieren, wozu und wie. Die Wende zum Initiatischen*. Freiburg, Germany: Herder, 2001.
4. Anthony Campbell, *Seven States of Consciousness: A Vision of Possibilities Suggested by the Teaching of Maharishi Mahesh Yogi*. New York: HarperCollins, 1974.

5.   Ken Wilber, *The Marriage of Sense and Soul: Integrating Science and Religion*. New York: Broadway Books, 1999.

Chapter 11. Anatomy of Consciousness

1.   For more information about the tree of life, see for example Hannah Nathans, 'The Enneagram and the Tree of Life: States of Consciousness'. *Enneagram Monthly*, February 2000.
     Good introductory texts include (to name only a few): Perle Besserman, *The Shambhala Guide to Kabbalah and Jewish Mysticism*. Boston: Shambala, 1997; Z'ev ben Shimon Halevi, *Introduction to Cabalah*. York Beach, Maine: Samuel Weiser, 1972; Aryeh Kaplan, *Meditation and Kabbalah*. York Beach, Maine: Samuel Weiser, 1982; Daniel C. Matt, The *Essential Kabbalah: The Heart of Jewish Mysticism*. Book Sales, 1997.
2.   A.H. Almaas, *Facets of Unity: The Enneagram of Holy Ideas*. Berkeley, Calif.: Diamond Books, 1999.
3.   See, for example, Howard A. Addison, *The Enneagram and Kabbalah: Reading Your Soul*. Woodstock, Vt.: Jewish Lights Publishing, 1998.
4.   Robert Assagioli, *Transpersonal Development*. Thorsons Pub., 1991.
5.   Maslow differentiated five levels, from physiological needs to self-actualisation.
6.   Robert Assagioli, *The Act of Will*. Baltimore: Penguin Books, 1973.
7.   Steven A. Fisdel, *The Practice of Kabbalah: Meditation in Judaism*. Northvale, N.J.: Jason Aronson Inc., 1996.
8.   More about Rumi in Mojdeh Bayat and Mohammad Alia Jamnia, *Tales from the Land of the Sufis*. Boston/London: Shambhala Publications, 1994.
9.   Eric van Praag, *Spiritueel leiderschap*. Deventer, the Netherlands: Kluwer, 1996.

Chapter 12. Working With the Levels of Consciousness

1.   See, for example, Hal Stone and Sidia Winkelman, *Embracing Ourselves*. Novato, Calif.: New World Library, 1985.
2.   Daniel J. Levinson, *The Season's of a Man's Life*. New York: Ballantine Books, 1986 (reissue edition).

Chapter 13. Determining the Type

1.   www.intl-enneagram-assn.org/ethics.html.
2.   Tom Condon, Jack Labanauskas and Liz Wagele, 'Questions and Answers'. *Enneagram Monthly*, March 1999.

3.   David Daniels and Virginia Price, *Stanford Enneagram Discovery, Inventory and Guide (SEDIG)*. Redwood City, Calif.: Mind Garden, 1997.

Chapter 14. Working Professionally with Others

1.   C.B. Truax and R.R. Carkhuv, *Towards Effective Counselling and Psychotherapy*. Chicago: Aldine Publishing Company, 1967.
2.   *ibid.*
3.   See, for example, Hannah Nathans, *Adviseren als tweede beroep: resultaat bereiken als adviseur*. Deventer, the Netherlands: Kluwer Bedrijfsinformatie, 1995 (2nd edition).

Chapter 16. Self-management and Working with Others

1.   In early gnostic Christianity, 'metanoia' meant the awakening of a common intuition and a direct knowledge of God. Peter M. Senge, *The Fifth Discipline: The Art & Practice of The Learning Organization*. New York: Doubleday, 1992.

Chapter 17. General Development Interventions

1.   See also, for example, Jürgen Gündel, *Das Enneagramm: Neun Typen der Persönlichkeit*. Munich: Wilhelm Heyne Verlag, 1997.
2.   Daniel Ofman, *Bezieling en kwaliteit in organisaties*. Utrecht, the Netherlands: Servire, 1992.
3.   Gareth Morgan, *Creative Organisation Theory: A Resourcebook*. Newsbury Park, Calif.: Sage, 1989.
4.   Shakti Gawain, *Creative Visualization: Use the Power of Your Imagination to Create What You Want in Your Life*. Novato, Calif.: New World Library, 2002.
5.   See, for example, Timothy Gallwey and Bob Kriegel, *Inner Skiing: Mastering the Slopes Through Mind/Body Awareness*. New York: Bantam Books, 1992 (reissue edition); also *Inner Golf, Inner Tennis*, etc. See also Hannah Nathans, *Adviseren als tweede beroep: resultaat bereiken als adviseur*. Deventer, the Netherlands: Kluwer Bedrijfsinformatie, 1995 (2nd edition) in Chapter 4.2, 'De kracht van de mentale voorstelling'; Hannah Nathans, 'Het gebruik van imaginatie bij visieontwikkeling; Opleiders in organisaties'. *Capita Selecta*, 32. Deventer, the Netherlands: Kluwer Bedrijfsinformatie, 1997.
6.   Jürgen Gündel, *Das Enneagramm*. Munich: Wilhelm Heyne Verlag, 1997.

7. R.F.W. Diekstra and W.F.M. Dassen. *Ik kan denken/voelen wat ik wil*. Lisse, the Netherlands: Swets & Zeitlinger, 1985.
8. After David A. Cooper, *Kabbalah Meditation: Judaism's Ancient System for Mystical Exploration Through Meditation & Contemplation*, audio cassette. Sounds True, 1997.
9. An exercise of Thomas Condon on the Internet.
10. Robert Assagioli, *Psychosynthesis: A Manual of Principles and Techniques*. New York: HarperCollins, 1990.
11. With thanks to Gila Nieuwenhuizen-Gerzon.
12. David A. Cooper, *Kabbalah Meditation: Judaism's Ancient System for Mystical Exploration Through Meditation & Contemplation*, audio cassette. Sounds True, 1997.
13. See, for example, Ralph Bakker and Roy Martina, *Vitaliteit! Geheimen van mensen die bruisen van energie*. Baarn, the Netherlands: Bigot & Van Rossum, 1993.
14. See, for example, John F. Thie, *Touch for Health: A Practical Guide to Natural Healing Using Acupressure Touch and Massage to Improve Postural Balance and Reduce Physical and Mental Pain and Tension*. Princeton: DeVorss & Co., 1979.
15. Helen Palmer, *Intuition Training with Helen Palmer*, audio tape. Boston: Shambhala Publications.
16. For more koans, see Yoel Hoffmann, *The Sound of the One Hand*. New York: Bantam Books, 1975.
17. See, for example, C. Klein, *How To Forgive When You Can't Forget*. New York: Berkeley Books, 1995.
18. E. Ginsburg, Elat Chayyim Workshop, Summer 1999.
19. See, for example, Alexander Lowen, *Bioenergetics*. New York: Putnam, 1975.
20. H. Zimmer and C.G. Jung. *Der Weg zum Selbst*. Zurich: Aasscher Verlag.
21. Hal Stone and Sidia Winkelman. *Embracing Ourselves*. Novato, Calif.: New World Library, 1985.
22. For exercises see, for example, Marcia Emery, *Dr. Marcia Emery's Intuition Workbook: An Expert's Guide to Unlocking the Wisdom of Your Subconscious Mind*. Englewood Cliffs, N.J.: Prentice-Hall Press, 1994; K. Hafkamp, *Intuïtieve managementvaardigheden*. Amsterdam/Antwerp: Contact, 1996; L. Keen and A. de Waard, *Intuïtie in je vingers*. Deventer, the Netherlands: Ankh-Hermes, 1994; Nancy Rosanoff, *Intuition Workout: A Practical Guide to Discovering and Developing Your Inner Knowing*. Boulder Creek, Colo.: Aslan, 1988; Marilee Zdenek, *The Right Brain Experience*. New York: McGraw-Hill, 1983.
23. D.W. Vaags, 'Where and How Do New Ideas Come From?' First European Conference on Creativity and Innovation, 1987.
24. See, for example, Patricia Garfield, *Creative Dreaming*. New York: Fireside, 1995 (updated edition), or Robert Moss, *Conscious Dreaming:*

A Spiritual Path for Everyday Life. New York: Three Rivers Press, 1996.

25. Hannah Nathans, *Adviseren als tweede beroep: resultaat bereiken als adviseur*. Deventer, the Netherlands: Kluwer Bedrijfsinformatie, 1995 (2nd edition).

26. Tom Condon, 'Steps to Change, Excerpts from The Dynamic Enneagram'. *Enneagram Monthly*, July/August 1999.

LITERATURE

Addison, Howard A., 1998. *The Enneagram and Kabbalah: Reading Your Soul*. Woodstock, Vermont: Jewish Lights Publishing.

Almaas, A.H., 1999. *Facets of Unity: The Enneagram of Holy Ideas*. Berkeley, Calif.: Diamond Books.

Assagioli, Robert, 1973. *The Act of Will*. Baltimore: Penguin Books.

Assagioli, Robert, 1990. *Psychosynthesis: A Manual of Principles and Techniques*. New York: HarperCollins.

Assagioli, Robert, 1991. *Transpersonal Development*. Thorsons Pub.

Bakhtiar, Laleh, 1994a. *Traditional Psychoethics and Personality Paradigm* (*God's Will Be Done*, Vol. I). Chicago: Kazi Publications.

Bakhtiar, Laleh, 1994b. *Moral Healer's Handbook: The Psychology of Spiritual Chivalry* (*God's Will Be Done*, Vol. II). Chicago: Kazi Publications.

Bakhtiar, Laleh, 1994c. *Moral Healing Through the Most Beautiful: The Practice of Spiritual Chivalry* (*God's Will Be Done*, Vol. III). Chicago: Kazi Publications.

Bakhtiar, Laleh. 'The Interfaith Enneagram.' *Enneagram Monthly*, February 1998.

Bakker, Ralph, and Roy Martina, 1993. *Vitaliteit! Geheimen van mensen die bruisen van energie*. Baarn, the Netherlands: Bigot & Van Rossum.

Baron, Renee, and Elizabeth Wagele, 1994. *The Enneagram Made Easy: Discover the 9 Types of People*. San Francisco: HarperSanFrancisco.

Bast Monaghan, M., 1999a. 'Tranformational Change in Organisations.' *Enneagram Monthly*, April 1999.

Bast Monaghan, M., 1999b. 'The Idealized Image and Stress.' *Enneagram Monthly*, July/August 1999.

Bayat, Mojdeh, and Mohammad Alia Jamnia, 1994. *Tales from the Land of the Sufis*. Boston/London: Shambhala Publications.

Benedict, Ruth, 1989. *Patterns of Culture*. Boston: Houghton Mifflin.

Bennett, J.G., 1983. *Enneagram Studies*. York Beach, Maine: Samuel Weiser.

Besserman, Perle, 1997. *The Shambhala Guide to Kabbalah and Jewish Mysticism*. Boston: Shambala.

Böhl, F.M.Th., 1949. 'Chaldeeën' in *Winkler Prins Encyclopedie*. Part 5. Amsterdam/Brussels: Elsevier (6th edition).

Briggs Myers, Isabel, and Mary H. McCaulley, 1985. *A Guide to the Development and Use of the Myers Briggs Type Indicator*. Palo Alto: Consulting Psychologists Press.

Campbell, Anthony, 1974. *Seven States of Consciousness: A Vision of Possibilities Suggested by the Teaching of Maharishi Mahesh Yogi.* New York: HarperCollins.

Chernick Fauvre, Katherine, 1995. *Enneagram Instinctual Subtypes: The 3 Drives That Fuel The Passion Of Enneagram Type.* Enneagram Explorations 1995, revised 1997.

Condon, Tom, 1998. 'In a Deep Trance.' *Enneagram Monthly*, June 1998.

Condon, Tom, 1999. 'Steps to Change, Excerpts from The Dynamic Enneagram.' *Enneagram Monthly*, July/August 1999.

Condon, Tom, Jack Labanauskas and Liz Wagele, 1999. 'Questions and Answers.' *Enneagram Monthly*, March 1999.

Cooper, David A., 1997. *Kabbalah Meditation: Judaism's Ancient System for Mystical Exploration Through Meditation & Contemplation.* Audio cassette. Sounds True.

Daniels, David, 1998. 'The Core Dilemmas of the Nine Types: A Key to Effective Therapy.' Enneagram talk, August 1998.

Daniels, David, 2000. 'Nature and Nurture: On Acquiring a Type.' *Enneagram Monthly*, March 2000.

Daniels, David, and Virginia Price, 1997. *Stanford Enneagram Discovery, Inventory and Guide (SEDIG).* Redwood City, Calif.: Mind Garden.

Daniels, David, and The Enneagram Business Alliance, 1999. *Papers The 9 ways of effective leadership.* Workshop Nederlands Studie Centrum 1999.

David, Oscar, 1999. *The Enneagram for Managers: Nine Different Perspectives on Managing People.* Lincoln: iUniverse.com

Delfgaauw, Bernhard, 1965. *Beknopte geschiedenis van de wijsbegeerte: van Thales tot Lyotard.* Baarn, the Netherlands: Wereldvenster.

Delft, Dirk van, 2000. 'De wereld om Mekka.' *NRC Handelsblad*, Wetenschap en Onderwijsbijlage, 8 January 2000.

Diekstra, R.F.W., and W.F.M. Dassen, 1985. *Ik kan denken/voelen wat ik wil.* Lisse, the Netherlands: Swets & Zeitlinger.

Doughty, Sterling, 1999. 'The Enneagram of Cooking Perfect Rice – The White Cloud Way.' *Enneagram Monthly*, April 1999.

Dürckheim, Karlfried Graf von, 2001. *Meditieren, wozu und wie. Die Wende zum Initiatischen.* Freiburg, Germany: Herder.

Emery, Marcia, 1994. *Dr. Marcia Emery's Intuition Workbook: An Expert's Guide to Unlocking the Wisdom of Your Subconscious Mind.* Englewood Cliffs: Prentice-Hall Press.

Fisdel, Steven A., 1996. *The Practice of Kabbalah: Meditation in Judaism.* Northvale, New Jersey: Jason Aronson, Inc.

Flautt, T. and J. Richards, 1999. 'Enneagram and MBTI: Their Relationship and Complementary Use.' Presentation to the 1999 IEA (International Enneagram Association) conference.

Friederiechs, Wilbert. 'Franciscus achterna.' *Koorddanser*, March 2000.

Gallwey, Timothy, and Bob Kriegel, 1992. *Inner Skiing: Mastering the Slopes*

Through Mind/Body Awareness. New York, Bantam Books (reissue edition).

Garfield, Patricia, 1995. *Creative Dreaming*. New York: Fireside (updated edition).

Gawain, Shakti, 2002. *Creative Visualization: Use the Power of Your Imagination to Create What You Want in Your Life*. Novato, Calif.: New World Library.

Ginsburg, Elliot, 1999. Elat Chayyim Workshop, Summer 1999.

Goldberg, Michael, 1996. *Getting Your Boss's Number: And Many Other Ways to Use the Enneagram at Work*. Metamorphous.

Grün, Anselm, 1999. *Der Himmel beginnt in Dir. Das Wissen der Wüstenväter für Heute*. Freiburg, Germany: Herder.

Gündel, Jürgen, 1997. *Das Enneagramm: Neun Typen der Persönlichkeit*. Munich: Wilhelm Heyne Verlag.

Gurdjieff, G.I., 1991. *Meetings With Remarkable Men*. New York: E.P. Dutton.

Hafkamp, K., 1996. *Intuïtieve managementvaardigheden*. Amsterdam/Antwerp: Contact.

Halevi, Z'ev ben Shimon, 1972. *Introduction to Cabalah*. York Beach, Maine: Samuel Weiser.

Halevi, Z'ev ben Shimon, 1990. *Adam and the Kabbalistic Tree*. York Beach, Maine: Samuel Weiser.

Hargrove, Robert, 1995. *Masterful Coaching: Extraordinary Results by Impacting People and the Way They Think and Work Together*. San Francisco: Pfeiffer & Co.

Hoffmann, Yoel, 1975. *The Sound of the One Hand*. New York: Bantam Books.

Hofstede, Geert, 1991. *Allemaal andersdenkenden – omgaan met cultuurverschillen*. Amsterdam: Contact.

Hurley, Kathleen V. , and Theodore E. Donson, 1992. *What's My Type?* San Francisco: HarperSanFrancisco.

Hurley, Kathleen, and Theodore Donson, 1998. 'The Enneagram: Key to Opening the Heart.' *Enneagram Monthly*, May 1998.

Ichazo, Oscar, 1982. *Interviews With Oscar Ichazo*. New York: Arica Institute.

I Tjing, het boek der veranderingen. Deventer, the Netherlands: Ankh-Hermes (1953).

Jorritsma, J., and W.J. van de Wetering. *Ontdek je sterke kanten*. Blaricum, the Netherlands: Andromeda.

Kaplan, Aryeh, 1982. *Meditation and Kabbalah*. York Beach, Maine: Samuel Weiser.

Keen, L., and A. de Waard, 1994. *Intuïtie in je vingers*. Deventer: Ankh-Hermes.

Kessels, Jozef, 1996. *Het Corporate Curriculum* (inaugural speech). Leiden: Rijksuniversiteit Leiden.

Kirton, Michael J. (ed.), 1989. *Adaptors and Innovators: Styles of Creativity and Problem-Solving*. London: Routledge.

Kirton, M.J., and P.P. van der Molen, 1990. *Programma en handleiding voor de licentietraining*. Amsterdam: Chain.

Klein, C., 1995. *How To Forgive When You Can't Forget*. New York: Berkeley Books.

Levine, Janet, 1996. *Nine Styles of Teaching: How Educators Teach*. Companion guidebook to video.

Levine, Janet, 1999. *The Enneagram Intelligences*. Westport, Conn./London: Bergin & Garvey.

Levinson, Daniel J., 1986. *The Season's of a Man's Life*. New York: Ballantine Books (reissue edition).

Lowen, Alexander, 1975. *Bioenergetics*. New York: Putnam.

Matt, Daniel C., 1997. *The Essential Kabbalah: The Heart of Jewish Mysticism*. Book Sales.

McInnis, E., 1998a. 'The Enneagram and Christianity', Part 1. *Enneagram Monthly*, November 1998.

McInnis, E., 1988b. 'The Enneagram and Christianity', Part 2, *Enneagram Monthly*, December 1998.

Moore, James, 2000. 'Gurdjieff, The Man and the Literature.' *Gurdjieff International Review*, Internet 2000.

Morgan, Gareth, 1989. *Creative Organisation Theory: A Resourcebook*. Newsbury Park, Calif.: Sage.

Moss, Robert, 1996. *Conscious Dreaming: A Spiritual Path for Everyday Life*. New York: Three Rivers Press.

Naisbitt, John, 1982. *Megatrends – Ten New Directions Transforming Our Lives*. New York: Warner Books.

Naranjo, Claudio, 1994. *Character and Neurosis: An Integrative View*. Nevada City: Gateways/IDHHB Inc. Publishers.

Nathans, Hannah, 1995. *Adviseren als tweede beroep: resultaat bereiken als adviseur*. Deventer, the Netherlands: Kluwer Bedrijfsinformatie (2nd edition).

Nathans, Hannah, 1997. 'Het gebruik van imaginatie bij visie-ontwikkeling; Opleiders in organisaties.' *Capita Selecta*, 32. Deventer, the Netherlands: Kluwer Bedrijfsinformatie.

Nathans, Hannah, 2000. 'The Enneagram and the Tree of Life: States of Consciousness.' *Enneagram Monthly*, February 2000.

Nolan, Vincent, 1987. *The Innovator's Handbook: The Skills of Innovative Management: Problem Solving, Communication, and Teamwork*. Sphere Books Ltd.

Nygaard, L., 1999. 'The Origin of the Enneagram.' *Enneagram Monthly*, March/April 1999.

Ofman, Daniel, 1992. *Bezieling en kwaliteit in organisaties*. Utrecht, the Netherlands: Servire.

O'Hanrahan, Peter, 1998. 'Working with the Instincts and Sub-types.' Part 1. *Enneagram Monthly*, July/August 1998.

Olffen, Woody van, and Arjen van Witteloostuijn, 1999. 'Marktgerichte universiteit levert niets op.' *NRC Handelsblad*, 5 July 1999.

Ouspensky, P.D., 1971. *The Fourth Way: An Arrangement by Subject of*

Verbatim Extracts from the Records of Ouspensky's Meetings in London and New York, 1921–46. New York: Random House.

Ouspensky, P.D., 1973. *The Psychology of Man's Possible Evolution*. New York: Random House (2nd edition).

Ouspensky, P.D., 1974. *In Search of the Miraculous: Fragments of an Unknown Teaching*. San Diego: Harcourt Brace.

Pacwa, Fr Michell, SJ, 1991. 'Tell Me Who I Am, O Enneagram.' *Christian Research Journal*, Fall 1991.

Pagano, Rolph, 1999. *Wie is hier de baas? Een boek over leiderschap, doelgerichtheid en communicatie*. Schiedam, the Netherlands: Scriptum.

Palmer, Helen. *Intuition Training with Helen Palmer*, audio tape. Boston: Shambhala Publications.

Palmer, Helen, 1991. *The Enneagram: Understanding Yourself and the Others in Your Life*. San Francisco: HarperSanFrancisco.

Palmer, Helen, 1996. *The Enneagram in Love and Work: Understanding Your Intimate and Business Relationships*. San Francisco: HarperSanFrancisco.

Palmer, Helen, 1998. *The Enneagram Advantage: Putting the 9 Personality Types to Work in the Office*. New York: Three Rivers Press.

Palmer, Helen (ed.), 1999. *Inner Knowing: Consciousness, Creativity, Insight, and Intuition* (New Consciousness Reader). New York: Tarcher/Putnam.

Palmer, Martin, 1998. *Yin and Yang: Understanding the Chinese Philosophy of Opposites and How to Apply It to Your Everyday Life*. London: Piatkus Books.

Piederiet, J.E., 2000. *Enneagram en outplacement*. Rotterdam: Van Ede & Partners.

Plato, schrijver, teksten gekozen en vertaald door Gerard Koolschijn [Plato, writer, texts selected and translated by Gerard Koolschijn], Bert Bakker, Amsterdam, 1998.

Praag, Eric van, 1996. *Spiritueel leiderschap*. Deventer, the Netherlands: Kluwer.

Riso, Don Richard, 1990. *Understanding the Enneagram: The Practical Guide to Personality Types*. Boston: Houghton Mifflin.

Riso, Don Richard and Russ Hudson, 1999. *The Wisdom of the Enneagram: The Complete Guide to Psychological and Spiritual Growth for the Nine Personality Types*. New York: Bantam Books.

Riso, Don Richard and Russ Hudson, 2000. 'The Imbalances of the Centers.' *Enneagram Monthly*, November/December 1999, January 2000.

Rohr, Richard and Andreas Ebert, 2002. *Discovering the Enneagram: An Ancient Tool for a New Spiritual Journey*. New York: Cross Road Publishing.

Roos, Alexander, 1997. *Alchemie en mystiek*. Cologne: Taschen/Librero.

Rosanov, Nancy, 1988. *Intuition Workout: A Practical Guide to Discovering and Developing Your Inner Knowing*. Boulder Creek, Colo.: Aslan.

Salmon, Eric, 2003. *The ABC of the Enneagram: Identifying the Different Forces that Energise Us*. Cumbria: Institute for Outdoor Learning.

Scott Littleton, C. (ed.), 1999. *Eastern Wisdom: An Illustrated Guide to the Religions and Philosophies of the East*. New York: Henry Holt & Co., Inc.

Senge, Peter M., 1993. *The Fifth Discipline: The Art and Practice of the Learning Organisation*. London: Random House.

Shank, D., 1998. 'The Diamond Approach to the Holy Ideas.' *Enneagram Monthly*, February 1998.

Starren, Harry, and Twan van de Kerkhof, 1999. *De 21 geboden van modern leiderschap*. Hilversum, the Netherlands: Teleac/NOT.

Stentzel, L., 1999. 'My Life in the School.' *Enneagram Monthly*, November/ December 1999.

Stone, S., and S. Winkelman, 1985. *Thuis komen in jezelf*. Haarlem: Mesa Verde.

Thie, John F., 1979. *Touch for Health: A Practical Guide to Natural Health Using Acupressure Touch and Massage to Improve Postural Balance and Reduce Physical and Mental Pain and Tension*. Princeton: DeVorss & Company.

Truax, C.B., and R.R. Carkhuv, 1967. *Towards Effective Counselling and Psychotherapy*. Chicago: Aldine Publishing Co.

Vaags, D.W., 1987. *Where and How Do New Ideas Come From?* Contribution to First European Conference on Creativity and Innovation, 1987.

Vollmar, Klausbernd, 1995. *Das Enneagramm. Praktische Lebensbewaltigung mit Gurdjieffs Typenlehre*. Munich: Goldmann

Vries, S. de, 1996. *Hindoeïsme voor beginners*. Amsterdam: Forum.

Vroon, Piet, 1989. *De tranen van de krokodil: over de snelle evolutie van onze hersenen*. Baarn, the Netherlands: Ambo.

Webb, Karen, 1996. *Principles of the Enneagram*. New York: HarperCollins.

Weggeman, Mathieu, 1997. *Kennismanagement: inrichting en besturing van kennisintensieve organisaties*. Schiedam, the Netherlands: Scriptum.

Wetering, Willem Jan van de, 1999. *Het enneagram als weg naar verandering: persoonlijkheids typologie*. Blaricum, the Netherlands: Andromeda.

Wieseltier, Leon, 1998. *Kaddisj*. New York: Knopf.

Wilber, Ken, 1999. *The Marriage of Sense and Soul: Integrating Science and Religion*. New York: Broadway Books.

Wolinsky, Stephen, with contributions by Margaret O. Ryan, 1991. *Trances People Live: Healing Approaches in Quantum Psychology*. Falls Village, Conn.: The Bramble Company.

Zannos, Susan, 1997. *Human Types: Essence and the Enneagram*. York Beach, Maine: Samuel Weiser.

Zdenek, Marilee, 1983. *The Right Brain Experience*. New York: McGraw-Hill.

Zimmer, H., and C.G. Jung. *Der Weg zum Selbst*. Zürich: Aasscher Verlag.

INDEX

Z
Zen, 53, 259
Zimmer, Heinrich, 261